TRAWLERS GO

Also by the same authors and in the NEL series:
PQ17 - CONVOY TO HELL

Trawlers Go to War

Paul Lund and Harry Ludlam

NEW ENGLISH LIBRARY
TIMES MIRROR

First published in Great Britain by W. Foulsham & Co. Ltd.
© Paul Lund and Harry Ludlam, 1971

*

FIRST NEL PAPERBACK EDITION JUNE 1972
Reprinted June 1972

*

Conditions of sale: This book is sold subject to the condition that it shall not, by way of trade or otherwise, be lent, re-sold, hired out, or otherwise circulated without the publisher's prior consent in any form of binding or cover other than that in which it is published and without a similar condition including this condition being imposed on the subsequent purchaser.

NEL Books are published by
New English Library Limited from Barnard's Inn, Holborn, London E.C.1.
Made and printed in Great Britain by Hunt Barnard Printing Ltd., Aylesbury, Bucks.

45001175 5

This book is dedicated to every 'sparrow' who passed through the Nest.

CONTENTS

		Page
Introduction		
	'Harry Tate's Navy'	9
1	The Death of 'Cocker'	11
2	A Nest of Sailors	17
3	The Fighting Fishermen	30
4	Where's Namsos?	40
5	'Gracie Fields is Making Water'	53
6	The Silver Badge Fleet	68
7	The Northern Patrol	81
8	The Terror of Tobermory	100
9	The Triumph of 'Lady Shirley'	120
10	'Don't Hang Your Bloody Heads'	133
11	From Tobruk to the USA	146
12	'Tally-Ho, Drive On!'	161
13	The Grim Run to Russia	177
14	One of Our Ships is Missing	191
15	'Sir, the Wheel's Come Off'	214
16	The Last of 'Lord Austin'	227
17	Take My U-Boat	243
	No Grave But The Sea	251
	Acknowledgements	253

Introduction

'Harry Tate's Navy'

The Royal Naval Patrol Service was a very special service indeed. It was, in fact, a navy within the Royal Navy, down to the unique distinction of having its own exclusive silver badge, worn by seagoing officers and ratings. Its unlikely headquarters was a municipal pleasure gardens by the sea at Lowestoft with the odd name of Sparrow's Nest. Its fighting fleet consisted of hundreds of coal-burning trawlers, drifters and whalers brought in from the fishing grounds and dressed for war with ancient guns, most of which had been used to fight World War I – and some the war before that.

Fish holds became messdecks, and trawls were swapped for mine-sweeping gear; asdic sounding equipment was fitted for anti-submarine patrol. Then off went the fishermen to the bitter waters of the Northern Patrol, to the Channel and 'E-boat Alley', to the Atlantic and Arctic convoys, to the U-boat ridden US east coast, Gibraltar and the Mediterranean, Africa, the Indian Ocean and the Far East. Vessels, many of them as old or older than their outdated guns, made astonishing journeys of thousands of miles, fighting in strange waters and braving heavy odds. Other Patrol Service men helped to crew the small nucleus of Admiralty-built trawlers which existed at the beginning of the war, and others as they left the shipyards, besides a variety of requisitioned craft including armed yachts, boarding vessels, and paddle-steamers converted for minesweeping.

To start with, the ships of the Patrol Service were manned almost exclusively by skippers, mates and men of the Royal Naval Reserve, except for communications ratings, who came from a white-collar world. The crews were fishermen, tugmen and lightermen, and their officers were skippers from the fishing fleets, with a leavening of senior ranks from the Royal Navy and RNR to ensure that a modicum of naval discipline was observed. But as the war dragged on, the huge expansion in Patrol Service shipping had to be matched in its crews, and so there poured into

Sparrow's Nest an ever-increasing flood of ordinary civilians from all walks of life, many of whom had not been to sea even on a seaside pier. As they went off to join their ships, their ignorance of nautical matters was a source of wonder to the fishermen, who also found it hard to understand what these men were doing in *their* navy, while the outlook, customs and language of the seamen produced no less wonder among the white-collar brigade. Yet somehow, with tolerance and good humour on both sides, the mixing process worked.

However, in spite of all the efforts of the naval men in charge and the great influx of newcomers, including RNVR officers, the casual, haphazard atmosphere of the fishermen's navy persisted, as did its fiercely stubborn independence, if not downright cussedness. The fleet of rust-stained, weather-beaten fishing craft – 'minor war vessels', in the official language of the Admiralty – earned the nickname of 'Harry Tate's Navy', after the famous comedian of the 1920s and 30s who was eternally confounded by modern gadgets and contraptions, the embodiment of the ordinary man struggling with irritations he could not control.

So the 'sparrows in the Nest', as Lord Haw-Haw called them, went forth from the efficient madhouse of their central depot to fight the war in many parts of the world, facing enemy planes and warships, U-boats, E-boats, mines and terrible weathers with a courage, skill, endurance and determination which won the admiration of their comrades in the big ships.

Grim statistics tell the measure of the contribution by the Patrol Service in World War II, for at the final count it had lost more vessels than any other branch of the Royal Navy.

Starting with 6,000 men and 600 vessels, 'Harry Tate's Navy' grew to 66,000 men and 6,000 vessels of all descriptions. One very green Ordinary Seaman who joined it was a bank clerk named Paul Lund, and it is from his experiences, together with those of more than a hundred officers and men who generously contributed their diaries, letters, papers, photographs and fresh personal testimony, that this book has been written.

It hopes to tell for the first time the eventful story of His Majesty's other navy, just how it was.

I

The Death of 'Cocker'

Anything less like a British warship it would have been hard to imagine. She lay in Tobruk harbour, HMS *Cocker*, an unlikely ship in unnatural waters, far, far from home.

Even her saucy name was unreal. She had been launched in the 1930s, all 300 tons of her, as the more prosaic *Kos 19*; for she was a sturdy Antarctic whaler, and had served her peacetime masters well in the most relentless of oceans, doing one of the toughest and bloodiest of jobs, that of killing whales. Now here she was, on a June day in 1942, lolling in warm waters, renamed and fitted out with guns, asdic and depth-charges, all the paraphernalia of war.

Requisitioned only the year before, *Cocker*, like others of her kin had been brought up from the bottom of the world for service in the Mediterranean as an anti-submarine vessel; but call her what you will, try to hide her under Admiralty grey paint, dress her crew in the rig of the day, still at sea doing a punishing fourteen knots, with her midship deck awash, she was an ugly duckling.

In her brief year of war so far she had been a maid of all work, escorting, towing, 'arse-end Charlieing', and had earned several commendations escorting supply ships along the North African coast on the Tobruk run.

On this day, as on many previous occasions, *Cocker* slipped out of Tobruk harbour just before dusk to carry out the necessary asdic sweep of the harbour approaches prior to the arrival of her charge, a single-funnelled freighter. Once the freighter appeared, *Cocker* and her infinitely more imposing companion ship, the naval corvette HMS *Gloxinia* – nearly three times her size – would take up escort stations, and as fast as *Cocker*'s tired reciprocating engines would allow, they would steam down to Alexandria and the 'big eats' at the Fleet Club which all the naval crews dreamed about.

On this night, however, there were snags. The wayward

freighter did not appear at the appointed time, so *Cocker* swept and re-swept, probing with her asdic for any sign of the underwater enemy, whose habit it was to sit quietly outside harbours for just such situations as this. Her crew, still at 'leaving harbour stations', began to get irritable when the skipper showed no sign of setting the watch, which would have allowed most of the men to have gone below.

By now it was quite dark, and tiring of the constant pressure, with the added danger of crossing courses with her sister escort in the blackness, *Cocker* hove-to and carried out a 360 deg. sweep. The air was like velvet, the ship blacked out, yet all men were aware of the intense urgency. Didn't the crazy, laggardly merchantman realise that by dawn they ought to be well beyond the German dive-bomber range? Apparently not, so they cursed her, the slab-sided bastard, for the longer they waited for her to appear, the more certain they were to have Stukas with their breakfast.

Then, 'Captain, sir – vessel passing through the boom!' reported *Cocker*'s sharp-eyed lookout. The whaler immediately stirred to life and, much to the surprise of her crew, took up station on the freighter's port quarter – her seaward side. *Cocker*'s more usual, and safer, billet was on the shoreside of the ship she was escorting, a position which took her comfortably along under the coastal cliffs. Now this station had been pinched by *Gloxinia*, pushing *Cocker* out to the fully exposed seaward side of the miniature convoy.

But at least with the watch now set and the comforting vibration of *Cocker* at her best 'seven-o' revolutions they were thankfully on their way. Among those on watch was Petty Officer Coxswain Bertie Male.

'I was relieved at midnight, and savouring the now cool air I went aft, where, following instructions that all off-watch personnel must sleep on deck while in this danger area, I had brought my camp bed up from below. Having set up the bed I stood eating a doorstep of a third-grade salmon sandwich before getting my head down to the pure bliss of, at the most, three hours' undisturbed sleep.

'The jangling alarm bells jerked us into life for action-stations. Then, as if driven by a monumental sledgehammer, an enemy torpedo rammed itself into the very vitals of *Cocker*. Instantly our ship and home was no longer either – she seemed to disintegrate, almost dissolve into the sea. A second explosion followed, probably a boiler going up. By the light of flickering flames it was obvious that the ship had been blown almost in two. This, and the effect of the engines being at full-ahead, had collapsed her at about midship point into a mass of rending metal.

'The stern half, still motivated by a revolving propeller, seemed now to be crushing forward and downward on to the rapidly sinking bow section. There was the noise of grinding metal, rushing water, steam gasping out of fractured pipes, bulkheads collapsing, the agonised cries of trapped shipmates. The stern began to rise clear of the water, the activating arm of the whistle on the funnel dropped forward and there began a long drawn-out wail that lasted until she died.

'I ran up the canting deck to the stern rail, climbing over the rail out on to what normally would have been the vertical plates of the stern. Now they were nearly horizontal, so steeply had she sunk by the head. There to my horror I saw the propellor still furiously turning at 'seven-o' revolutions. So *that's* what 70 revolutions looked like. My racing thoughts were now playing me tricks, and I recalled in absolute detail the day when, as a boy, wilfully playing with a chaff-cutting machine in a friend's farmyard, I accidentally cut off another boy's thumb. I thought, was I now to be chaff for these great revolving blades?

'Although I had seen similar disasters overtake a dozen other ships I still could not believe that it had actually happened to us. But the noise was real, and so was the flotsam now swirling past, and men in the water gasping with the shock and immersion in fuel oil. My brain cleared. I had only seconds to get clear, not only of the revolving scythe but also from the ship's depth-charges. We had forty charges in the racks and some of these were primed and at the ready, which meant that when the mangled ship had sunk to a certain depth they would go up.

'In a frenzy I stripped off all my top gear, but a navy blue roll-necked sweater recently arrived from home defied all my efforts to get it over my head. Coolly now I selected a space among the floating debris and jack-knifed into the hole, surfacing in thick oil, gasping and conscious of the sodden weight of the sweater. Try as I would while treading water, I still could not get the sweater over my head, nor could I swim a yard with it on. There was nothing else for it but to cut it off, which I did, blessing the fact that I had kept my knife on me and wondering oddly at the same time what my sister would have said at her knitted labour of love being cut to ribbons. Then I swam like the devil as far as I could get from the ship's suction and the slowly sinking depth-charges.

'It was hardly minutes since the torpedo had struck, though it seemed a lifetime. In the darkness I could hear men talking in the sea quite close to me. I eased my swimming pace and looked back at the remains of the ship now bolt upright in the water, with the propeller still slapping round. She began to slide, accompanied by the never-to-be-forgotten death noises of a ship broken and doomed. Bulkheads were crashing, great bubbles of air vomiting up to the surface – the nudity of those parts of a ship normally seen only when she was in dry dock was as starkly shocking as one's first view of female nudity. Above all this I heard a voice nearby call out in agony, "I can't swim! I can't swim!..." and a callously matter-of-fact voice from another direction answer "You've left it bloody late to learn, chum!"

'*Cocker* vanished in a welter of volcanic eruptions, leaving a sudden heavy silence, and those of us struggling in the sea began the soul-destroying task of finding out who was left. The fuel oil was warm and smooth to the touch, but tasted vile – choking coughs in the darkness began to indicate the presence of survivors. There seemed to be a fair number of us in the water, but sound at sea-level is deceptive. Calls of men to their mates, and the shouts of others telling what wreckage they were hanging on to confused the air; it seemed that half a Carley float was the best there was to offer. Then we were aware of the thud of approaching propellers, and pent-up feelings gave way to rousing cheers – it seemed as if half the ship's company had survived and were intent on making themselves heard.

'But then our shouts and cheers died away miserably as it slowly began to register on us that the approaching vessel, the *Gloxinia*, was not bent on rescue, but at full-ahead was, with regret carrying out the newest Admiralty Fleet Orders – that the enemy must be sought out *regardless of survivors*. We were now consumed by a slow build-up of hatred for the men in the fast-coming corvette, who in seconds would be hurling depth-charges among us; yet, bitter as we felt, we knew that this was a captain carrying out his instructions.

'*Gloxinia* came hounding on at a great pace, and as more men in the water realised what was about to happen great oaths were hurled at the ship which only half an hour before we had chatted with via the Aldis lamp. "Swim away – get out!" cried my brain, and being naked except for my khaki shorts I struck out in the water as fast as I was able. And here, for me, fate took a hand.

From close by came the panic-stricken screams of a young seaman, all tangled up with what he thought was some undersea monster. I stopped swimming to help him; it turned out that his belt had broken and his trousers had slipped down around his legs, hindering his leg movements. By great good luck we came upon a dan buoy which had been spewed out by *Cocker* and I hoisted him up on to this, following quickly myself and getting the buoy under our stomachs with our legs still dangling in the water. We had only just made it when *Gloxinia* fired a pattern of depth-charges.

'I have never been kicked in the rudder by a mule, but that is the best way I can describe it. Three pairs of depth-charges, three mule-like kicks which, beginning at my tailbone, travelled up my spine and clamoured to get out of the top of my skull. It was sheer hell, but being halfway out of the water we were relieved of the full force of the explosions and so survived, while others around us died horribly.

'Afterwards it went strangely quiet, no chattering voices or calling to shipmates. It seemed that each of us still alive was now afraid to call in case he should find himself the lone survivor from the assault of the corvette, which had vanished into the darkness to continue her search and escort duties. . . .'

Gradually *Cocker's* survivors did come together. There were only a dozen of them, including the skipper (Lieutenant John Scott, RNVR) whose own escape had been one of the narrowest. He was in his cabin, dazed and going down with his mutilated ship, when he heard quick voices above saying 'The Old Man's dead!' This roused him and he rallied and managed to slither out through the porthole, which had only been enlarged three months before for just such an emergency. But the following blast from the depth-charges rammed the skipper hard in the stomach and paralysed him from the waist down.

The survivors now struggled on in the sea, some twelve miles from shore and twenty miles from Tobruk.

Coxswain Male: 'We had only the half of a Carley float, into which we packed the injured until it settled so low in the sea they were sitting up to their armpits in water. The remainder of us kept off the float, as in this condition the injured had just positive buoyancy. Here our messdeck comedian came into his own to equal even this situation, as with great deliberation he said: "If Noel Coward were here I suppose he'd be singing 'Roll Out The Barrel'. Well, I bloody don't feel like singing – not even 'Show Me the Way To Go Home'!" It was about four hours to dawn and we could only hope that *Gloxinia* had wirelessed our position and that daylight would bring a rescue ship before the Stukas found us.'

The initial shock and the effect of the depth-charges slowly wore off; men began to chatter a little, and some in answer to questions disclosed that they had injuries, the true extent of which would only be made apparent by daylight and death; one man's head was so torn open that the brains were showing.

The waiting hours to dawn, and the uncertainty of what might or might not arrive with it, proved too much for one man. From out of his utter all-night silence he suddenly went berserk, thus seriously endangering the precariously situated inhabitants of the damaged liferaft. It needed great courage for one of the other survivors to save the rest by hitting the crazed man with a piece of debris. The man slipped away and sank, to join those who had already died.

It was nearly noon before the remaining exhausted survivors were picked up by a British motor torpedo boat.

Cocker's skipper, Lieutenant Scott, recovered from his ordeal to return to sea in command of one of the bigger frigates. Awarded the DSC, he later added a bar to this when he destroyed a U-boat.

Coxswain Male, who had joined the Service as an ordinary seaman and progressed to leading seaman and then petty officer, went on to take a commission and reach the rank of Lieutenant, RNVR, with his own command – an unusually talented rise from rank to rank.

And *Cocker*? Her death added yet another hard statistic to the appalling losses of the trawlers, drifters, whalers and other craft that comprised the unlikely warships manned by the Royal Naval Patrol Service – 'Harry Tate's Navy'. Nearly three hundred such ships had been lost to date; by far the largest losses of any section of the fighting Fleet.

It had all begun in the grounds of a seaside council's pleasure gardens, three years before. . . .

2

A Nest of Sailors

It was a sunny August day at Lowestoft in 1939. Though the storm clouds of war were about to break, the little Suffolk fishing port and holiday resort seemed as yet untouched. In the walled municipal pleasure gardens called Sparrow's Nest, overlooking a flat beach lapped by a lazy North Sea, all was peace. Green lawns, bowling greens, colourful flower beds and lily ponds, strolling holidaymakers and others lolling in deckchairs.

It was a brochure picture of the most easterly town in Britain, 'first in the land to greet the rising sun.'

Next day all was abruptly changed, as into the Nest strode the Navy.

Telegrams had gone off to retired officers standing by for the emergency. Now in they came to Lowestoft to take over Sparrow's Nest as a transit depot for the Royal Naval Patrol Service. Trawlermen already in port, members of the Royal Naval Reserve, hurried to report there. One of the first to arrive on that day – August 24th – was William Thorpe, mate of a Lowestoft trawler just docked.

'It was eleven o'clock on a brilliantly sunny morning when I got to the Nest. Sunning themselves in the deckchairs on the main lawn were Elsie and Doris Waters – "Gert and Daisy" – and members of the cast of their seaside revue showing at the Nest's concert hall, but there was no show for them that night. By the afternoon there were several of us there, besides some naval Regulars from Chatham. We took the seats out of the concert hall, altered all the stage, and stowed beds and blankets where we could, working on till midnight. Next day more RNR men arrived and we all slept there. On the third day we were made up into crews, given £5 each to post to our wives and sent off by bus to Hull. There we took over six trawlers and sailed them down to Dover to convert them into minesweepers.'

At the Nest, the idle summer was ended. Gert and Daisy's revue vanished overnight, the only reminder of it being a parcel of props in the centre of the stage marked 'To Be Forwarded'. So swift was the takeover that the local newspaper went to press carrying an advertisement for next week's shows at the concert hall, shows which could never take place. But it did manage to get in a rushed paragraph on another page which explained, rather mysteriously: 'Sparrow's Nest Closed – Owing to last-minute developments the shows at Sparrow's Nest, advertised on another page of this issue, have been cancelled. All the other entertainments will be as usual.'

That was the last notice about the Nest the newspaper carried, and while the fishermen, as they arrived in port, streamed to its gates, the other entertainments did go on as usual, notably at the cinemas, showing such popular new films as Robert Donat in *Goodbye Mr Chips*, Ronald Colman in *Lost Horizon*, and Gracie Fields in *Shipyard Sally*. Holidaymakers still abounded in the town and the local regatta went on as planned, though a small item in the *Lowestoft Journal* reported that sailings of steam trawlers for the North Sea fishing grounds had been stopped, and that those at sea were being recalled by radio.

By August 29, when the order went out for general mobilisation in Britain, Sparrow's Nest was already flying the White Ensign. Many more men like William Thorpe had joined the Navy's requisitioned fishing vessels and were busily stripping them for conversion to war service. Into Lowestoft by every train came a fresh influx of RNR men from other ports; seamen from the coal-burning trawler and drifter fleets which fished around Britain's coasts and out on the Dogger Bank, and others who went farther afield in their deep water trawlers to the icy Barents Sea and remote Bear Island. All well experienced men, they were passed quickly through the Nest and on to ships hurriedly converted and armed, and given a white, instead of a red, ensign to fly.

On September 3, officers and men at the Nest paraded on the lawn before the naval officer commanding. To the younger RNR men he seemed so old as he leaned, puffing, on his stick, and told them the dramatic news of that morning: 'Gentlemen, I have ... (grunt) to tell you ... (grunt) ... that we are now at war with ... (grunt) our old friend ... er – enemy, Germany. ...'

Men from the main fishing ports of Milford Haven, Fleetwood, Grimsby, Hull and Aberdeen now flocked to the Nest, arriving in a hundred different ways.

Some heard of the emergency at sea. Like Skipper John Harwood of Aberdeen, a veteran of the Patrol Service in World War I. 'I was fishing off the Minch, and was changing grounds to a position off the Butt of Lewis when I heard on my wireless that the liner *Athenia* had been torpedoed by a U-boat. The same day I saw a number of naval ships making for Cape Wrath. I knew then it was war, and made tracks for home. I didn't see any other ships all the way to Buchan Ness, so I decided to go on to harbour at Aberdeen. It was packed with ships, all awaiting mobilisation. Within a week I was sent to the Nest to await an appointment.'

Some men were already in port when they answered the call. Like Douglas Finney, an engineman trawling out of Aberdeen, who the morning war was declared, was at home recovering from dermatitis. 'All my relatives in the RNR were getting their call-up papers and knew they were due to leave, but there was no word of my papers. My wife became convinced that the recruiting office hadn't heard of me, and she promptly marched me down there. The RNR commander told me not to worry, that I'd be called up in due course, and to get off home again. I *was* called up in due course: they were at the door with my papers the very next morning, and I left for the Nest the same evening, arms bandaged and all. My relations in the RNR didn't leave until about a month later. So much for a patriotic wife!'

The RNR men were fishermen of all ages who had each undergone three weeks' annual naval training. For other men now wanting to join up with their colleagues there would have been sore disappointment had it not been for the experience of Skipper Sidney White, of Hull. When the first trawlers were being requisitioned, Skipper White, who had been at sea since the age of sixteen, volunteered for the RNR but was told that the age limit was 35, and he was two weeks over age. The skipper went to his MP and questions were asked in the House of Commons, with the result that the rule was speedily altered to allow men over 35 to join up.

Throughout September the numbers of men arriving at Sparrow's Nest increased daily. The Nest's incongruous name, which came from its wealthy former owner, named Sparrow, was replaced by the temporary ship name of HMS *Pembroke X*. There were sentries with fixed bayonets at the gates now, but men could still walk in or out at any time, and inside there was no Service discipline, nor would it have worked had there been. To help kill the boredom of men waiting for ships – and to get them out of the hair of the overworked administrative staff –

route marches were devised; but although these started out in orderly fashion, when the marchers got back a good many men would have disappeared. The one time everyone turned up in strength was on pay day.

These Patrol Service fishermen were tough men. Out trawling they thought nothing of working sixty to seventy hours on deck without sleep; they could carry on gutting and washing fish automatically, and fall asleep at meals eaten while on the job. Like the man who was given his breakfast of fish and fell asleep over it; his mates took it away and replaced it with a plate of fish-bones. When the fisherman woke up he carried on with his work immediately, thinking he had eaten his meal.

Skippers and mates of the fishing trawlers were all-powerful and had to be obeyed. The dictum was if the skipper could stick it, so could the rest; though there was the certain Norwegian skipper who, for a respite, would tie his scarf round the bridge voicepipe, put his woolly cap on top, and return to his cabin, hoodwinking the crew into believing he was still up on the bridge.

Most skippers were uncommonly stubborn, many were thoroughly harsh men. There was the trawler master on an Arctic trip who, after calling all hands on deck to shoot trawl, suspected one of his crew of feigning illness, and flushed him out of his bunk with jets of icy water from the ship's hose. But the man really was ill, with a high temperature, and died as a result of the brutal treatment. After a court of inquiry this same skipper was a changed man, and if any crewman was ill or hurt he couldn't do enough for him. Once, when a deckhand got a septic hand from a wire cut, the skipper took him on the bridge, dressed the wound and told him to stay there until he was better and to do no more work. The skipper then departed to his cabin and brought up a music-stand and a violin, which he played for the sick man between conning the ship; an experience worse, said the deckhand afterwards, than the pain from his throbbing hand.

Mates were required to command absolute authority over their crew, even to fighting them if necessary. There was the skipper who, when one of his bigger deckhands was polishing a ventilator, told the mate, a small man, to order the deckhand to do the job over again ... and again ... and again, until the deckie lost his temper and challenged the mate to a fight, in which the mate received a terrific thrashing. While getting beaten up, the mate saw the skipper roaring with laughter on the bridge. Afterwards the skipper told him: 'Well, Mr Mate, you needed taking down a peg or two. . . . ' The mate discovered that the big deckhand was a former champion boxer, and the skipper had put him up to the whole thing.

Rough and tough, and little time for lyrical romancing about the sea. These were the trawlermen. Skippers and men went fishing for one purpose only, to earn themselves a livelihood. A £700 catch was a good trip, and the skipper took ten per cent of this, but he had to pay all manner of expenses out of his money, including use of radio and baskets, watchman's fee, electricity, water, 'stage' expenses, and food for everyone aboard. Often, after paying out all the bills, he would be left with only £10 for himself after three weeks' Arctic trawling; sometimes he would actually owe the company money, which would be deducted from the proceeds of his next trip.

The mate got 7⅝ per cent of the catch. He and the skipper were the only shareholders of the ship's company, which gave them certain powers of action. One hard-up skipper sold his anchor and cable for a little ready cash, which was quite legal as skippers had the right to sell gear if they wanted to.

The true measure of a skipper was his ability to 'smell' fish, which he did without instruments and purely from his own intuition, plus the contents of his little 'Black Book'. This was the book which all skippers kept, in which they entered, and kept to themselves, the knowledge gained of fish movements from year to year. The true North Sea skipper scorned the use of charts and was reputed to be able to tell where he was at any time merely by dipping his finger in the sea and tasting it, or by observing the nature of the seaweed. If a crew ever saw the Old Man studying a chart they would believe the worst – that they were really lost. For a skipper's pursuit of a catch might take him long distances to bitter waters in some of the fiercest weather to be found anywhere in the world. It was not unusual for a weather-battered trawler to run out of coal and finish up burning deckboards, cabin bunks, pannelling, anything, in order to get home.

These, then, were the kind of skippers, mates and men who came to Sparrow's Nest dressed in their once-a-year RNR uniform, or with it stuffed in their seabags. The majority went off to join trawlers converted to shoot out minesweeping gear as they had formerly shot trawl, for the great need in these early days was for minesweepers. Other men joined trawlers fitted out with asdic apparatus for anti-submarine patrol, 'pinging' the depths to detect the presence of U-boats.

Men from the Nest were very quickly in action in the Channel, in the North Sea, and off the north coast of Scotland, guarding the waters between the Orkneys and Iceland. It was here in October, after the first few weeks of war, that the trawlers suffered their first casualty. The *Northern Rover*, patrolling from Kirkwall in the Orkneys, suddenly vanished without trace. Later the *Barbara Robertson* was sunk by gunfire from a U-boat off the Hebrides.

Other trawlers fell victim to enemy mines laid in the Channel and off the Thames estuary, where Hitler's 'secret weapon', the magnetic mine, had begun to wreak havoc among shipping. Even with the threat of mine and U-boat, however, the stubborn habits of the fishing skippers died hard.

The Fleetwood trawler *Gava* was given an old 12-pounder gun and took a naval lieutenant aboard when she went out with a sister trawler, similarly armed, to guard six other trawlers while they fished. But *Gava* and her companion ship began to fish too, and were taken unawares when an Aberdeen trawler steamed up to say she had sighted a U-boat. *Gava*'s naval lieutenant gave orders for immediate action to protect his small convoy. 'Chop away your gear, skipper,' he commanded. But *Gava*'s skipper, with little regard for the danger they were in, bluntly replied: 'Not so bloody likely – I'm not chopping a good set of gear away!' He coolly had his men haul it in. 'Now,' he said, 'we'll go and pick up the marker buoy, and after that we'll attend to the U-boat.' Fortunately the German was never sighted.

Nor could hoisting a White Ensign sweep away old superstitions, as the non-fisherman telegraphist sent to another aged trawler soon found.

'We had a black cat, which all our fishermen crew thought was very lucky, and once when we were due to sail they all stepped on to the jetty at Harwich and refused to go to sea, because the cat was mssing. After a thorough search of the ship we found the cat in the provision locker lying under a sack of potatoes, nearly flattened but otherwise unharmed. And off we went to sea.

'We always wore our lifebelts at sea and the cat was the only one aboard without one. So one of the seamen got a Durex, blew it up and tied it round the cat's neck. It looked so funny, but we got used to it, and the cat went around like that for months. It really seemed the ideal thing.'

This old trawler was early in action during the bleak period of fighting the magnetic mine. In the space of five days in mid-November, mines accounted for fifteen merchant ships as well as two minesweeping trawlers and a destroyer. One of the merchantmen to go down was the Japanese liner *Terukini Maru*, sunk off Harwich. The old trawler steamed out with other ships to pick up survivors.

'It was a terrible sight seeing this big ship go down. The sea was littered. But most people were picked up, and among them was a woman from Cheshire. At Christmas she sent £20 to our trawler group of five ships to buy ourselves a Christmas dinner. This was a lot of money then, and it was divided £4 to each ship

'We were going to sea on Christmas Eve, so some of us took our £4 to the NAAFI to buy a turkey, a leg of pork and some vegetables. We had a cook who couldn't cook, no rarity then, and on Christmas morning our purchases were still lying around. A slight collision in the fog forced us to anchor, so I tried to get the crew busy. They chopped the head and legs off the rurkey and I told them it would need stuffing. One man broke a loaf up into filthy crumbs and was about to stuff the lot in when I told him to mix it with water first. The result turned out rather like black plaster on the galley bench. One man then held the turkey while another stuffed in the breadcrumbs, but as fast as he stuffed them in, they came out of its neck. So I told them about skewers. A seaman got his jack-knife and hacked bits off the coalbox, sharpened them, and skewered the bird.

'I put the leg of pork on the galley bench and chopped the trotter off. This caused an uproar – "Friday, and a pig on the bench!" They thought it by far the unluckiest thing that could happen, and every man of them rushed to heave the trotter over the side. Later that day a pigeon came from nowhere and settled on the gun platform. This, they thought, was great – a lucky omen – and were soon up there feeding the bird on bread and saucers of tinned milk. Apparently its arrival was considered enough to wash out our earlier bad luck.'

Not all the early trawler crews were exclusively fishermen, there were already some cases where 'outsiders' had turned up in force. One RNR fisherman from Hull, still only nineteen but with years of hard experience of trawling behind him, went from the Nest to a trawler in which most of the crew had never been to sea before. Her skipper and coxswain were both RNR, as were her chief engineer and second engineer, but the other officer was a raw sub-lieutenant RNVR, fresh from officers' training at Skegness.

We were at Milford Haven, with four of our flotilla out in the Haven, and our ship in dock behind the lock gates. The skipper and coxswain were in the nearest pub. When they finally rolled on board the coxswain immediately collapsed and had to be carried below, while the skipper, who was three sheets to the wind, staggered up to the top bridge. I was in the wheelhouse as his surprise order came down from the bridge – "Let go for'ard, let go aft – full-ahead!"

'We were only a hundred feet from the dock entrance and pointing directly at the lock gates, which were closed. I sang out that the Chief wasn't ready to start engines yet, and managed to delay us to give the harbourmaster time to get the gates open.

'Eventually I eased her out into the Haven. The other four trawlers outside had got their "picks" up and were heading out to sea at half speed to allow us to catch up – we were going to the Clyde for a big refit, and home for Christmas. However, our skipper's next order was to stand by to drop anchor! Our poor sub-lieutenant, who had come into the wheelhouse to be out of the skipper's way, said desperately: "What the hell are we going to do?"

'I told him to go to the foc'sle head, and when the skipper shouted "Drop anchor!", let it drop just to the waterline, but not into the water, and leave the rest to me. I blew down the voicepipe and warned the Chief of our predicament and told him that whatever I did with the telegraph he was to ignore the signals and keep the engines going at slow-ahead.

'Down came the skipper's next order, "Stop engines!" which I dutifully rang up, then the second order, "Drop anchor!" and the Sub did as I had told him. After a short time the skipper shouted to the Sub: "Where's she heading?" The Sub pointed straight ahead, so the order came down "Ring off!" and I rang "Finished with engines" on the telegraph. The skipper then staggered down to tell me to keep a good lookout and to call him at breakfast – though it was still only half-past four in the afternoon. He lurched off to his berth just below the wheelhouse and I gave him a quarter of an hour to doze off, still moving the ship slow-ahead. When I judged him to be asleep I signalled to the Sub to get the anchor up again quietly and blew down to the Chief to ease her on to full-ahead, as I didn't want to wake our skipper with any bells ringing or sudden vibrations.

'In the meantime the leader of our flotilla had been flashing at us impatiently with his Aldis. We had no signalman – the skipper or coxswain did that job – and when I asked the Sub to reply he confessed miserably that he could neither send nor receive morse. I tried what little I knew but I was dead slow, and after a few attempts the man at the other end must have thought "There's a right idiot over there" and slowed down to my speed. He was sending "What's the trouble ? Get into your appointed position." I asked the Sub, "For God's sake, what's our position ?" But he said he didn't know that either. "Hell," I said, "you'd better get to the skipper's berth and find the orders – but don't wake him up!"

'After what seemed an eternity he came back empty-handed – "Can't find a thing – what are we going to do ?" I'm sure he could see his newly-won braid going for a Burton. However, I finally hopped the ship along until I got her into position No. 2 in line, and as no one said anything I assumed I had found the right place.

'We arrived at the Clyde the next day and the skipper was duly called at breakfast. He didn't say a word, no more did we.'

On Christmas Day the Hull trawler *Loch Doon*, minesweeping off Blyth struck a mine and sank with the loss of fifteen men. She was the last of fourteen trawlers and drifters to die in 1939. Most were sunk by mines, along with them a little drifter by the name of *Ray of Hope*. She was part of a very strange and special Patrol Service flotilla.

During the first days at Sparrow's Nest, Skipper Sidney White and five other RNR skippers reported to the concert hall to be told they were going on secret work, and could pick their own crews of twelve from men willing to volunteer for a private mission. They were then to report to Commander Charles Hammond, DSC, RN, in his 'office', a tumbledown shack on the Lowestoft dockside.

The skippers found that the ships allotted to them were six small wooden herring drifters, all much less than 100 tons. Skipper White: 'We refitted and commissioned in about 14 days, with a lot of cajoling and swearing from "Bill" Hammond over the length of time it all took. Our ships were to comprise the Mine Recovery Flotilla, formed to undertake special mine recovery duties for HMS *Vernon*, the Navy's shore-based research establishment at Portsmouth.'

Skipper White took command of *Silver Dawn*, and the other drifters in the flotilla were *Ray of Hope*, *Jacketa*, *Lord Cavan*, *Formidable* and *Fisher Boy*. The little boats, their only armament consisting of a few rifles, were fitted with a small trawl sweep to drag along the sea bottom to recover ground mines, though every rock threatened to carry the trawl away. It was hoped they might recover intact one of the magnetic mines which were hitting at shipping so mercilessly, and bring it back for examination. To this end, although their first base was at Margate, the drifters were sent anywhere that a suspected magnetic mine was reported to have been dropped, according to reports of enemy ships or parachutes seen off the south-east coast. No magnetic mine was actually swept up by them or anyone else, though at last, in late November, two were found on mudflats in the Thames estuary, where they had been dropped from aircraft. They were recovered intact for the experts at HMS *Vernon* to examine and find a counter measure.

Skipper White was among the selected few taken by closed truck to the secret naval research section near Havant, where a motley crew of boffins in beards and sandals were locked in for weeks to work on the magnetic mine problem and produce an answer to it. When, near Christmas, Winston Churchill announced that 'The magnetic mine is being mastered', it was in fact still taking heavy toll among shipping.

It was the engineer officer of Grimsby base who first thought up the idea of 'degaussing' the ships – having them set up their own magnetic field to foil the mine. Initially this meant running some three miles of copper wire round a ship's scuppers, but this wire was often knocked and damaged. Later the idea was improved to fitting a single wire, powered by the ship's dynamo, in a casing round the outside of the ship.

But all this took time to evolve, and in the meantime the drifters of the Mine Recovery Flotilla, or 'Vernon's Private Navy' as they were quickly called, carried on with their hazardous fishing for mines. In December they were working from Ramsgate when two vessels were called for to tackle a specially dangerous job. Skipper White of *Silver Dawn* and Skipper Walter Hayes of *Ray of Hope* volunteered, and went out to shoot their trawls some five miles east of the swept war channel used by the convoys. The two drifters took it in turns to sweep, the other standing by, in waters where parachute mines had been seen to drop.

All went well until *Ray of Hope* got her sweep fast on the bottom. Skipper Hayes heaved on the winch, drawing his ship back, but in reversing she passed over a magnetic mine, which was promptly triggered off by the metal of her engine and fittings. *Ray of Hope* went up immediately in a terrific explosion, blowing Skipper Hayes from his bridge. The skipper and his second hand, John Bird, were the only survivors, and were picked up by *Silver Dawn* along with two or three bodies of dead crew. Though a southbound convoy was passing at the time, no help was forthcoming from its escorts, who would not venture into the dangerous waters. The remainder of the flotilla steamed from Ramsgate to help search for the lost men, but their efforts were fruitless.

The disaster was not taken lightly by bluff, bearded Commander Hammond. He was a perceptive man who worked by a frank and simple code: 'You can't drive a fisherman, but a little leadership and understanding and they'll win the war for you.' Immediately following the loss of *Ray of Hope* he called a meeting of the crews above decks in Ramsgate harbour, in sight of the distant sea where the drifter had perished, and told them that in view of the loss, any man, repeat *any man*, could opt out if he chose and return to Lowestoft. They were to think of their families and domestic commitments; he preferred uncommitted men and would not blame anyone for quitting the flotilla.

The invitation was something unheard of before in the Navy. Only about half a dozen men did choose to leave, which pleased Hammond very much. This was the situation when a new party of volunteers from the Nest came to join the flotilla, among them two RNVR signalmen. One was Signalman Bev Smith.

'At the Nest we volunteered for "special dangerous service", having romantic ideas about blockships or some such thing. Romance went by the board when we arrived at Ramsgate in the dark, at low tide, to find five scruffy little steam drifters tied up to the wall. The majority of us found we were required for *Fisher Boy*. We clambered down to find the ship occupied by a stoker, a deep sea trawlerman, who told us that only he and the skipper remained of *Fisher Boy*'s crew. The skipper himself left shortly afterwards and we were taken over by Skipper George Brown, a very able Yarmouth fishing skipper.

'My signalman companion joined *Silver Dawn*. In the whole of the flotilla there were only us two signalmen which made communications between ships difficult, as all we had were a pair of hand flags and an Aldis lamp.

'The method of sweeping devised by Commander Hammond and the skippers after the *Ray of Hope* disaster was that in future two drifters would tow one trawl along the bottom of the sea bed. In the event of something being picked up in the trawl, one ship would pass her end of the trawl over to the other, which would then steam in to a gently shelving beach until she virtually went aground. She would then slip both ends of the trawl attached to a wire with a buoy, and steam off to anchor safely offshore while a dinghy party went out to haul the trawl up on the beach with the aid of any suitable towing vehicle they could find. Then the trawl was carefully opened and the contents examined.

'We trawled many a time in snowstorms, and on one occasion when there was a big fall of snow and the decks were covered, Commander Hammond was leaning out of the wheelhouse window with watchful eye when, as our two ships came together, the crews started snowballing each other. I couldn't help thinking how tolerant the old Commander was, with his RN background, to allow his two minesweeping crews to skylark in this manner. But no doubt with the *Ray of Hope* affair still very fresh in his mind he was disposed to be tolerant with us all at that time. We were an easy-going, pretty rough-looking crowd, many of the fishermen having brought with them their old fishing gear of oily jerseys, fearnought trousers and seaboot stockings.

'We hadn't a cook on *Fisher Boy* and the galley stove was cracked. Several people had a go at cooking and the whole thing was a pretty miserable business. Commander Hammond eventually arranged for us to buy a new cooker or coal burning range for the galley from a local ship's chandler. This was duly installed, and the next time we sailed from harbour the old stove was ceremoniously slung overboard.

'We swept for six or seven days after this without catching anything in the trawl. Then came a day when we found by the way the ships were moving that something had been picked up, and we went through the whole performance of beaching the trawl. What with the tenseness that always went with this procedure and the opening up of the trawl, everyone's feelings may be imagined when we found we had recovered our old galley stove.

'Christmas Day came. It was bitterly cold and we hadn't been paid since we joined the ship. One of our crew had been ashore in the morning and found a pawnshop, where he'd been able to hock some odds and ends and raise a few shillings. We had secured from the base a joint of pork, which was bunged into the oven, and we were all sitting in the little after cabin feeling pretty miserable. At this time rum was not being issued to the ship, probably because the depot at Ramsgate was not properly organised.

'It was my first Christmas away from home and I was feeling pretty dejected, when a lad from one of the other drifters came down and said Commander Hammond had sent a message round for us to call up at his office. We went up there to find that the ladies of his village had got together and baked a cake for every crew, besides sending us pairs of knitted socks and other comforts. All of which helped to brighten our day, plus the fact that the Commander told us that if we went into the local pub there was a pint of beer waiting for everybody. It was typical of the way he always thought of and looked after his men. I must say it went a great way to livening up our Christmas Day, and somehow or other, having got into the pub, we all seemed to manage to get hold of more than one pint, and came back feeling that perhaps things weren't quite so bad after all.'

3

The Fighting Fishermen

It was January 9, 1940. Around dinnertime. The trawler *Calvi* was busy minesweeping off the North Foreland when a big convoy began to pass slowly by in the swept war channel. A routine scene. But suddenly there was a tremendous explosion as the second ship of the convoy, the 10,000-ton liner *Dunbar Castle* triggered off a magnetic mine and blew up right under her bridge. She sank within minutes close to the North Goodwin Lightship, where the tip of her mast was to mark her grave for the duration of the war.

Calvi was quickly to the rescue along with other ships and picked up two lifeboats of survivors. There were 73 of them, including women and children, two nuns, and some completely naked firemen. In one of the boats was the body of the liner's captain, who died in the boat even as rescue came. Every other occupant of this boat was quickly hauled out except one dazed man, severely shocked, who refused to budge. All aboard the trawler yelled to him to make a move and grab a willing hand, but even as they called, he sat there in his terrible stupor and died.

Calvi ran out of rum trying to comfort her big load of distressed passengers. Men and women were shocked and injured, children were sick all over the ship, and through it all the nuns remained calm.

After taking her survivors safely into Ramsgate harbour, *Calvi* kept the two lifeboats as salvage, and later towed them into Dover harbour and sold them for £14.

It was just another day's incident in the sea war, now five months old, in which the ships of the Patrol Service were ever prominent, patrolling and minesweeping, and adding their names to the spiralling casualties; blown up by the mines they were seeking to clear, or devastated by bombs from raiding enemy aircraft. Like the trawler *Valdora*, an aged survivor of World War I, which was sent to the bottom by German bombers off Dover; and three trawlers which met with similar fate in the North Sea. The *Robert Bowen*, swooped on by Heinkels while minesweeping out of Aberdeen, broke in half and sank with all hands; her companion ship, *Fort Royal*, sank in minutes. *Fifeshire*, a big new trawler which had seen scarcely any fishing time before she was given a gun, died off Copinsay, in the Orkneys, under a pall of flame and smoke from Heinkel bombs. She sank rapidly under the feet of her captain, a naval sub-lieutenant only twenty years old, leaving only one survivor to tell the tale.

Other trawlers and drifters limped back to harbour heavily damaged by bombs or carrying the bodies of crew killed by the spraying machine-guns of raiding aircraft. But it was not all one-sided. In a spirited action off the north of Scotland, three patrolling trawlers, *Arab*, *Gaul* and *Stoke City*, determinedly attacked a U-boat which tried to escape by lying on the sea bottom; they banged away in turn with their depth-charges until they had completely broken up the U-boat and collected evidence of their 'kill.'

Just prior to this, in dirty weather early in January, two other trawlers, together with a small destroyer, had run a U-boat on to the South Goodwin Sands, a bold action which earned each of their skippers the DSC. The trawlers, *Cayton Wyke* and *Saon*, were working from the Dover Patrol. There was a break in the Goodwin Sands where a ship could get through on a good tide, and this gap was protected by an electric loop cable. On a dark night with a strong gale blowing, the trawlers received a coast-guard alert that a crossing had been detected on the loop. The three vessels steamed up and down the break in the sands, dropping 82 depth-charges, and eventually drove the U-boat on to the west of the Goodwins. Commanding *Saon* was Chief-Skipper William Mullender.

'We went in and saw the U-boat stuck fast on the sands, but couldn't approach it because of the strong gales. A cable ship came out and joined us as we waited for the weather to ease before trying to save the U-boat, for it would have been a great prize if captured intact, the first of the war. But as we watched and waited, the sands slowly swallowed the U-boat up, and its crew.'

Little 'Billy' Mullender, five feet of pluck, was without a doubt the embodiment of all the finest qualities which the Royal Naval Reserve skippers brought to the war at sea. His private battle had begun at a very early age, for he was born such a delicate child that he was not allowed to go to school. He was plagued by an illness which cost the lives of a brother and sister, and when he was nine years old the family doctor told his father, a Lowestoft fisherman, that there was only one thing he could do, and that was to take the boy to sea on a kill or cure basis. So the ailing young Mullender began his life at sea in a sailing smack, sleeping on the upper deck with only a canvas screen between him and all weathers. It cured him. By the age of 21 he had obtained his skipper's ticket and was running his own ship, after teaching himself to read and write along the way. The outbreak of war had found him, in his late thirties, the only skipper on the coast to be master of two ships at once, running a pair of colliers between Blyth and Lowestoft; the ships had separate crews and he captained one ship at a time as the other was being unloaded – and he'd been doing this for 12 years. Like whipcord was Billy Mullender.

Back at Sparrow's Nest in the early months of 1940 activity increased tremendously. Landladies of Lowestoft who were evacuated when the Navy declared the port depot a restricted area, had to be speedily brought back to their homes to provide billets for the sailors, who now thronged the town. As the trainees generally returned to their boarding houses for mid-day dinner, it meant that regularly, four times a day hundreds upon hundreds of men were either converging on the Nest or passing out of its gates on their way home. To avoid congestion in the town's main street they were ordered to walk along the seafront. Enemy planes over the North Sea became aware of this practice and fighters on sneak raids would skim in from the sea or swoop over at rooftop height, machine-gunning as they went, causing the ratings to fling themselves under any cover available. There was many a man who lay with his face in the grass and numbly asked himself: 'Am I going to be killed before I even get to sea?' On the lighter side, down into unwritten history went such incidents as that of the man who emerged from the lavatory in his billet with his trousers round his ankles, quite dizzy from going round and round dodging a richocheting Jerry bullet that had sought to keep him company.

Basic training was going ahead now. 'Square bashing' was done at the Oval, the former sports ground only yards away from the Nest on the seafront. Here the stokers were marched across from the Nest by a Scottish chief stoker who played the bagpipes as they went. On the now dishevelled cricket ground the hardened stokers derisively shovelled pebbles into dummy furnaces – square holes – to simulate their future work at sea.

Already there had appeared some tough, gritty characters among the Patrol Service instructors, and perhaps none more so than Chief Petty Officer Edward Pugh – or 'Ted the Bastard' as he became known to all and sundry. Ted, a trawler chief engineer from Milford Haven, had been called up to the Patrol Service at the war's outbreak. He was in his late forties, now an instructor at St Luke's, the big hospital on the seafront where engines removed from ships had been set up for training engine room personnel. Brought up under the strong discipline of a military father, Ted had been a young Royal Artillery sergeant in World War I, winning the Croix de Guerre for gallantry at the Battle of the Somme. At the Nest he was a holy terror on parade and knew his nickname full well. He sent home to his wife for his birth certificate, and on its arrival had it framed and mounted on his office desk. He then fell in the 'Awkward Squad', his more charitable description for the latest batch of recruits and made them line up to read it, after which he bellowed: 'So I'm "Ted the Bastard" am I? But only on the parade ground with a shower of mechanical crabs like you bloody lot!...'

Among the recruits coming to Lowestoft now, besides the fishermen, tugmen and lightermen, were many men who had volunteered for 'special service' with the Royal Navy and so were sent to the Patrol Service. Frequently the reason for a man volunteering in this way was from a desire to escape the tedium of life in the bigger warships; sometimes it was as a matter of expedience when in high desperation. For instance, many naval trainees at HMS *Royal Arthur*, the Butlin's camp at Skegness, were so desperate to quit the camp under practically any terms that they opted for the Patrol Service as a quick and thankful means of exit. The trouble with the Skegness camp was that it took the full brunt of the bitter winter of 1939-40, when, although temperatures tumbled well below freezing point for long periods, there was no heating in the chalets, the walls of which became coated with ice from the breath of their occupants. The only heating for the trainees was in the lavatories, and this provided by coke braziers made of buckets punched out with holes and stood on a couple of housebricks. Several ratings died, either as a result of huddling over the braziers to keep warm, or through taking the braziers into their freezing chalets. Men who chose to escape through the Patrol Service were highly relieved to bid the place earthy farewell and unroll their hammocks on the floor of the concert Hall at Sparrow's Nest.

However, many an unknowing volunteer from Skegness was in for a surprise when finally drafted from the Nest to his 'warship'. Like Seaman Robert Muir.

'We were ordered to Dover to join the *Nautilus*. We thought she was a destroyer, but when we walked along the quay at Dover and asked a man where the *Nautilus* was, he replied: "You're standing right over her!" And sure enough, as we looked over the quay at low water, there she was, a little motor fishing drifter. Still, she was nice and comfortable after we got used to her.

'Her job at that time was going out with the paddlesweepers and laying the dan, or marker buoys, also shooting and exploding mines as they were swept up. Our armament consisted of one Lewis gun and two rifles. To combat the magnetic mine we were given a "skid", a small raft with coils of wire on it, which we towed behind us when sweeping. A "skid" could cope with about three mines, after which it sank.

'Following this we became a mark-ship for one of the minesweeping aircraft brought in to help in the fight against the magnetic mine, which was still doing a great deal of damage. The plane had a big hoop right round it from wing-tip to tail and nose, and had to fly at about 25 feet above the water for the contraption to be effective. We hove-to at one end of the sweep, flying an extra large black flag, while the plane swept in over us, making something like 50 runs until it had cleared the area. Of course, if we had happened to anchor over a magnetic mine it would have been our bad luck!'

Came the day *Nautilus* was selected for an important cloak-and-dagger operation. All very hush-hush.

'We took on extra stores and six extra jars of rum, and prepared a berth for a naval commander. When he came aboard we sailed from Dover under secret orders. These were opened three miles out and simply told us to proceed to Sheerness for further orders. When we arrived there, the commander went ashore for his secret instructions, and on his return we moved out into the harbour and anchored. The whole crew was invited to the wardroom, and all six of us went down to find a rum jar ready opened on the table. After we'd had a liberal tot, the commander broke it to us. We had been selected to put the blockships into Zeebrugge. Our job would be to lay the dans after the sweepers up to the mole, after which we were to carry on to the mole, go alongside and find out if the lock-keeper was a fifth columnist. If he was, we were to shoot him and give the blockships the go ahead. The commander added that anyone who wanted to cry off could do so there and then and he would be replaced. None of us stepped out. "Thank you, gentlemen," he said – "I am proud to sail with you."

'Well, we made three attempts to get over there, but on each occasion, after covering about twenty miles, we were recalled, as the time was not right. By this time we had knocked back three jars of the extra rum. After the third attempt the Admiralty decided that the poor old *Nautilus* was too slow with her seven knots and took us off the job. We were left wondering what eventually happened to the lock-keeper.'

When you came from civvy street as a clerk, underwent a crash course as a telegraphist and found yourself in an old trawler with a crew of ex-fishermen, you were also due for some surprises. Like Telegraphist Thomas Burn, who had never in his life seen such hard days.

'We had to coal the ship, all hands. 180 tons shovelled through the little deck coal-holes, and we worked all night. We had very little money but broke off about 9 p.m. and went to the dockside pub for a pint. The cook was a proper rogue and flogged the little carpet out of the skipper's cabin for his beer. He later flogged his hammock, which he didn't need as we slept in bunks. We went nine weeks without pay, through moving around; no cigarettes or anything. It was a real lean time.

'We couldn't get any proper signal pads. I had a sheaf of square lavatory papers in my kitbag and this was all I could use to write my signals on for the first few weeks. There was no ship's clock and my pocket watch had to keep me in touch with the world. I controlled the radio set from the wireless room below, and if anyone on the asdic bridge wanted to pass an R/T message he had to ask me to switch on. One day as an enemy plane flew over us the skipper, up on top, snatched up his handset and bawled: "Bloody German bomber flying south-east!" The message didn't go out as I hadn't switched on, just as well, considering we had been strongly warned against using plain language; there were code groups to cover such messages.

'The crew had no idea of naval discipline. In harbour we were supposed to keep deck watches in case of prowlers, but they never did – I think I was the only one to stick to the rules! Luckily I was deck watchman late one night when two of the crew fell over the side as they were coming aboard drunk; I called the rest of the lads and we fished them out, or they'd have been gonners.

'We were working with a convoy in the North Sea in horrible weather when the destroyer in charge of the escort called us up by lamp, but as the skipper couldn't read the signals he called me up top and I staggered from one well, to deck, to well, to get the message. The destroyer was ordering us: "Proceed with consort to search area – suspected U-boat in the vicinity." The skipper said to me: "What the hell does he mean – what's a consort?" I told him, and we went off with the other trawler escorts. It was a terrific sea but we got a good contact, attacked with depth-charges and saw some commotion, though whether it really was a U-boat no one ever knew.

'Depth-charging by some trawlers could be murderous. There was one skipper who foolishly stopped his ship to do depth-charge trials, and blew half the stern off! Some skippers just hadn't a clue when it came to naval drill, either. To position their ship alongside, many depended on the jetty stopping them, and at one time it was reported that they'd done £9,000 worth of damage at Harwich. After that they were ordered to tie up to buoys in mid-stream.

'For a time my trawler escorted convoys up the east coast and we were based on the Tyne. We were in harbour one wild night, pitch dark and stormy, all ready to escort a south-bound convoy formed up outside, when the NOIC came on to the jetty and called for our skipper. I went up with the skipper, and this RN commander called from the jetty: "You've got a change of destination, skipper, can you read morse?" The skipper, knowing I was beside him, bellowed "Yes!" The commander then said we were to proceed with a convoy going north, not south, and he spelt out its destination in dot-dash fashion, in morse: ".-../././-/...." I whispered to the skipper "Leith," and he shouted out to the commander "LEITH!" The commander choked with fury. "You silly bugger!" he yelled. "What the hell do you think I gave it to you in morse for?" Just to add to that poor commander's sorrow, as we moved from the jetty the skipper put our sharp bow into the bows of a Norwegian passenger ship lying close by. We could see light showing through the hole.

'At sea in this old trawler we got an awful lot of water down the hatch into the messdeck, the former fish hold. This had a sloping deck, and invariably, in spite of baling out, we had about six inches of water lying at the bottom end. It swished around night and day and when the ship rolled, the water was three feet deep at the "deep end".

'The pump in the crew's lavatory never worked, so all business was done over the side. This apparently was nothing to our hardy fishermen, who said it was normal practice with them. In peacetime they reckoned that when the weather was bad they just performed on the fish, and they solemnly advised me never to eat fish. I've seen us stop a minesweeping trawler on occasion and swap them some tobacco for a basket of fish, but none of our fishermen would eat it.'

The long fight against the magnetic mine continued, now with pairs of steel-built trawlers dragging thirty magnets between them on a sweep. And still engaged on its risky task of mine recovery was 'Vernon's Private Navy'. Two of the five wooden drifters, *Fisher Boy* and *Silver Dawn*, left Ramsgate to sail down the Channel and work off Falmouth, sweeping the war channel and outside it, towing their 'catches' into the mouth of the Helford river. Here they ran their ships ashore and warped the sweep wires round riverside trees, so as to bring the catch ashore between the ships in case it blew up.

In this way they caught some ordinary mines, but none of the magnetic type, and mostly, just shellfish.

One morning at Helford, after *Silver Dawn*'s crew had enjoyed the respite of a day's shore leave, oysters appeared on the breakfast table; the hands, while ashore, having scooped them up with nets and buckets. During this splendid meal in walked Commander 'Bill' Hammond.

'What the hell are you eating?' he demanded.

'Oysters, sir.'

'I should think they're bloody oysters!' said the commander. 'Don't you know this is the Duke of Devonshire's estate and these are the King's oyster beds? You'll all be for the high jump over this – fry me a bloody plateful!'

Far from the 'high jump' however, Skipper White of *Silver Dawn* found himself awarded the DSC, along with Skipper Wally Hayes, for the operation in which *Ray of Hope* was lost. Commander Hammond at the same time received the DSO. Skipper White:

'The air raids made it a long wait at Buckingham Palace and we were not allowed to smoke. We began fidgeting, and I asked the Equerry for the lavatory. "Tch, tch!" he said irritably – "Follow me." We followed him upstairs and he opened a door.

"This is the Queen's toilet – as the West Wing is being redecorated I suppose you'll have to use it."

'We all got in, it was a large room, and lit our cigarettes and took our turns, but then we couldn't find the chain to flush. The Equerry returned to find the place full of smoke. "Tch, tch!" he said, "you could all be shot according to the ancient laws of the land!" I told him we couldn't find the chain, and with a sigh he went up to the lavatory, which had two lionesses for arms, pressed the nose of one and flushed the pan.

'We were then led through room after room to the Throne room, where stood the King with a senior officer from each of the three Services. For us, an Admiral had to hand each decoration on a velvet cushion to the King, who then put it on a hook already sewn in place on our tunics. A petty officer had rehearsed us for this every time we were in harbour. The drill was to take three paces forward, receive the medal, take three paces back and say "Thank you, Your Majesty." Being a small man I found that after three paces I was still not within the King's reach, so I had to shuffle up to him. The King began: "I-I-I-. . . .h-h-h-h-h. . . . " He took ages to get the words out and they were very embarrassing moments for all of us. When he finished at last, I boobed and said: "Thank you, sir – I mean, Your Majesty." As for Commander Hammond, he fell over the cushion going backwards.'

Coxswains John Bird of *Ray of Hope* and Harry Bunce of *Silver Dawn* were each awarded the DSM. The decoration of Coxswain Bunce was memorable in that he was the only man in the war to have two actual DSMs pinned to his chest. He was presented with the first one by the Duke of Kent. Not long afterwards Bunce marched out on to a parade ground again to be presented with a second DSM, all because of a records department mix-up. Humour never being far from bravery he treated it all as a huge joke, one he told rather than the citation for his award – that, although a poor swimmer, he had dived into the sea and saved two lives.

After the decorations there was an unkind relegation for another vessel of the flotilla. It happened this way. One day when the drifter *Formidable* got into port, her skipper, the ship not having had any mail for some time, sent his leading hand across to the mail office. After an hour or so had passed he began to get anxious, but eventually the leading hand reappeared, towing a GPO trolley piled high with letters and parcels. *Formidable*'s skipper looked up incredulously from the bridge of his little drifter, which lay well below the level of the jetty. 'Hell!' he exclaimed – 'That's a lot of mail for eight men!'

Eagerly they pulled the mail on board and sorted it, only to find that not one letter bore the name of a member of the crew. Suddenly they realised that all the letters and parcels were addressed not to His Majesty's Drifter *Formidable*, but to His Majesty's Ship *Formidable* – a newly launched aircraft carrier. Despondently they had to tie the mail up again in neat bundles, rebag it and get it on its way to the proper vessel.

Shortly afterwards *Formidable*'s skipper received instructions that, to avoid further confusion, his ship was being renamed ... *Fidget*. It was a blow from which he never fully recovered.

4

Where's Namsos?

One day in April 1940 as signals, far too many of them for his inadequate staff to decipher, kept streaming in from the Fleet, the harassed Duty Commander at Combined Operations Headquarters at Donibristle, Fifeshire, suddenly spotted the name of "Namsos" mentioned in one of them. Puzzled, he checked the big operational map on the wall, but Namsos was not there. The map stopped halfway up Norway.

'Good God!' he exclaimed – 'it's not even on the map Anybody got a map of Norway?'

Someone produced a school atlas, and they found it. Namsos, a small coastal town about 100 miles north of German-held Trondheim.

If the Combined Ops staff knew little about Namsos, the non-fishermen among the crews of the trawlers hurriedly despatched there knew even less. But they were soon to find out as a strong contingent of ships of Harry Tate's Navy took on their first major concerted action of the war. In all some thirty trawlers joined in with the Fleet of warships to aid the British Expeditionary Force sent belatedly to assist the Norwegians against the fast advancing Germans. The British troops landed north of captured Trondheim at Namsos, Narvik and Harstad, and south at Aandalsnes. The trawlers were to provide anti-submarine protection for the troopships and also to help ferry the troops ashore. But as it transpired, in one of the swiftest turnabouts of the war, they were soon to revert to the more dismal role of assisting the hasty evacuation of Norway.

Eight big trawlers of the 15th and 16th Anti-Submarine Striking Force sailed from Scotland to Namsos to find that it wasn't very much of a place at all. White wooden houses and a wooden pier, reached twenty miles up Namsen Fiord; a small fishing and timber town whose inhabitants were far fewer than the 5,000 Allied troops landed there. In the course of a week's bitter fighting, however, Namsos became an inferno, and three trawlers were so badly damaged by the fierce attacks of German bombers that they had to be abandoned and sunk.

During the hours of daylight the slow moving trawlers everywhere in the Norwegian operation were constant targets for the marauding enemy planes. At each alert the ships would make at full speed for the nearest cliffs under which they could shelter, thanks to the deep water even at the edge of the fiords. Wherever possible, crews went briefly ashore to chop down small firs and branches from the larger trees, and uproot evergreen shrubs; all the greenery was then draped over the decks and rigging as a camouflage against the searching bombers. Soon a number of trawlers were steaming about the fiords looking like mobile Christmas trees. But still their losses mounted under the relentless air attacks.

Here, there and everywhere in the thick of events at Namsos, was the Hull trawler *Arab*, commanded by Lieutenant Richard Stannard, RNR, an ex-merchant officer. *Arab* was always at hand to aid her sister ships in trouble and she also rescued the survivors of a bombed and burning sloop. Her outstanding moment came when Lieutenant Stannard put his trawler against the blazing pier at Namsos and resolutely fought the fire that threatened any moment to ignite an ammunition dump and send it sky high. For this action Stannard won the VC – the second naval VC of the war – together with awards for four of his crew.

After the week of desperate fighting Namsos was evacuated. On the last day at the battered town only three trawlers remained to nose alongside the shattered pier in the dark and ferry the remainder of the French troops aboard the waiting transports and a warship. Then a stop to bury the dead, including the commander of one of the trawlers, before moving off for operations elsewhere.

Meanwhile, more than 300 miles north of Namsos, *Northern Spray* and other trawlers had arrived at the naval and army operational headquarters at Harstad. They were under air attack within half an hour of their arrival, and saw half the jetty blown away. The advancing Germans, they were told, were already 'just over the hill', while to the south, in bitterly contested Narvik, there were some two thousand of the enemy and more arriving hourly. *Northern Spray*'s captain, Lieutenant-Commander D. J. B. Jewitt, RN, was group commander of the five trawlers including *Spray*, which formed the 12th Anti-Submarine Striking Force. He stationed two trawlers in Vest

Fiord, the main approach to Narvik, to observe movements and challenge any vessels moving in or out, the latter proving to be refugee craft carrying escaping Norwegians.

The trawlers generally remained stationary, sheltering under the high cliffs to escape attack from the enemy planes which swooped down in the pale light of the midnight sun.

Northern Spray took up patrol in calm and broad Ofot Fiord with her sister ship *Northern Gem*. Among *Gem*'s crew was young ex-trawlerman Sid Kerslake, RNR.

'*Spray* took the port side of the fiord and *Gem* the starboard. This became our regular beat, with an occasional run into Lödingen in the Lofoten Islands, for coaling and supplies. Once, while we were alongside at Lödingen, the alarm went and we tumbled on deck to see a Hurricane chasing a German plane. We were delighted to see the frantic enemy fly straight into a cliff face, and wildly cheered the Hurricane as it flew back performing a victory roll.

'Shortly after this, when patrolling Ofot Fiord in the early morning in thickly falling snow, we received a signal that destroyers and a heavy unit, believed to be hostile, were moving up the fiord. We were ordered to challenge them. Some time later we were horrified to see these ships emerge out of the snow. But challenge them we did, in true naval fashion, being greatly relieved to find that it was the *Warspite* with her covering force of destroyers on the way to stir things up in Narvik. This they proceeded to do almost every morning with clockwork regularity, and it made us feel safer to know they were around. It gave us all a great feeling of patriotism, for at this early stage of the war it was still a sort of game and we did not realise that people actually could be killed – you always thought it couldn't happen to you.'

Hearing the heavy gunfire and seeing all the naval vessels going about their deadly business set *Northern Spray*'s Commander Jewitt stamping impatiently about the bridge. At last he could bear it no longer. He ordered: 'Hoist battle ensign and get all H.E. ammunition up at the ready,' and set course for Narvik. There was mist, smoke and snow all around. Soon a warship signalled *Spray*: 'What ship and what do you want?'

Jewitt answered: '*Northern Spray* – am coming to join in the bombardment.'

Back came the reply: 'Fuck off!'

And there was the passing sloop that took a good look at *Spray*'s camouflage of fir trees and signalled: 'The decorations look pretty – when is the wedding?'

But *Spray* and *Gem* were soon involved in an action of their own. Seaman Kerslake: 'On the evening of May 8 we were having tea in *Gem* when the alarm went and a German plane shot over the mountains on *Spray's* side of the fiord. *Spray* fired a fierce burst at it, but by the time it was in sight of her it was also past her, as both ships lay within feet of the shore edge and were almost overhung by the sheer rock walls. From *Gem* we saw that one of the plane's engines was on fire and smoking badly. We gave the plane a full broadside from our two twin-Lewis guns, all we had time for before it passed over and disappeared beyond the steep rock wall, losing height rapidly.

'*Gem* signalled: "Have you seen our bird?" To which *Spray* replied: "You mean OUR bird!" The plane was obviously making for Narvik, so the trawler crews stood down and went back to their tea. An hour later a Norwegian "puffer" – a small motor fishing boat – entered the fiord and went alongside *Spray*. It was crewed by three Norwegians who, unable to speak English got their message across with the greatest difficulty: they had seen the plane come down and would take men from the trawlers to the spot, which was just by Ae Fiord, not far away. Lieutenant-Commander Jewitt decided to put half a dozen men from each trawler aboard the puffer, with orders to capture any survivors and bring back confidential books and codes; the plane was assumed to have a crew of about three. The seamen concerned were not asked to volunteer, they just happened to be about on deck at the time and all were very keen to go.' *Gem*'s contingent included Seaman Kerslake.

'We were armed with .303 rifles and wore our tin hats, but on a lovely evening we had on only various old clothes, myself wearing a fisherman's jersey and a muffler and ordinary shoes. After all, it was always flat calm in the fiord, no need for seaboots, and we were only going after a crashed plane's crew – or so we thought.

'The puffer nosed down the fiord and we lost sight of our two trawlers on turning into Ae Fiord. After a few twists and turns we rounded a small headland and there was the aircraft. It had crash-landed on the island shore with part of its port wing under water. The ground from the shore rose up 2,000 feet and was covered with fir trees and bushes, rocks and snow. If there were any survivors from the plane they were somewhere in hiding.

'*Gem*'s gunner, Fred Powell, a retired RN gunner called back to service, lay on deck on the puffer with his Lewis gun resting on the stem-post, covering the area. We nosed into the shore, but the boat touched bottom some six yards from dry land, so we had to jump in and wade ashore with the water up to our waists. Eight of us followed in line behind the officer-in-charge from *Spray*, a small, bespectacled skipper from Grimsby.

'We were laughing and joking about our unexpected "paddle" when Gunner Powell suddenly shouted: "They're up on the hill – I'll give them a burst over their heads!" I guess he thought they would then give themselves up, but he had only fired a few rounds before the Germans opened up with a Spandau firing explosive bullets and blew away half his head.

'Our shore party dived across the shingle for the sheltering rocks, the enemy bullets whistling over our heads. I levelled my rifle at a German up on the hill, but in the excitement I hadn't slipped the safety-catch. In the second or so before I could release it, Jack Sullivan, *Gem*'s asdic operator, said urgently: 'Don't look now, Sid, but there's a dirty big Jerry behind you!' I then felt a bayonet at my back, and that was it. We all surrendered, being overwhelmed by German Troops. Too late it was realised that the plane was a troop carrier and their casualties on crashing had been small. But one of us did escape. This was our officer, who hid in the water behind some rocks and later crawled away unseen.'

All three Norwegians aboard the puffer were killed by the German's hail of fire, leaving the boat going round in circles. Every other man on board – all from *Spray* – was wounded, some very seriously, but despite being shot up in both ankles, and in great pain, Asdic Rating Sid Gledhill courageously struggled into the wheelhouse, pulled aside a dead Norwegian whose body was jammed in the wheel, and steered the boat away.

Seaman Kerslake: 'It was all over in minutes. We saw the puffer disappearing stern first out of the fiord, and the Germans gathered our rifles and threw them in the water. Then they searched us. They were a company of crack Alpine troops from a Jaeger battalion, thirty-five strong, plus the plane's crew. Taking us up to the top of the hill, where they had set up an emergency camp, they got a fire going and gave us some bread and a hot drink of ersatz coffee. After being questioned we were allowed to settle down on the ground on rocks that were free of snow. We were all bitterly cold and shivering as our wet clothes were beginning to freeze on us, but we would have felt far worse had we known that the survivors on the puffer, on their return, reported that we had all been killed.'

The plane had initially been damaged by a Skua aircraft from the *Ark Royal*. The German pilot. although with one leg completely shattered, had brought the plane down to a forced landing just short of the water's edge without a single extra casualty. They had then made their high camp commanding a clear view of the plane far below, and the entrance to the fiord.

Seaman Kerslake: 'We had been in the camp for about three hours when we saw a British destroyer come in and land a party of Marines. At this the Germans decided it was time to be off. The Unteroffizier gave us German greatcoats to warm us, and ordered us to carry their equipment, including guns, boxes and bandoliers of ammunition, and the machine-gun. We were warned that we would be shot if we tried to escape, after which we began a march inland across the hills. The Germans planned to strike directly across the island to a tiny village on its opposite coast, where they hoped to seize a boat to take them to the mainland. And so we set out, the wounded pilot being carried on a door from the plane rigged up as a makeshift stretcher.

'All the time we marched a brutal-looking little man in uniform took photographs. An officer of the plane's crew told me this was the Nazi of the group, and they all had to jump to his orders. He warned that if we tried to escape the Nazi would kill even those who made no attempt to do so. When we had walked a considerable distance waist-deep in snow, crossing streams of icy water, I was desperate for a "slash" and asked permission from this crewman. He told me not to be more than a minute or he would be obliged to shoot, as my move would be taken as an attempt to escape. I had my quickest "slash" ever! Afterwards we talked as we marched and he told me he had flown to London in civil aircraft pre-war and liked London very much.

'It was daylight when we reached the opposite coast, and to their dismay the Germans saw that *Northern Spray* had rounded the island and was steaming at sea off the village shore. She opened fire and shells began thudding into the hillside above us, far too close for the nerves of the Germans. They hurriedly put us in a shepherd's hut together with their wounded flyer, and cleared off. We lay low during the shelling. At last it stopped and we heard rifle and machine-gun fire close by.

'Our signalman in *Gem*, Charlie Keen, opened the hut door cautiously, and there facing him was a hefty Marine with bayonet fixed, all ready to skewer him. 'A bloody Jerry!' yelled the Marine, and only Charlie's dire mouthful in the most violent English caused him to stop the bayonet in mid-air. We all ran out waving madly and shouting that we were British matelots.'

Events had moved swiftly since the return of the puffer, which was a distressing scene. In the darkened hours of late evening, Telegraphist Eric Bardsley, of *Northern Spray*, had looked down on its arrival from the trawler's wheelhouse veranda.

'From the returning boat came a flashed SOS, repeated again and again. Commander Jewitt was suspicious and ordered the gun crews to cover the boat. When it arrived alongside, the scene on board was one of utter shambles and horror. *Gem*'s gunner lay dead in the bows, and the three Norwegians, all dead, were jammed in the wheelhouse. There was blood everywhere, with every man aboard wounded and in pain. Our own gunlayer had a nasty wound in his back, and Sid Gledhill, who had been sending the SOSs, was suffering from the wounds in his ankles. Seaman Yardley was shot in the leg, while Seaman Wood had a huge hole in his back and was carried aboard spreadeagled with his shirt off, showing all the extent of the hole. He called out jokingly to his helpers, "They got me, pal!" Harry Peak, a Hull fisherman, was the worst injured, he had been raked by bullets and the whole side of him from thigh to ankle was laid open.

'We now had six badly wounded men aboard with only rudimentary medical supplies and medical knowledge, so we had to act quickly. We made for Lödingen, which was only a few miles away, towing the damaged puffer to hand over to the Norwegians there. We flashed the sloop *Stork* for a doctor, but her reply was that we should proceed to Skanland. We did so and found the *Resolution*, flagship of the FOIC Narvik. It took us two hours to reach her with our badly wounded laid out in the wardroom. Harry Peak was in a dreadful state, stretched out on a couch. Ramsden was kneeling beside him and saying: "Harry, can't we harmonise 'Somewhere In France With You'?" and in spite of his great pain Harry managed to sing it with his chum.

'All the wounded were taken aboard *Resolution* while 150 Marines came aboard *Spray* with the object of rounding up the German force. The question was, where had they gone, and how? It was a desolate, untracked area. The major in charge of the Marines guessed that they would try to obtain a boat, so we went along Ae Fiord inquiring at each village, but without result. We almost gave up, but then decided to visit a small, uninhabited place called Skjellesvik, on the far side, and there we found the Germans up on the hillside. The Marines put ashore parties which made a pincer movement on the hut, another squad approaching from the rear in case of escape that way. From *Spray* we could see them crawling up the ground on either side of the hut while the gunners on board fired thousands of rounds from the Maxim at anything else ashore that moved. The Germans were seen leaving the hut and moving up the mountainside, and when the hut was stormed the Marines found only the prisoners from *Gem* and the wounded pilot.

'During this action we received a signal from *Resolution*, "Where are the Royal Marines?" so on our way back we signalled a brief report. We reached *Resolution* to find the Marine Band on deck playing "Life On The Ocean Wave" and all on deck gave three cheers for the Royal Marines and the RNR. At this moment an enemy plane flew over and was shot down by *Resolution*'s ack-ack guns, at which there were three more cheers!

'Poor Harry Peak died after having his leg amputated, and he was buried in a civil ceremony at Skolund. We now had a very depleted ship's company of only 22 fit men.'

As for the Germans, the Marines captured nearly all of them and handed them over to a company of French Alpine troops. Seaman Kerslake: 'The French, we learned later, stood all thirty-four Germans up against the rocks and shot them, their explanation being that they did not take prisoners.'

Next day *Northern Gem* was ordered to shell the island village, in case any more Germans were in hiding. This she did with her ancient World War I four-inch, also spraying Lewis gun shot over the entire area. But there was no sign of a living thing until suddenly a Norwegian puffer appeared from the land side of the jetty and made off at speed along the coast. *Gem* hailed her to stop but she did not, so the trawler gave chase and fired a warning shot across her bow.

Seaman Kerslake: 'The puffer then came alongside us, throwing out a line for'ard and another aft, which we made fast. Our replacement gunner, together with a seaman and an officer – our leader on the plane party – dropped on board the vessel to investigate for Germans. But immediately they set foot on deck the man in the puffer's little bridge put his engines full ahead and simultaneously the two men at the ropes cut them through – and away she went.

'We dared not shoot for fear of hitting our own men, who were fiercely attacked with knives and axes by five Germans (so we thought) dressed as fishermen. Eventually our three men, after shooting two of the attackers, jumped overboard. As we picked up the gunner he laughed, said "Thanks", and died immediately. The seaman was severely cut, but our bespectacled officer was a terrible sight. He had been chopped with an axe right between the shoulder blades, and there it stuck. Our deck ran with blood, and it was a miracle he survived.

'We chased after the puffer, firing with machine-gun and Oerlikon until she stopped. She was riddled like a cullender when we drew alongside, there were four dead men on deck and another shot to bits in the wheelhouse, which had been blasted to a shambles. This time our men who boarded the boat did so with caution, and hearing a noise down in the foc'sle one man fired a round down the hatch and yelled: 'Come up – out, out!' At this a very old man and a very old woman came up on deck, followed by a young woman carrying a baby in her arms.

'I can't describe the silence that followed. I thought all the crew were going to cry – I certainly felt like it myself. We brought the frightened trio and the child on to the *Gem* and sank the puffer. Only after questioning did we learn that the old people and the young mother and baby were the survivors of two families of Norwegians joined by marriage. When we had fired on the village their menfolk thought we were Germans and decided they should all make a dash for it in the boat. Why they had not recognised our White Ensign was a mystery.

'One of the men we had killed was the young woman's husband. We had a whip-round the crew for her, it was all we could do.'

On *Northern Spray* in the quiet hours of the night they began to pick up German wireless transmissions in morse. Regularly every night at 2 a..m the same station broadcast a half-hour "programme" in the German language and in groups of cyphers, always signing off with "Heil Hitler." Telegraphist Ken Edwards, with his schoolboy knowledge of German, managed to understand one word in twelve and also recognised Norwegian place names from that area. The first part of each message appeared to be in the form of a navigational report, the word *fyr*, Norwegian for lighthouse or lightbuoy, being repeated often, while the last part of the broadcast seemed to be a weather report. Commander Jewitt was informed, and at the next 2 a.m. "broadcast" *Spray*'s wireless cabin was filled with people listening in with the loudspeaker switched on. At a guess, they placed the transmitting station as being about twenty miles away. Commander Jewitt alerted *Resolution*.

One night shortly afterwards, as *Spray* was alongside a small village, the German station came in as usual and "flooded the dial" – they were right on top of it. *Resolution* took a "fix" with direction-finding equipment, and confirmed that the mystery station was in the village. The next night an armed party went ashore and captured the enemy operator, a Norwegian fifth columnist. Jewitt was complimented on the vigilance of his wireless staff, which might well have saved the lives of many troops in the hard fighting which was still going on.

For both *Northern Spray* and *Northern Gem* there now followed a welcome break from weeks of almost ceaseless patrol, as each ship went for a week's boiler clean at Svolvaer, the chief town of the Lofoten Islands. Here the friendly and hospitable people could not do enough for the trawler crews, and there were parties galore during their stay. *Northern Gem's* arrival at Svolvaer was auspicious enough. All her ammunition spent, she was about a mile from the port when an enemy bomber zoomed to the attack. The trawler could only retaliate by firing starshells from her four-inch, but fortunately this was enough to drive away the German. *Gem* drew in to the dockside to be greeted by most of Svolvaer's inhabitants, who had watched the duel. They were led by the smiling mayor, who presented the trawler's skipper with the case of one of the star-shells she had fired; it had landed in the local cemetery close to where the mayor and his friends had stood watching the fight at sea.

The hospitality of the people of Svolvaer made *Gem*'s return to Svolvaer soon afterwards, during the evacuation from Norway, all the more bleak.

The trawler was ordered to escort to the UK a small Norwegian passenger ship, the *Ranen*. This coastal vessel had become a buccaneering auxiliary of the Royal Navy armed with Oerlikon and Bofors guns and crewed by an enthusiastic motley of naval ratings, Marines and soldiers. She was skippered by Commander Sir Geoffrey Congreve, RN, who had promptly taken the ship over after losing his trawler, the *Aston Villa*, to enemy bombs.

Ranen and *Gem* left Lödingen together, steaming out of Vest Fiord with the object of doing as much damage as they could to what was now virtually enemy held territory.

As they approached Svolvaer *Gem* was challenged and fired on by a vessel which seemed to be an enemy trawler. *Gem* replied immediately with her starshells and started a fire on her attacker, at which the mystery ship went behind some rocks and vanished completely; neither *Gem* nor *Ranen* could discover any further sign of her, or any wreckage.

The two ships then steamed to Svolvaer and, with *Ranen*'s

piratical crew in their element, pumped lead and shell into the harbour installations, blowing up all the oil tanks and setting fire to the jetties. Then, the very last ships to leave the Narvik area, they started off for home.

Halfway across the North Sea a dozen enemy planes, evidently ignoring the *Ranen*, swooped down on *Gem* and for the next five hours gave her hell. Time after time the planes, in turn, roared over her, dropping a single bomb on each run – and missing. Finally one plane dropped low to the sea and made two vicious wave-top machine-gun attacks, spraying the decks, windows and waterpipes and wrecking both the trawler's smallboats, but incredibly in this hail of explosive bullets containing tiny steel darts, and with one twin-Lewis out of action, *Gem* did not suffer a single casualty.

Her luckiest escape of all came when the frustrated enemy plane flew low again and dropped what looked to be an aerial torpedo about twelve feet long; as *Gem* heaved over to starboard the menacing object literally slid down her port bow – if the ship had rolled to port instead, it would have dropped square on the foc's'le head and probably finished her. The plane flew off with smoke pouring from one engine – a good hit from *Gem*'s Oerlikon, bolted to railway sleepers on the foredeck.

And so back to the UK. Both *Gem* and *Ranen* were supposed to steam for Scapa, but *Gem*'s skipper quickly knocked that instruction on the head. As he acidly observed: 'Once you get to that damn place you never know when you'll get out!" So instead he headed for Aberdeen, where his war-weary crew secured an immediate two weeks leave.

Fourteen trawlers were lost in the Norwegian campaign, all falling victim to enemy planes. Among those were some so badly damaged that they could not make the crossing home and had to be sunk by British forces. The Germans, however, were able later to salvage seven of the trawlers and sail them again under the enemy flag.

One of the earliest losses was the *Larwood*, sunk at Narvik, and one of her wounded survivors was none other than Ted the Bastard – Chief Petty Officer Edward Pugh, back at sea again as a relief from suffering the raw recruits at the Nest. He escaped the Germans and came back to Britain in the cruiser HMS *Glasgow*, which brought King Haakon and Crown Prince Olaf to safety.

On the lighter side was a cameo of Harry Tate's Navy retained by men of the warships. When all the destroyers were speeding out of Ramsdal Fiord, a trawler signalman with a small, battery-operated signal lamp stood on top of one of the cliffs asking the first destroyer for instructions for the asdic trawlers. Owing to the speed of the destroyers and slowness of his signalling, each destroyer down the line got a piece of the message. . . .

As a further instance of what the individual trawlers went through there was the *St Cathan*, which survived no fewer than twenty-nine attacks by enemy bombers while operating in Vest Fiord. *St Cathan* went to Norway armed with one Lewis gun, 350 rounds of ammunition, and her four-inch. Like several others she came away loaded with guns, her crew armed to the teeth; and with other "loot" besides. For with the Army retreating so fast, culminating in the complete evacuation of Norway, equipment of all kinds had to be abandoned – headquarters gear, the contents of officers' messes, radios, staff cars, and a whole assortment of supplies. Much of this abandoned gear was hustled on board by trawlers taking off Allied personnel and Norwegians wanting to escape to the UK. Towards the end the scramble of men and goods became chaotic.

Fitted carpets found their way on to trawlers' messdecks; even Austin motor cars of the wartime utility type were swung aboard and later used by the ship's officers – until reclaimed. Some other items came from shattered shops and buildings, for in Jack's fair reasoning nothing was stolen but merely saved from the advancing enemy.

When *Arab*, the VC trawler, steamed triumphantly back to her base at Belfast it was her multitude of scroungings that seized the eye. A seaman who saw her come in describes the fantastic sight.

'She came into Pollock Basin late one grey day, to the whistles and cheers of trawlers tied all around, a heroine ship, with the star performer on the bridge, the captain himself. But the really interesting thing was her appearance, for she looked like a Robinson's removal van. One forgot to look at the bullet holes, the dangling radio aerial and halyards and other marks of battle, because rivalling them in attention, and in the end completely overshadowing them, were the contents which this pantechnicon from Norway had brought back with her.

'She looked like a second-hand shop, with every conceivable item of movable equipment loaded all over her decks. On the well-deck some musical matelot strummed out "The Fleet's In Port Again" on a brand new grand piano. Leaning against it were numerous new motor cycles and next to them some prams. The remaining welldeck space was thickly covered with tables, chairs, mattresses, rolls of lino, deck chairs, and all the contents of an ironmonger's shop. More gear lined the port and starboard gangways and the after end, with the lighter, smaller bits stacked up all over the engineroom casing. But all this was extra to what was hidden below decks, where enough was stored to start up several shops.'

The humour, however, could not disguise the melancholy at the sudden withdrawal. As Telegraphist Bardsley of *Northern Spray* noted: 'We are amazed by the news that units of the Navy, the NWEF, and certain French and Norwegian army units are being completely withdrawn from Northern Norway. Narvik has been destroyed by the Allied forces so as to render it useless to the Germans for some time to come. A great proportion of Germany's light naval forces are at the bottom of the fiords and scores of her planes lie wrecked on the mountains, but the cost has been heavy for us, too. History may never know of many of the gallant deeds done on bleak mountainside or along the calm fiords, but from French Foreign Legionnaire to Grimsby trawlerman, all have put their whole heart and soul into the bitter struggle to save Norway.'

The trawlers' last loss of the campaign came with the tragic end in action of *Juniper*. On June 7 *Juniper*, commanded by Lieutenant-Commander Geoffrey Grenfell, RN, sailed from Tromso, far north of Narvik, escorting the tanker *Oil Pioneer*. At dawn next day she sighted heavy warships, and wirelessed an urgent signal reporting her discovery. Then, ordering the tanker to sail independently, she bravely turned and challenged the big ships. Back came the reply from one of them that she was the British cruiser *Southampton*. But she was not, she was the German *Hipper*, and her heavy guns proceeded to blast *Juniper* out of the water. Only four of her Patrol Service crew survived, and were rescued from the water along with a score of men from the tanker, to be taken to German prison camps.

Even before the tragedy of *Juniper*, however, other ships and men of Harry Tate's Navy were fighting and dying in a bigger and more dismal evacuation. Dunkirk.

5

'Gracie Fields is Making Water'

In May 1940 the five wooden herring drifters of 'Vernon's Private Navy' were all together again at Ramsgate, but working under the temporary command of Lieutenant-Commander A. J. Cubison, RN. He was a man with an orderly turn of mind and, unlike his predecessor, decided that his first duty was to organise the flotilla on proper RN lines. This included trying to improve the drifters' rather haphazard system of communicating with each other at sea.

Signalman Bev Smith of *Fisher Boy*: 'I was landed with the job of devising a simple code of signals that the skippers could easily understand. I managed to compile one and it was typed out by Commander Cubison's secretary. To give some idea of its extreme simplicity, the signal flag letter "A" meant "Form single line ahead," while flag "C" followed by a number gave the true course on which to steam; and so on.

'Having distributed the code to all the skippers, Commander Cubison importantly hoisted his first signal somewhere off Ramsgate harbour, and sure enough the drifters got into a line. He then hoisted a course signal. The response was that some of the ships altered course as soon as the signal was hoisted, while some decided to stay in line and change course in line ahead. The result was that in an astonishingly short time he had the five ships of the Mine Recovery Flotilla spread out from the North Foreland pretty well to Dover. But he wasn't deterred and tried two or three times to get these signals right, though really with little success. Shortly afterwards we had other things to think about when little coasters from Holland and Belgium started to arrive in Ramsgate harbour carrying a mixture of civilians and Dutch and Belgian seamen. We heard that things weren't going too well in France.

'One day Commander Cubison was observed standing on the steps of his office with a handkerchief in each hand, waving like fury at our little fleet moored across the other side of the harbour. Someone alerted me to the fact that the Commander was "doing something a bit odd on the steps" and I realised he must be trying to send a semaphore message. It read: "All ships raise steam immediately and prepare for sea." He came down to us very soon afterwards, had a quick word with the skippers, then joined *Lord Cavan* and hoisted his now famous signal "A" – "Form single line ahead." We steamed out perfectly and took a short cut across the Channel, regardless of minefields, to Dunkirk harbour.

'We were to go in, bring off British troops and load them on to transports which would be lying off Dunkirk. When we got into the Dunkirk Roads there were some noisy bangs and flashes which had us all pretty frightened. With the sky lit up from the glare of burning fuel storage tanks, our flotilla milled about off the harbour, undecided. I was at the helm of *Fisher Boy* with little Skipper George Brown standing beside me. *Fidget* closed us and her anxious skipper hailed across to ours: "What are you going to do, George?" Promptly George Brown pushed his head out of the bridge window and bawled: "I'm a-going in, boy!" And with that he told me to bring *Fisher Boy* well over and we steamed for the harbour, the other drifters deciding to follow us in.

'I was smoking Craven A cigarettes and gave one to Skipper Brown, who, I noticed, was trembling violently. He popped the cigarette into his mouth the wrong way round and made three attempts to light the corked tip end before I saw what he was doing and told him to reverse the cigarette. He was an amazing man. I was just as frightened as him – we all were; none of us knew what had happened so far at Dunkirk and for all we knew the harbour was already occupied by German troops. But George Brown always visibly shook with fright in such cases, which made it even more courageous the way he would go into any danger. I never knew him to do anything other than carry out his instructions, regardless of how he felt at the time. He was a very brave man.

'It was something of an anti-climax getting into Dunkirk harbour. We managed to make fast to the mole, then looked around for soldiers but couldn't find any. However, we worked our way down into the general harbour installations, found some troops and encouraged them to come aboard. They were very weary and were glad to join us. Our cook was kept busy making tea for thirsty mouths. We finally left the harbour with about 250 troops crammed aboard and went out to find one of the transports supposed to be waiting outside. Seeing the silhouette of a ship in the distance we steered for her, and promptly went aground on a sandbank. Too late we found that the ship had been hit and abandoned, and was in fact sunk. Fortunately the tide was making, so we came off the sandbank without too much trouble.

'George Brown now searched around to see if any other ships were available, and finding none, decided we'd have to take the troops back to Ramsgate ourselves. We were all relieved to get back and see the troops safely ashore, but were none too happy when a naval officer ordered us to load up again with stores and get back to Dunkirk forthwith. This we did, in daylight, and though we had a few shocks we made the crossing without harm. This time we took scaling ladders made by Ramsgate carpenters to help the troops climb down from the mole on to our little drifters.

'By now Commander Cubison had established the *Lord Cavan* in Dunkirk harbour as a command vessel, and was terribly busy about the place. I was up on the mole with him and two or three others, trying to encourage more troops to come aboard down the scaling ladders, when we heard sudden great crashes and bangs as the German big guns shelled the harbour. The troops, being quite used to this by now, smartly dropped flat on their faces – and as we felt they knew what they were doing, we got down beside them pretty quickly. But Commander Cubison remained standing amid the shellfire and gave us one hell of a coating – told us to get up and get on with it. He seemed to have absolutely no fear at all, in fact one almost felt he revelled in things getting so lively. We loaded troops aboard *Fisher Boy* until it was impossible to move anywhere on deck or to remove the scaling ladders from the mole, so we just steamed away leaving them there.

'*Fisher Boy* was still in one piece when we got back to Ramsgate on this run, though the main steam valve was leaking badly and I doubt if we were making more than four knots. We were terribly low in the water with all the troops on board, but fortunately the weather was calm and somehow or other we stayed afloat. The troops sat on their haunches and as a destroyer raced by, her wash caused us to roll, the water seeped on to our deck and thoroughly soaked their backsides; but they were so packed that they were unable to stand up, and too tired to worry much about it anyway.

'All our drifters were by this time working independently.

Silver Dawn struck an obstacle in Dunkirk harbour which took a chip out of her propeller, and she vibrated and throbbed in the most hair-raising fashion all the way back to Ramsgate, but they got their troops back.'

It was *Silver Dawn*'s only trip to Dunkirk because of this damage.

'Things were now getting too lively to continue going into Dunkirk in daylight so the rest of *Fisher Boy*'s trips were timed so that we arrived after dusk. On each journey we took additional scaling ladders with us, as we were piling so many troops aboard that we could never recover the ladders. Night after night we steamed there stocked up with tea, cigarettes and full water tanks to recover our biggest possible quota of exhausted troops.'

The drifters had originally been instructed to limit their loads to a hundred men each, but this rule was forgotten from the start. The astonishing loads they did carry were made possible only by a generally calm sea.

At Dover the old minesweeping drifter *Nautilus* received orders to make for Dunkirk with her sister ship, the drifter *Comfort*. But they were only halfway across when they ran into trouble. Petty Officer Robert Muir, of *Nautilus*:

'It was a pitch black night and suddenly an E-boat loomed out of the darkness. We had the sauce to engage it with our full armament – one Lewis gun. I suppose it thought we weren't worth bothering with, for it pushed off at full speed. Our skipper was rather pleased with our performance, but shortly afterwards there was a terrific explosion and next moment there were men in the water screaming for help. We stopped and managed to pick up nine men as they were swept by us on the tide. *Comfort* picked up about sixteen. They were survivors from the destroyer HMS *Wakeful*; the same E-boat we had brushed with had put a couple of torpedoes into her. Her captain was among the survivors picked up by *Comfort*.'

Wakeful had been returning from Dunkirk with a load of troops below decks when she was struck amidships. She broke in half and sank immediately, taking most of her hundreds of soldiers down with her.

Comfort was ordered to take her survivors back to Dover, but in a night of chaos she was doomed to be the victim of a terrible confusion. Shortly after the sinking of *Wakeful* the destroyer *Grafton* was similarly torpedoed, and she and the Fleet minesweeper *Lydd* both opened fire on *Comfort*, thinking the drifter to be an E-boat. Finally *Lydd* rammed *Comfort* and the drifter's men were fired on in the sea. It was a cruel and ghastly mess. The captain of *Wakeful* was picked up from the sea for the second time that night; there were few other survivors from *Comfort*.

Nautilus escaped the horror because her orders were to carry on to Dunkirk and put her survivors aboard the cruiser *Calcutta*. Petty Officer Muir:

'We located the *Calcutta* and went alongside her to discharge our survivors. We hadn't been alongside for many minutes when she decided to fire an eight-inch broadside inland. I was down in the mess having breakfast when she fired the first rounds. We were lying right below her after turret, the messdeck hatch open, and the flashback seemed to come right down the hatch. I was up on deck in two seconds flat and after that went down again and changed myself.

'We pushed off inshore – *Nautilus* had a very small draught – and anchored off the beach. There were all sorts of craft around and lines of soldiers on the beach, and we could see there wasn't much organisation at that time. Stukas were dive-bombing and machine-gunning everything in sight. We were lying close to the destroyer *Greyhound* and her captain decided to go ashore to try to get things organised, so my mate and I were detailed to take our smallboat and ferry him to the beach, bringing back a few soldiers on the return journey. Away we went, nursing a jar of rum in the bottom of the boat. We arrived at the beach, put the captain ashore and never saw him again. We picked up four soldiers, all we could manage in the boat, gave them a good tot, had a couple ourselves and then made for *Nautilus*. But we arrived to find her ablaze from stem to stern, with ammunition shooting off all over the place. Apparently she was hit by a bomb in the engine room and had begun to sink, so the skipper set fire to the ship's papers down in the wardroom and the ship, being all wood, caught blaze. The crew were picked up by *Greyhound*.

'So my mate and I carried on and took our four troops to one of the paddlesweepers, then headed back to the beach for more. We got to within 200 yards of the beach when over came the Stukas again and a bit of shrapnel from one of the bombs they dropped went right through the boat's bottom and sank us. It was quite a swim, but we made sure to take the jar of rum with us, it was our saviour. We made the beach and found an abandoned lifeboat fitted with Robinson's gear – its propeller worked by man-power on the handles. We got this afloat, then had another good drink from the rum jar, which was getting pretty low by then. We picked up eight soldiers, set them to work on the handles turning the propeller, and got them across to the paddlesweeper with the others. We then turned the boat to go back for more, but were unlucky again, for as we neared the beach there was another raid and bang! – two holes in the boat and down we went. Once more we had to swim ashore – after rescuing the rum jar.

'We decided to empty the jar and look for something else that would float, but there was nothing. Then a small naval landing craft came in to the beach to pick up troops, and we asked its commander to take us as crew. We were lucky, he needed extra hands and we were detailed to drop the kedge-anchor aft so that the boat could pull itself off again after loading up. After about two or three trips I noticed that the commander kept taking a swig out of a bottle which I thought contained water, and being thirsty I asked if I could have a drop. He said certainly, and I had my first introduction to gin. He didn't get much more after that as my mate and I nearly cleared the lot.

'Conditions on the beach were getting worse; we saw soldiers go mad and threaten to stab their pals. Eventually our landing craft was almost out of fuel and had to cease operations. The commander had no room for us on the return crossing but offered to put us on board the paddlesweeper *Gracie Fields* to take us back to Dover. We said we'd rather go on another paddler, the *Sandown*, as she was due to sail about midnight, so he took us to her on his last trip. It was the best decision we ever made. We knew some of *Sandown*'s crew and they bedded us down in their quarters with a bottle and a couple of sandwiches. I didn't remember anything else until we arrived in Ramsgate and they told us that the *Gracie Fields* had been sunk on the crossing.'

No one was likely to forget the grimly humorous signal that went out above the hell of Dunkirk: 'Gracie Fields is making water in Dunkirk harbour and requires immediate assistance.'

She was one of some thirty river and seaside paddlesteamers which had been taken over to help with minesweeping, painted battleship grey and showing only a number. *Gracie* came with the first paddlesweepers on the scene, from Dover; they arrived each day at dusk, spent the early night hours filling up with troops and tried to sail before midnight.

It was on her second trip that *Gracie* was bombed by enemy planes and hit in her engine room. The old naval minesweeping sloop *Pangbourne*, returning to Dover jam-packed with troops, tried to tow her with the sweep wire but *Gracie*'s rudder jammed and she sank slowly. *Pangbourne* was able to save all her crew and passengers.

The paddler *Sandown* had a charmed life. On one occasion thirty-seven dive-bombers made a mass attack on her and failed to score a hit – though just one bomb would have been enough to sink her. And there was the old *Emperor of India*, another from *Gracie*'s flotilla, which made four trips to and from Dunkirk, once towing twenty small craft astern: lifeboats, yachts, motor boats, and a rowing boat with an outboard motor which had picked up two soldiers from the beach.

But other paddlers besides *Gracie* were lost. *Brighton Queen* went down under heavy gunfire, and *Devonia* was bombed and beached, while *Brighton Belle* struck a wreck on her first return passage. As she was sinking, another paddler from Dover, the *Medway Queen*, went alongside and took off survivors. The *Medway Queen* herself, in an unbroken week of nightly visits, brought a record 7,000 troops back to England.

A terrible disaster overtook *Waverley*, one of four paddle-sweepers from Harwich. On her first day, *Waverley* had embarked 600 troops and begun her return passage when twelve Heinkels swooped down on her in a concentrated attack. She fought back strongly, but a bomb struck her on the port quarter and crashed right through the bottom of the ship, leaving a gaping hole. The troops kept up rapid rifle fire and no more bombs hit the ship, but she would not answer to the wheel and began to sink rapidly by the stern. Within a minute of the order being given to abandon ship she had vanished, taking nearly 400 troops down with her. The survivors, including her captain, were picked up by a French destroyer and several drifters.

The three others of *Waverley*'s flotilla, *Marmion*, *Duchess of Fife* and *Oriole*, their crews working for four days and nights without sleep and almost without food, between them brought nearly 5,000 troops safely home. But yet another paddler, the *Crested Eagle* was lost, and her story comes later.

At Dover, Second Hand William Thorpe took over the trawler *Calvi* and steamed her to Dunkirk. To help him, he had the ready assistance of Sub-Lieutenant Everett, a very popular young officer fresh from officer's training at King Alfred. Thorpe took *Calvi* in and moored alongside the jetty with two other trawlers. But the berth quickly became *Calvi*'s grave, for in the heavy air raids which immediately followed she never really stood a chance.

The destroyer *Grenade*, berthed ahead of *Calvi*, was the first victim. In spite of all her guns she was soon severely hit and ablaze from stem to stern. *Calvi's* crew were among those who, in the confusion, helped to drag survivors from the oily water. Another of the trawlers managed to tow the blazing *Grenade* away from the jetty out into the harbour, where she continued to burn all night, erupting with frequent explosions until she finally sank. Before this, however, one of the trawlers with *Calvi*, the *Polly Johnson*, after being hit by bombs which killed her gun-crew, broke adrift and sank near the harbour entrance. And then *Calvi* herself began a fight for life. Second Hand Thorpe:

'I was firing the port Lewis gun, the steward loading the pans for me, when we saw a bunch of bombs coming down very close to us. We ran to take shelter in the wheelhouse, but as I opened the door to go in, the blast from the exploding bombs blew me inside, down the skipper's hatch, and before blacking out I saw everything in the cabin thrown up on the deckhead. I don't know how long I was unconscious, the next thing I heard was the steward calling me. By this time *Calvi* was near to settling on the bottom and we staggered out of the wheelhouse to find ourselves down in the water on a level with the rail of the next ship, the trawler *John Cattling*.

'A bomb had gone through *Calvi*'s counter-stern and exploded beneath her, and most of our crew had scattered. Our second engineer was in the water, and two men helped me to get him out. He was badly cut about and we stayed with him, giving him morphia tablets, till we got back to Dover in the *John Cattling*, which was well loaded up with soldiers. On muster we found we had lost only three of our company, including Sub-Lieutenant Everett. We had about forty troops aboard when we were hit, but what happened to them in the confusion we never knew.'

One of the three men missing from *Calvi* was Leading Seaman Ernest 'Lofty' Yallop. He escaped from the sinking trawler to find himself near the *Crested Eagle*. The paddler, heavily laden with troops, was about to push off and he had just time to swing his legs over the side and get aboard before she was away. Morale was low on *Crested Eagle*, two captured Germans were shot out of hand and the gunners had panicked and left their pom-poms as screaming, diving Stukas came down so low that their tails almost touched the water.

Yallop had just gone below decks when one of the planes dropped a bomb between the funnel and the engine room.

'There was a huge explosion and she started to turn over on

her side, making horrible noises. We were trapped as we stood, about thirty of us, for wreckage was strewn all over the funnel and the upper deck and we could not climb out. We all, sailors and survivors of other ships, put our arms round each other's shoulders and sang "Roll Out The Barrel." She continued to roll over to port, very slowly, with the sea creeping up to the closed portholes. Just when it seemed we were done for we managed to smash some portholes and let the air in. They worked like demons on deck to pull us up through the wreckage, the lucky ones of us. I got out to find a terrible mess. The troops had been packed tightly aboard so there was no escape from the bombing. When I came on deck it was like being in the fish hold of a trawler, except that it was humans squelching underfoot instead of fish. Blood ran everywhere and it was so slippery I could hardly keep my feet. I passed a soldier with a huge hole in his side, he was all screwed up and shaking his fist in the air at the Stukas. The ship was starting to go up in flames. Troops jumped for the water too quickly, putting their arms up in the air as they jumped, with the result that their lifejackets jerked up as they hit the water and broke their necks. A Dornier came down and machine-gunned those still alive, about thirty or forty of them, killing them as they struggled in the water.

'Sitting among the mess on deck I found Sub-Lieutenant Everett – he'd also managed to get to the paddler before she sailed. He was nursing a badly injured foot, but when I went to help him, waved me off, saying "I'm all right, Lofty – you look after yourself." The ship's bridge had gone. I scrambled to find the captain and asked him what I could do to help, but he said there was nothing that could be done and told me to get over the side immediately and try to swim across to a small troopship. As I jumped from *Crested Eagle* the flames were shooting high. After swimming for some distance I looked back and saw a man hanging on under the paddlers. It was my great pal, Johnny Stone, the ship's steward, and he couldn't swim. He was a man full of life and jokes, and now he clung on below the paddles, yelling for me to come back – I think he had hurt his spine. But I couldn't swim back to help him, it was impossible, with the ship already a blazing inferno. He kept calling to the end and I was helpless and could do nothing.'

Crested Eagle sank only minutes after *Calvi*, taking down with her more than 300 troops.

The armed fishing trawler *Gava*, her crew not yet Patrol Service men but still civilians, had just landed her catch at

Fleetwood, when she was told to steam for Ramsgate and there received naval orders to make for Dunkirk. Gunner Amos Sumner:

'It wasn't until we pulled nearer the bigger ships anchored outside that we felt the atmosphere of war. The noise of battle was loud and there was a lot of shouting. Our naval lieutenant ordered us into the harbour. There was a slight lull in the fighting as we went in, which was most uncanny. There were bodies floating all around among the debris.

'We tied up alongside the jetty and had begun to take on board the remnants of a French tank corps when suddenly there was a loud humming. We looked up and the sky seemed black with Stukas. While we were still loading the Frenchmen the planes began to dive-bomb us. It seemed a hopeless task but we kept blasting away with our old 12-pounder for all it was worth.

'I was only a lad and I was scared, and I certainly wasn't alone. Fortunately the Stukas didn't dive too low, and they took it in turns to run over us rather than coming down in force. Eventually they gave up, luckily for us, as we were getting flash-blind from the continual pounding of the gun. We were both surprised and delighted to learn afterwards that we had actually shot down three of the planes.

'We managed to rescue 376 French soldiers, but one French officer refused to sail with us. Nobody really knew why, it seemed he felt it more patriotic to remain on French soil. He stood to attention on the quayside and saluted his comrades as we sailed away.

'Outside Dunkirk we picked up the crew of a French destroyer which had been dive-bombed. Several troops aboard her fell into the water when the destroyer sank and three of our crew unhesitatingly dived in and saved them, a brave rescue for which each of them received the OBE. We finally steamed for Ramsgate well down in the water, carrying more than 500 troops and survivors – there was hardly any room to move in the old ship. One of the French soldiers we'd pulled out of the sea appeared to be dead, so we covered him with a tarpaulin. On our arrival outside Ramsgate someone accidentally stood on him; he gave one big moan and sat up – what a shock!'

By dawn on what was to be the last day of the Dunkirk evacuation – June 2, 1940 – a score of trawlers and drifters had added their beaten and sunken hulks to those of the paddle-sweepers and other requisitioned craft operated by men of the Patrol Service. On this last day the asdic trawler *Arctic Pioneer* was patrolling the channel being used by the crowded ships crossing from France to England when through very thick fog she heard a distress signal. Powerless to help in these pre-radar days, having no idea of the stricken ship's whereabouts, she sadly fished from the sea later, a Kisbee lifebelt belonging to the trawler *Blackburn Rovers*.

The grim fate of this trawler was bound up with two others. *Blackburn Rovers* was leading *Westella* and *Saon* on patrol of the waters crossed by the ships from Dunkirk when *Blackburn Rovers* made an asdic contact. Commander Rex English, RN, senior officer of the group, who was aboard her, felt sure she had contacted a U-boat, and took her in after it. But Chief-Skipper Billy Mullender in *Saon* was convinced that *Blackburn Rovers* was, in fact, 'pinging' on a wreck, and more importantly, in going in to investigate was running right over a British minefield. He flashed urgently to *Westella* not to follow, but she did.

Blackburn Rovers erupted on a mine so suddenly and disastrously that her crew never knew what hit them. She blew up in the magazine, broke in half and sank at once. As she did, her depth-charges went off among the survivors struggling in the debris-strewn sea. *Westella* began rescue work, but then she also struck a mine. Her bows were blown off and she began to settle. Now the *Saon*, already battered from an earlier action, was forced to enter the minefield to rescue survivors from both vessels. Chief-Skipper Mullender:

'We saved thirty-six men in all from the two crews. Many of *Blackburn Rovers*'s survivors were suffering from internal haemorrhage as a result of being caught in the depth-charge explosions. The messdeck of *Saon* was like a slaughterhouse, with blood running everywhere.

'*Westella* was sinking gradually by the head, and I realised she could not be allowed to sink in her own time, as her asdic dome was still intact and this equipment was secret. I thought I heard a man cry out aboard her, and her skipper confirmed that one of his crew might still be in the ship. I called for two volunteers to go off in the smallboat to try to find this man, though I told them I couldn't wait for their return as I must go at once to Dover with the injured. My asdic-rating and steward, both Grimsby men, immediately stepped forward and were soon on their way over. I told them to put all depth-charges to safe as soon as they got aboard, in case the ship went down under them, then to make a thorough search for the missing man. They knew I had given instructions for *Westella* to be sunk by gunfire from another ship as soon as they had left her, which meant they would be left adrift in mid-Channel in a rowing-boat. But this did not deter them in any way. It was two months before I saw them again. Then I learned that they'd found the missing rating under the anchor chain for'ard, his leg broken. They got him into the smallboat and after being adrift for some time, at last hailed a tow which brought them to Margate.'

One survivor from *Blackburn Rovers*, after being rescued by *Westella*, was plunged back into the sea again when she was hit. 'I found myself with another man clinging to the large wooden nameplate which had previously been attached to *Westella*'s bridge. That was just after 4.30 p.m. We clung to that nameplate and floated for two days and nights before being picked up, pretty well done in, and landed at Dover. There we lay for some hours in a quayside shelter before being taken off to hospital, where my injured legs were put in plaster.'

Commander Rex English was among the survivors picked up by *Saon*. He, like so many others, was suffering from internal bleeding after the depth-charge explosions. Chief-Skipper Mullender:

'Because of being such a mess, he wouldn't allow a steward to attend to him. So I bathed him myself, dressed him up in my own underwear and shirt, and eventually managed to get him to go to hospital.'

As this unhappy episode of the three patrol trawlers was being enacted out in the Channel, the drifters of 'Vernon's Private Navy', which had been crossing to and fro from Ramsgate with their mercy loads of troops, each made their last journey. Signalman Smith of *Fisher Boy*:

'On the last day of the evacuation, things having got pretty desperate, *Fisher Boy* made her way to Dunkirk in daylight. But before we got to Dunkirk harbour, out in the Roads, we came upon a big troopship, the *Scotia*, which had been blasted by German bombers and lay on her side in the sea, burning fiercely.

'There must have been two thousand French soldiers struggling in the water, and there were hundreds more standing on the side of her hull, all being continually machine-gunned by enemy planes. We were the only other ship in sight, but Skipper Brown did not hesitate. We steamed in, never feeling so small with our crew of thirteen, and two or three lads went off in a dinghy to drag exhausted men out of the water while I and another of the crew slung heaving lines and hauled aboard those who could grab hold of them.

'There were hundreds of tin-hats floating on the water, and when you came up to them you saw that they were really French soldiers, who had donned small Board of Trade type lifebelts, kept on their helmets, greatcoats, bandoliers, field boots and other gear and jumped trustingly into the water in the belief that these little lifebelts would keep them safe, the result being that they now floated dead in the water with just their helmets showing. It was a tragic sight which scarred us all mentally.

'When our crowded little ship got back to Ramsgate we heard that the evacuation was finished, and Dunkirk had fallen. In a way it was lucky we had come upon the *Scotia* and stopped to work among the survivors rather than going on, as George Brown would have done, into Dunkirk harbour, and probably falling victims to the Germans.'

Two other drifters *Fidget* and *Jaketa* also picked up some survivors from *Scotia*. The final casualty on that day was the 'command' drifter, *Lord Cavan*, from which almost until the last minute, the indefatigable Commander Cubison had continued organising the beach rescue work.

An hour before *Lord Cavan* was due to sail a shell smashed through her wooden side and exploded against the harbour wall. She quickly sank. All hands got off safely and were brought back to Dover by a destroyer.

Signalman Smith: 'The crew were especially sad about the loss of *Lord Cavan* as she was well stocked up with cigarettes and other little items which they had "won" from NAAFI lorries and so on while working in and around Dunkirk.'

When the final count was taken, Cubison's little drifters had rescued no fewer than 4,085 troops from the beaches and waters of Dunkirk, and brought them safely home. *Fisher Boy*, in seven trips, had ferried one-third of these – more than 1,350 men. A truly remarkable achievement by a herring boat.

Two weeks after Dunkirk another evacuation was being attempted hundreds of miles to the south-west, at the port of St Nazaire on the Bay of Biscay. Here nearly 100,000 British and French troops and some civilians, including women and children, were awaiting ships to rescue them from the half-ruined town under bombardment from the Germans. In one convoy which arrived to help in the pick-up was the asdic trawler *Cambridgeshire*. She was a Grimsby trawler, and her commander, Skipper W. G. 'Billy' Euston, RNR, and chief engineer, George Beasley, were both Grimsby fishermen.

On the calm and sunny afternoon of June 17 1940 *Cambridge-*

shire was anchored with other ships off St Nazaire. George Beasley had just come off watch and was in his bunk when the trawler was shaken by a terrific explosion from across the water. He rushed up on deck to see the 16,000-ton troopship *Lancastria* listing right over after being attacked by German bombers. The planes had scored at least four direct hits on the huge ship and she was sinking fast with more than 6,000 passengers aboard.

Skipper Billy Euston did not hesitate for a second, steaming *Cambridgeshire* at full spead for the *Lancastria*. 'Masses of men were climbing over the ship and jumping from her as she turned, and when we were still some distance away we could hear them defiantly singing "Roll Out The Barrel!".'

The great liner sank in less than twenty minutes, and during the horrific scene of her dying and for long afterwards, in spite of repeated bombing attacks and the machine-gunning of survivors in the water, *Cambridgeshire*'s small crew of sixteen men doggedly pursued their rescue work. George Beasley:

'As we closed up to the sinking liner the sea was black with men and we started pulling them aboard from all sides, some covered in thick, slimy oil, and others wounded and badly burnt. It was a terrible sight, a terrible mess, yet there was no panic at all. Some men sitting on the keel of *Lancastria* were still singing just before she went down, they certainly had plenty of pluck.'

Man after man was hauled aboard the trawler, which under their weight settled dangerously low in the water. They were packed in like sardines, crowding the hold, the stokeholds and engine room, until there was hardly any room to move.

Skipper Euston: 'We stayed until we had loaded far more men than we could reasonably carry, and to our regret could take no more. We left our lifeboat and threw over the side all our liferafts and lifebelts, everything that was floatable, to help those we could not take on board. When we had finished we were packed solid, every inch of space below was full and the decks were just a solid mass. We nearly capsized under the weight, but managed to steam alongside the *John Holt*, one of the transports, and transfer everyone safely to her.'

All 1,009 of them – nearly half the total survivors. For between 3,000 and 4,000 men died with the *Lancastria*. It was an appalling disaster, made all the more bitter by the mystifying neglect of other ships to come to her assistance. Had others acted as promptly as the trawler, the staggering death roll must have been much less. Instead, the casualty figures were so shocking that Churchill forbade publication of the news, on the grounds that the British public had already been fed more disaster than it could stomach.

But work was not yet over for *Cambridgeshire*, the heroine of that terrible day. The same night she steamed quietly into St Nazaire under the guns of the German bombardment, with orders to take on Army personnel for passage to the UK. Skipper Euston:

'I was not able to leave the bridge until we were several hours out of St Nazaire, and it was then I discovered that our passengers were, in fact, the General Staff of the British Expeditionary Force, headed by the commander of the Second Army, General Sir Alan Brooke. I jokingly asked if he and his staff could all swim, and when he asked why, pointed out that we had no life-saving equipment on board, having thrown every last thing we had to the *Lancastria* survivors. He just smiled and said, "We shall not worry about that".'

Nor did they have to. Gallant *Cambridgeshire* sailed them all safely home to Plymouth.

6

The Silver Badge Fleet

Even before Dunkirk, Churchill's top secret instructions had gone out to various commands for a withdrawal to Canada if Britain should collapse. After the Dunkirk evacuation Patrol Service skippers received similar secret orders which they were not supposed to open, but which, of course, they did. The orders were that in the event of overwhelming invasion they were to steam as far away as their coal and food would allow, and if possible to make their way across the Atlantic to Canada or the US, and carry on the fight from there. There was many an emotional scene on ships of Harry Tate's Navy when they received their special recognition signals – six feet square, made of canvas and painted in red and white stripes – together with these depressing orders.

Men talked it over on the messdecks. Some, especially the married men, swore that in the event they would disobey orders and slip back home somehow rather than leave their wives and children to the mercies of the Germans. Others found themselves in two minds, not wanting to desert their parents and families, but recognising what would be a desperate need to fight on. They were days of agonising personal decisions.

Not that any ship yet was actually poised to run, all were far too active. Many trawlers and drifters, besides a host of other craft, were taken from minesweeping and anti-submarine duties to form an Auxiliary Patrol against invasion, steaming close off Britain's shores to give the alert should an enemy force sneak past the 'front line' of warships.

In early July 1940 Churchill was able to note with satisfaction that the Admiralty had 'over a thousand armed patrolling vessels, of which two or three hundred are always at sea', and that a surprise crossing 'should be impossible'. Among this vigilant thousand were the redoubtable drifters of 'Vernon's Private Navy', still operating from Ramsgate. Signalman Smith of *Fisher Boy*:

'Ordered to take up anti-invasion patrol for the time being, we were equipped with a radio and transmitter, two Hotchkiss guns and two Lewis guns. We'd managed to get quite a few other odds and ends of armaments while at Dunkirk, so *Fisher Boy* was bristling by this time. We were also equipped with six small mines carried in two coffin-like boxes over the stern. Each mine was linked to the other by a length of grass line, and our instructions were that in the event of sighting an invasion fleet we were to steam across their course of approach and drop these mines into the water. They would float just under the water and the invaders would foul the grass line, so bringing the mines into contact with their hulls.

'The whole thing seemed to be a pretty dodgy operation and thank God we never had to put it into practice. We did, however, spend many hair-raising evenings not far off the coast of Calais listening and watching for an enemy assault. Working round Ramsgate and Dover during that summer meant that we saw a tremendous amount of the Battle of Britain and we also on many occasions engaged enemy aircraft with our Lewis or Hotchkiss guns, all 1914 vintage.'

In these dark days immediately following Dunkirk heartening news came from overseas of a triumphant sortie by one of His Majesty's trawlers – one of the few that had sailed early to the war in the Middle East. It happened only a few days after Mussolini's braggartly entry into the war following the debacle of Dunkirk; an encounter in which the little Hull trawler *Moonstone* brought swift humiliation for the Italian Navy out in the waters off Aden.

Moonstone had begun life as the fishing trawler *Lady Madeleine*. She was bought and put into commission by the Admiralty early in 1939, before war began. For this reason her crew were general service ratings, and her captain a warrant officer of the Royal Navy, Boatswain William Moorman.

In Mid-June *Moonstone* was working from Aden on anti-submarine patrol when a submarine, believed to be one of several Italian boats operating from Massawa, in the Red Sea, became active. The trawler joined with other vessels in an extensive asdic sweep of the area.

During the night of June 18 one of the searching ships, the destroyer *Kandahar*, was surprised to detect the submarine surfaced and busily transmitting its daily report back to the Massawa base. *Kandahar* gave chase, but the submarine dived in the dark and escaped, nor could it be traced again by searching aircraft.

Next day, just before noon, *Moonstone*'s asdic operator reported a strong submarine echo and the trawler immediately steamed to the attack, dropping depth-charges; but again the enemy escaped. Then, barely an hour later, the trawler regained contact and dropped more depth-charges. The explosions had scarcely subsided before the submarine, a big ocean-going boat, suddenly heaved itself to the surface a mile astern, streaming the Italian flag from a pole above its conning tower.

Moonstone wheeled hard round and steamed full-ahead with all guns firing, some of the crew even joining in with rifles as the distance between the two vessels narrowed. Though the submarine, which was fully three times the size of *Moonstone*, quickly returned fire, the hail of lead and shell from the trawler prevented the Italians from getting to their big gun, and finally *Moonstone*'s four-inch crashed a shell into the conning tower, killing all inside it. Some of the Italians began to wave white clothes in surrender, while others scrambled into the wrecked tower to haul down the flag.

There were far too many Italians for the trawler's small crew to handle, so after warning the enemy commander not to scuttle or she would reopen fire, *Moonstone* stood off while *Kandahar* raced in to take the prisoners aboard and fix a tow to the big submarine, the *Galileo Galilei*. Much to the mortification of the submarine's crew the confidential papers which they had hurriedly thrown overboard failed to sink and were fished from the sea by the destroyer's boarding party. *Kandahar* then towed *Moonstone*'s prize to Aden.

There was a grisly sequel. On arrival at Aden *Kandahar*'s captain cleared lower deck and asked his crew to keep strict silence about the captured papers. Next day *Kandahar* and two other destroyers, acting on information from the papers, set sail and were scarcely an hour at sea before they took a surfaced Italian submarine completely by surprise. *Kandahar*, then no more than half a mile from the submarine, fired a warning shot over its conning tower to give the Italians a chance to surrender. But to the amazement of the British ships the submarine began to return fire. Aboard *Kandahar* was Seaman Edmund Carroll.

'The combined armament of our three destroyers was eighteen 4.7 in. guns and the Italian commander must have realised that he hadn't a snowball's chance in hell with his single gun. We manoeuvred in such a way that he couldn't bring his torpedoes to bear, after which a couple of well-placed shots blew the Italian gun and its crew into oblivion. The submarine slowly settled on an even keel and the crew were already abandoning her when to our horror we saw the dorsal fins of dozens of sharks weaving in and out of the poor wretches. We heard screams and shrieks as they were eaten alive.

'All our boats were lowered at speed. I was on the point-five machine-guns and the captain ordered me to fire short bursts to drive the Italians back on to the submarine, which was still afloat, and so save them from the sharks, but this only made more men jump from the submarine into the sea as they misinterpreted our captain's intentions.

'As our boats picked up what survivors there were, only the conning tower of the submarine was still visible; one boat went alongside and our big, burly coxswain reached over and dragged the Italian commander out of it. On our return to Aden the *Kandahar*'s wardroom was used as an operating theatre and our surgeon did wonderful work to ease the pain of the Italians, some of whom were horribly mutilated. He was later decorated.'

As for the *Galileo Galilei*, for whose splendid defeat Boatswain Moorman won the DSC and accelerated promotion to lieutenant, it became a permanent, active insult to the Italian Navy, being promptly refitted, commissioned and sent back to sea as one of HM submarines.

In Britain at this time, survivors of Patrol Service ships sunk at Dunkirk and just after, returned to Sparrow's Nest to find it had been given a new name – HMS *Europa*. There were new buildings and extensions, and the old house of Sparrow's Nest had been transformed into barrack-like administrative offices. Nissen huts for training classes had sprung up around the Oval, and other classes were under way in empty schools. A former secondary school was converted into a fully-manned and equipped hospital. Inside the Nest, air-raid shelters were dug on the lawn. The order was always 'Muster on the lawn', though every blade of grass on it had long vanished under the tramping of thousands of boots. With the threat of invasion, holes were cut in the Nest walls for rifles to shoot through, and the adjacent ravines and scores were mined, to be set off in an emergency by press-buttons in The Cottage, the Commodore's office. In this cottage, while alterations were being made, old copies of *The Times* were found under the wallpaper, including one of 1805 giving an account of the Battle of Trafalgar.

As HMS *Europa* the Royal Naval Patrol Service took on its full and complete independence as a separate navy within the Royal Navy. Promoted from transit depot to a full drafting and holding depot, *Europa* assumed absolute responsibility for training men for His Majesty's 'minor war vessels' – the Admiralty's description – and set up its own promotions roster. It made its own rules. It was still under the general regulations of the Navy, but with adaptations proposed by the Commodore, Lowestoft, and approved and published by the Admiralty.

The Patrol Service even acquired its own special badge, a unique distinction which gave the final endorsement to its separate identity.

The badge came into being in a roundabout way. It had originally been suggested for the many civilian seamen who, in the first emergency, crewed vital auxiliary minesweepers as temporary naval volunteers, wearing their usual sea rig. The badge was intended both as a special emblem for them, and as a protection should they be taken prisoner, thereby ensuring military prisoner-of-war treatment. But by the time the badge reached the design stage, a strong plea had been made for the men of the anti-submarine trawlers; that they, too, should be afforded recognition along with the minesweepers. And so the badge was designed to cover both these divisions of the Royal Naval Patrol Service and, in fact, became exclusive to it.

The silver badge, about the size of a shilling, was in the form of a shield which showed a sinking shark transfixed by a marline spike (representing the anti-submarine service), against a background of a fishing net containing two trapped enemy mines (the minesweepers), the whole surrounded by a rope with two fishermen's bend knots and topped by a naval crown. Below was a scroll bearing the letters 'M/S – A/S'.

The badge was awarded after a man had served a minimum of six months on anti-submarine or minesweeping service in the RNPS, or less in special cases. It became the most prized 'medal' of the war, as men felt that six months sea-time in a minesweeping or asdic trawler really *was* sea-time under the worst conditions of danger and discomfort. The fact that naval general service men could not wear it was one of its main attractions. It was exclusive to the RNPS – and only to the men who served at sea. No shore-based man could have it.

It was worn on the left sleeve, four inches from the cuff, and when a Patrol Service rating became an officer, he could still wear it in the same place on his officer's jacket. No matter how many other 'gongs' its wearer might earn, the silver badge remained his proudest possession.

Throughout the long, hot, grim summer of 1940 as Britain stood alone, losses among the 'minor war vessels' manned by the Patrol Service mounted with alarming regularity and out of all proportion to the losses of any other naval craft. From June 1940 to the end of the year, more than ninety vessels were lost, half of them blown up by enemy mines. Some twenty others sank under the attacks of bombing aircraft, the rest went down to torpedoes and gunfire, or were wrecked in collisions or foundered in punishing seas.

During the invasion scare, reinforcements for the little ships in the south came from all directions. Down from the Clyde, in spectacular formation, steamed the five paddle-steamers of the 11th Minesweeping Flotilla, or 'Churchill's Secret Weapon – the Fighting 11th' as they were called, mainly because they had seen no actual fighting but had hitherto spent their time daily sweeping the Clyde estuary. Now they took over the sweep from Dover, combined with anti-invasion patrol at night.

The five steamers, which in peacetime sailed the Clyde, had been commissioned early in the war; they were fast, with speeds of 14 to 17 knots, and had a shallow draft, which was good for minesweeping. Their crews were a mixture of Patrol Service men, RN and RNVR ratings, and RN pensioners. Among them were hardened deep-sea trawlermen and real tough stokers from Glasgow. Their canteen messing was designed to save as much money as possible to spend on beer, which left many a man always hungry.

For weeks the five paddlers swept in front of the Channel convoys by day and went out on patrol every night. Telegraphist Leslie Clements, RNVWR, was in HMS *Scawfell*.

'We were armed with a 12-pounder gun which had the date 1898 stamped on the breech – it was said to have been made as a field-gun for the Boer War. We also had a Lewis gun with two mountings, one on each paddle-box.

'After a few weeks at Dover we went to Portland, and were in harbour there during the first heavy air-raids. We were on the spot when the *Foylebank*, a merchant ship converted to A/A cruiser, was sunk by enemy bombers. After this the paddlers earned a great reputation with the people ashore for our terrific A/A defence of the town! In *Scawfell* we shot down a Junkers 52 with our old 12-pounder, at which our crew leaped about the deck for joy. In another raid our sister ship HMS *Goatfell* was hit by a bomb. It landed on her 12-pounder mounting, killing several men.

'It was a period of considerable strain and one of our own seamen died of heart failure. Several men hardly ever went below decks, and we fired our gun so much that the supports under the deck were buckled.'

After a few weeks of this the 'Fighting 11th', real fighters now, were ordered back to resume their minesweeping on the Clyde.

The trawler *Marconi* steamed up from Torquay, where she had been under repair, to join the minesweepers operating from Harwich in 'E-boat Alley', the dangerous stretch of sea running from the Thames estuary north to Flamborough Head. Her first, ominous sight as she drew in to Parkeston Quay was that of the ancient, 1914 built trawler *St Olive*, so badly damaged that she looked like a pepper-pot. She had been attacked by planes the previous night, had seven hands killed and others wounded.

Marconi herself was no newcomer to danger, her recent repairs being the result of a fierce encounter with three dive-bombers. She was now put in a flotilla with three other trawlers and began her duties at once. This consisted of sweeping the war channel by day, both ways, before the convoy came through, and then patrolling the convoy route each night, keeping a sharp lookout for mine-laying planes and marauding E-boats. She was the new ship of Petty Officer Robert Muir.

'We followed this double drill for four days and nights at a time, having a break of two days and nights in harbour after each spell. During the four days it was hell on earth. We were continually at action-stations, being bombed and machine-gunned. After four months it was decided the strain was too much for us, as a lot of men were going round the bend and had to be sent off to hospital. So to give us some protection against the enemy planes we switched to doing our sweeping at night. We would leave the inside anchorage at about 8 p.m. and anchor about eight miles offshore till midnight, then make our way to the Orfordness lightfloat and patrol off there till 4 a.m., after which we swept the convoy route and steamed back to the inside anchorage off Felixstowe at about 8 a.m. The Ipswich patrol trawlers used to come out at midnight just as we were weighing anchor and patrol the outside line till dawn, then return to Ipswich.

'Night sweeping was still a hazardous job. We had to cope with E-boats in the dark, and having our sweeps down we weren't very manoeuvrable in an emergency, in fact we were sitting ducks. But for a time the switch to night sweeping foxed the enemy and we were not attacked quite as often.'

Not that any trawler was ever backward in showing her teeth. When *Red Gauntlet*, sweeping off Harwich, sighted an enemy bomber flying low with its deadly load for London, she manfully let go with her 12-pounder. She was the new ship of Second Hand Thorpe: 'We just missed him, and he got so annoyed that he turned round and came in to attack us. Our young gunner on the aft gun brought down the mizzen-boom in keeping him off and was worried to death about what the skipper would say, but I told him he could bring down the mizzen mast just as long as he could keep that plane off. The bomber pilot seemed to lose patience, for he finally dropped all his bombs at us at once – about 12. They fell to one side, shook us up a good deal but did no real damage. At least it meant twelve fewer bombs fell on London that day.'

What some trawlers managed to achieve with their meagre armament was nothing short of a marvel. Had they possessed the sharp teeth of some of the refugee vessels from the Continent which joined Harry Tate's Navy they might have done so much more.

Three French trawlers which escaped across the Channel at the time of Dunkirk each boasted the somewhat fantastic armament for those days of three 100mm. guns, one on the foc'sle and one each on the port and starboard sides; plus two 10mm. A/A guns in the port and starboard wastes, and two twin-Hotchkiss on the bridge.

These trawlers, *L'Atlantique*, *L'Istrac* and *Ambrose Pare*, were fitted with asdics and depth-charge throwers in Devonport dockyard and sent on anti-submarine patrol in the Channel with a mixed British and French crew under an RNR skipper and mate. They were big boats, but slow, and to those who sailed in them it seemed that after a few depth-charge attacks they might drop to bits. But two of the vessels clung on to life. The third, *L'Istrac*, met a quick and tragic end while on patrol when she ran into the guns of a German destroyer, which picked her off at leisure. Her commander was shot while on a liferaft.

L'Istrac had been working from Portsmouth along with other trawlers including the flotilla leader *Lord Wakefield*, commanded by Chief-Skipper John Harwood.

'We had many escapes during the heavy bombing at Portsmouth. One near-miss for us was when the Navy tugboat got a direct hit and just disappeared. We were berthed across from her, and in the explosion we went up in to the air and dropped down to the bottom of the harbour. None of the crew was hurt, but the ship – what a mess. It landed us in dock for quite a spell, during which time the bombing was fairly continuous. One day I counted about 80 bombers over Pompey, and two squadrons of Hurricanes and Spitfires chased them right out of the sky. Several times we were attacked while at anchor, but thank God we suffered little damage except for our balloon being shot down and a few holes in our funnel.

'Another of our group, the *Warwick Deeping*, was not so lucky, meeting with a similar fate to that of *L'Istrac*. She was about 25 miles south-west from St Catherine's Point when she was gunned down and sunk by enemy destroyers.

'In *Lord Wakefield* we saw the tragic end of the destroyer *Acheron*. She was heavily bombed while in dry-dock at Portsmouth, and I think most of her officers were killed when the stern was blown to pieces. She was repaired and re-commissioned, and set sail to some west port. She passed us westward of Nab Tower, but only got as far as the Isle of Wight when she was blown to bits on a mine. We picked up two of her Carley floats, but I did not get any bodies, only pieces of sailors' clothing. Oil was everywhere and bodies were not easy to see in the mess.'

It was at Portsmouth that a memorable clash occurred between an exasperated RNR skipper and an RNVR lieutenant. The skipper, a gentle giant of a man, brought his minesweeping trawler, which had an edge of speed, into harbour ahead of the lieutenant, who was senior officer. The lieutenant reported him. By way of reply the big fisherman took hold of the startled officer by the underarms, hoisted him in the air like a baby and threatened: 'I'll hang you from the bloody cross!' The skipper was afterwards court-martialled. An unfortunate episode, but Harry Tate's men were contemptuous of 'bull' and only asked to be allowed to get on with the job in hand.

So many ships were engaged on anti-invasion patrol at this time that shipping losses in the depleted area of the Western Approaches mounted. The situation so worsened that numbers of trawlers had to be released from patrol to take up service as convoy escorts. One of these escorts was the *Cape Argona*, whose lot it was to be involved in a rescue operation following the greatest single merchant shipping disaster of the war. Aboard *Cape Argona* was Sub-Lieutenant Geoffrey Dormer, RNVR, who describes the events of October 26.

'We were on our way home with a couple of other trawlers from a convoy dispersal point about 300 miles west of Ireland, when a plane signalled that a ship was on fire about fifty miles away. We turned and made for her at full belt, pouring oil and water on our plummer blocks (the bearings through which the main propeller shaft runs), for we had a bent propeller shaft, the result of near misses at Norway and Dunkirk, and of a mishap with a depth-charge.

'We saw a great column of smoke from about 40 miles away, and it took us four hours to get there with our machinery literally red hot. Eventually a mast appeared and then another, so far apart that we thought it must be two ships, but on steaming closer we saw that it was indeed one, the liner *Empress of Britain*, the third largest ship in the world. She was burning well with a slight list, and had seven or eight lifeboats near her.'

The magnificent luxury liner, pride of the Canadian Pacific Fleet, was in service as a troopship, carrying 643 people including troops and their families. That morning as she steamed for Britain, enemy bombers had swept down on her out of the sun. The liner's gunners fought back until all were killed or disabled by the machine-gun fire which raked her decks. Then the planes swooped in to drop high explosive and incendiary bombs. Soon the liner was ablaze midships, some of her boats burning fiercely as they swung on the davits. Her master, Captain Charles Sapworth, stayed on the bridge until it burned away beneath him, manoeuvring the ship to minimise the effect of the flames.

Sub-Lieutenant Dormer: 'We made for one lifeboat and picked up 66 people, including women, children and wounded. The coxswain of the lifeboat was the brother of one of our seamen – they hadn't met for a couple of years – and they had two other brothers also in the *Empress*, who were picked up by other ships. As we came up to the boat the survivors were singing "Roll Out The Barrel".

'I learned long afterwards that a U-boat was watching the *Empress* but was deterred from attacking by our arrival. There was a Jacob's ladder hanging from the liner's foc's'le which seemed clear of the fire. Some of us wanted to board her and try to take her 42,000 tons in tow – enormous salvage! But the CO vetoed this idea and later two destroyers arrived.

'One of our survivors had both legs broken and a bullet through his foot. He sat in the scuppers, smoking, surrounded by children who were much amused by the funny shape of his legs. A boy of eleven and his sister of eight were specially fascinated by one or two bodies floating in the water, they seemed in their innocence to be thoroughly enjoying the whole thing. We had an eleven months old baby too, but the saddest case was a young girl whose fiancé had been killed before her eyes.

'Luckily the weather was calm for once and the casualties were soon under morphia. Some of our tough young men were violently sick over moving them, but the children never turned a hair. The crew gave up most of their spare clothes to the survivors, who also helped themselves to a few things along the way, but we in return acquired all the lifeboat's equipment.

'We eventually transferred 61 of our survivors to one of the destroyers, which already had a number of dead laid out aft. We kept aboard only two women who were too ill to be moved, and an RAMC colonel, together with two nurses to look after them. One of the women, a Maltese Service wife, was soon to have a baby. She had both arms broken, both legs badly cut and burned and a couple of bullets in her from the Focke-Wulf that had bombed the ship and then machine-gunned the survivors. Yet she both survived and produced her baby successfully.'

The severely damaged *Empress of Britain* was taken in tow by the Polish destroyer *Burz*, but was torpedoed and sunk by a shadowing U-boat, the largest Allied merchant ship to go down in the war.

As for *Cape Argona*'s final memory of the disaster – 'There was a horrible smell and mess in the Subs' cabin afterwards, blood and dressings all over the place, and it took time to get used to sleeping there again.'

The following month of November 1940 saw 26 trawlers and drifters go to the bottom – very nearly one a day. Some sank under enemy bombs, the majority were torn apart by enemy mines. Like *Amethyst*, an asdic trawler operating from Parkeston Quay on patrol for the East Coast convoys. Steaming in the Barrow Deep on a beautifully fine and quiet November day she hit one of the very early acoustic mines – Hitler's latest 'secret weapon'. When the ship blew up at the stern, wounding seven men, all thought they had been bombed. *Amethyst* took ten minutes to sink, which allowed everyone to get off safely. They were picked up by the trawler *Le Tiger* and taken to Southend pier, where, adding insult to injury, they were promptly taken in charge by suspicious police, who had earlier arrested the survivors of a little Dutch schoot which had also hit a mine and sunk. It took *Amethyst*'s crew half an hour to convince the police of their identity before they were released, and attention turned once more to checking the bona fide nature of the Dutchmen.

The acoustic mine was a new menace which gave shipping a thoroughly bad time. Minesweeping trawlers would sweep the convoy route for the usual mines, including the magnetic type, and then the convoy would come through. A number of ships might steam by unharmed, then, bafflingly, the fourth or fifth ship in the column would be blown sky-high. When it was realised exactly what was going on, the sweepers were fitted with 'A' Frames and The Bucket, an electrical hammer device calculated to set off an acoustic mine about a mile away.

One of the test ships to go out with the first Bucket was the small trawler *Refundo*, an old veteran of World War 1. She got well outside the harbour, lowered her Bucket into the water, started the hammer and began to sweep. In less than half an hour she got a mine, but not where expected: it blew up under the bow, killing two men on the foc'sle head. The severely damaged ship was towed inshore, where she sank. This was on December 18.

From such mishaps were the lessons of the acoustic mine learned, until eventually all sweepers were fitted with reliable gear, an innovation which meant that they were now equal to dealing with three different sorts of mine.

The year 1940 ended with Harry Tate's Navy having lost well over 140 vessels since the outbreak of war. Among those which added a last sad statistic to the total was the aged trawler *Pelton*, torpedoed and sunk by an E-boat as she was sweeping off Great Yarmouth on Christmas Eve.

Christmas Day found the Clyde paddlers of the 'Fighting 11th' returned south to clear a minefield near Tuskar Rock, off the southern Irish coast. This was a tough, dangerous job in winter, especially for ships which, in peacetime, were only allowed in the upper Clyde and not in the open seas.

By Christmas Day *Scawfell* had swept up 25 mines and her crew ate their Christmas dinner of corned beef between runs over the minefield. *Scawfell* was working close to *Mercury*, whose crew had cheerily issued their own Christmas card. It showed Popeye the Sailor sweeping up a mine with a broom, and bore the message:

'HMS *Mercury* – we make a clean sweep of everything except our friends.'

Before the day was out *Mercury* got a mine tangled in her sweep, and as the wire came in the mine blew up astern. The explosion buckled *Mercury*'s stern and she began to sink. Efforts were made to shore up the bulkheads and pump her out; If she stayed afloat, *Scawfell* was to escort her into Wexford. This led to much speculation as to whether they would be interned by the Irish for the duration.

But the water could not be pumped, and at 9 p.m. *Mercury* was abandoned and quickly sank.

Merry Christmas.

7

The Northern Patrol

The Northern Patrol. There was a certain bleakness about the name and a bleak life it could be, as the many men drafted to it quickly discovered.

The Northern Patrol was a special force of ships steaming up and down lines of patrol between the Faroes and Iceland, their main purpose being to prevent German raiders slipping out unseen into the Atlantic to attack the homing convoys. They also challenged all vessels using the northern waters, and kept a lookout for U-boats.

During the first months of the war, armed merchant cruisers had made the patrol, with small trawlers acting as armed boarding vessels. But they met with heavy losses. An early disaster was the sinking off Iceland of the merchant cruiser *Rawalpindi*, gunned down by the German battlecruisers *Gneisenau* and *Scharnhorst*. This was followed by the loss of nine more merchant cruisers, the majority torpedoed by U-boats while patrolling off Iceland and Ireland.

So naval cruisers took over the watch on northern waters, but they could not be spared for long, and in any event they suffered a great deal of damage from the appalling weather conditions. Destroyers, also in short supply, did not have the endurance, but the coal-burning trawlers were found to be ideal for the job. Their duty was to report enemy sightings before being blown to Kingdom Come, unless they could slip away before being detected. They were painted in anything but pusser warship grey, generally a valiant black and tan, for it was not intended that they should hide behind camouflage. The reasoning appeared to be that they were eminently more expendable than big, expensive warships.

And so the trawlers, all based on Kirkwall, ancient capital of the Orkney Islands, steamed to and fro on their lines of patrol between the Faroes and Iceland for eight to ten days at a time; six knots back and forth, in some of the roughest seas imaginable.

On the Northern Patrol a novice seaman soon found that trawlers did not 'plough' seas, they rode them. As one rating describes it:

'Imagine the traditional Wild West bucking bronco enlarged to some 400 tons and fashioned like a ship and you have a good idea of a deep-sea trawler in a northern gale. She does everything in her power to throw you off your feet, hurl you against bulkheads and ship's fittings, stop you working, eating, sleeping, washing, shaving, dressing, even carrying out calls of nature. She seeks to stun you, maim you, hurl you overboard, destroy you utterly. She strikes at you when you are least prepared and off your guard. In everything you do, you battle against her relentless will to break you.

'She has two main weapons, the pitch and the roll; sometimes she uses both at the same time. Let's take them in turn. First the roll. On deck you reel drunkenly along, hanging grimly on to the lifelines or any solid structure. If you let go, she'll fling you off your feet to roll into the scuppers while icy water pours over you; and a nicely timed big sea may wash you over the rails into oblivion. Below decks you must struggle for everything. Getting yourself clothed to go on watch is a feat in itself. You are hurled from side to side of the messdeck as you let go for a moment to put on a garment. It takes two hands to put on a seaboot stocking, so you wait your chance. As you pull it on while sitting on your bunk, a sudden lurch flings you to the deck, cursing roundly, so that you have to pick yourself up and start all over again. The operation of getting dressed for watch, which in calm weather you could complete in three minutes, may take ten minutes in a gale.

'Eating is just as difficult. The messdeck table down aft runs thwartships and the eaters sit on two benches on either side. The fiddles are on the table to wedge the plates, but soup or any other fluids have to be taken with a certain technique. The bowl must be held in the hand, kept level, and spoonfuls taken when the roll levels out. You need both hands to hold it on the roll, then you let go one hand and spoon up rapid mouthfuls between rolls. As the ship rolls, all the eaters slide heavily, one on top of the other, first to one side and then the other, each man hanging on to his plate with both hands. Much cursing follows, the favourite remark being: "Roll right over, you fucking old bastard, and come up the other side!" The messman struggles to reach down the heavy pans from the galley above without scalding himself to death, while up in the galley the cook fights a desperate battle with his steaming pots and pans, which threaten to run amok if left for a second. Ship's cooks are notoriously temperamental, and in heavy weather are driven almost to the limits of endurance and patience. At times they may drive out all the galley hangers-on with a carving knife. The greasy galley deck can start a slide for the unwary which will send him skating three or four times from end to end with a fanny of hot tea in his hand before he can get a handhold.

'When at last you reach your bunk, you find that this rolling demon will not easily permit you to sleep. The bunks are fixed but your body is not, so you roll steadily from side to side and it's not easy to sleep in this state of constant motion. In a hammock the body sways with the bed and this is much more comfortable, but hammocks are used only when bunks are too few, and hammocks are awkward beasts to lash up and stow in heavy weather.

'The pitch is more violent than the roll, but it is easier on the eaters and sleepers. The mass-sliding game is gone from meal times, the sleeper's body is stationary in the bunk, though the sensation of being on a roller coaster in reverse takes some adjustment at first. You sleep head-to-bow, so that as the ship climbs steadily up each huge wave, your body comes towards the upright position. Then, as she tops the crest and plunges down the other side into the trough, you have the sensation of standing on your head. But this does not disturb sleep like the body-roll; in fact it can, in time, actually induce sleep, with a gigantic rock-a-bye-baby effect.

'However, the pitch is harder on the lookouts and the men working on deck, because in addition to the bucking and crashing of the bow into the troughs, there comes the lashing of faces and hands by icy spray; you are drenched, stung and blinded by it. Normally simple jobs become nightmares of frozen, fumbling hands and sliding feet. You can anticipate the roll much better than the pitch, with its sudden, violent intensity.

'In heavy weather jobs about the deck can be dangerous as well as frustrating. A seaboat breaking adrift from its lashings can endanger the lives of those who have to secure it again. In really bad weather it is foolhardy to attempt to cross the open deck, lifelines or no. Only in cases of emergency, such as enemy action or damage, is it attempted. When darkness falls in a full gale those aft stay aft, and those for'ard stay for'ard, till daylight.'

Typical of the smaller trawlers which first steamed on the

Northern Patrol was *Aquamarine*, a thirteen-year-old fishing vessel of some 350 tons. She began as an armed boarding vessel attached to Contraband Control at Kirkwall, her job being to intercept neutral ships.

Her crew were mostly RNR. The engine room staff were 'T.124' engagements – civilian seamen in uniform who did not consider themselves under naval discipline, not having undergone any service training. They were characters all, like the chief engineer, who once went off to visit his opposite number in a trawler shortly leaving for Aberdeen, had a glorious bender and woke up well on the way to that city.

Others of *Aquamarine*'s crew came from the Western Isles and used Gaelic as much as English. Some of the younger seamen were local, from the Kirkwall district and were great hands at 'the dancing'.

The quiet nature of the older seamen from the Islands and remoter parts of Scotland, who were to be found in most of the trawlers, was a feature that never failed to impress their messmates. Most were deeply religious men and kept a Bible under their pillow, reading from it before going to sleep, and saying their prayers regularly. Aboard one trawler there was an Islander who each night before turning in used to kneel in the middle of the messdeck and say his prayers, while the rest of the crew hurled not only abuse at him, but seaboots and any other heavy articles they could lay hands on. The Scot never wavered, but continued to say his prayers, and as time wore on the attacks grew less and less, until at last he was left entirely in peace to say his nightly prayers. He had won the respect of every man.

Another characteristic of the Stornowegians particularly was their gift of extraordinarily keen eyesight. Unsophisticated and uncomplicated, almost childlike men, they had pale blue, rather dreamy eyes, with which they could detect an object at great distances long before other eyes could discern them. Many was the trawler steaming in bad visibility in dangerous waters whose Stornowegian was called to help save her from harm. It was uncanny the way those dreamy eyes could spot a floating mine or a small object like a buoy minutes before anyone else could catch a glimpse of it. Up on the bridge an officer might train his glasses in the direction indicated and take a full minute or more to spot the object which the Stornowegian's hawklike eyes had detected unaided.

Many Stornowegians could not bear to be cooped up aboard a ship of war. Like big Jim Reid, a whaler in peacetime, who would never go below decks in his trawler; he ate all his meals standing up in the galley and slept in a Carley float alongside the funnel. In a rare moment of confidence he told a shipmate: 'I'm no afeared o' dying, but when I do, I want to feel the fresh sea breeze on my face, not be caught like a rat in that hellhole of a messdeck.'

There were many other men who, like big Jim, pondered on their doubtful chances should the ship go down suddenly. But one with singular confidence was *Northern Duke*'s wireless operator. At 'Up spirits' time, when the trawler was in harbour, he rashly bet that in an emergency he could escape through the messdeck porthole. He had plenty of takers, and got down to the job; but he finished up stark naked half in and half out of the porthole, stuck fast. As there were two other trawlers tied up alongside he had quite an audience when, after a good greasing, pushing and pulling, he was freed. Thereafter, that particular Sparks was always missing at rum time.

Among *Aquamarine*'s representative crew were such fearsome Scots as 'Lofty' McDonald, a giant of a ghillie, who could lift a two hundredweight sack with ease, and who spat violently at the very mention of the name of 'Campbell'. There was also a professional yachtsman, a yachtmaster and the usual sprinkling of larger-than-life personalities. Signalman Gordon Hooper:

'There was a Manxman, Bob Holmes, a real "old un" who was said to have been round the world with a tug-master's ticket, but had fallen on hard times – he had no kit at all. He would go ashore on the booze then flop into his bunk with the excuse that he was suffering from malaria. His great pal was a little bald-headed Scot called McGregor, and it was Bob's great delight to wait until McGregor was asleep and then draw all over his bald head with an indelible pencil. At night Bob would wait until McGregor was on the wheel and then crawl through a scuttle at the back of the wheelhouse and quietly grab the bottom spokes of the wheel so that poor old Mac couldn't tell whether the wheel had jammed or what. Bob led Mac an awful life, but they were the greatest of friends.

'We also had a rather boisterous Irish Sparks – or "That bloody mad Irishman!" as the captain used to call him. *Aquamarine* had been at sea for a fortnight and we hadn't received a single W/T message, Sparks maintaining that "nothing had come through". But the captain got suspicious and contacted the next ship. They handed over a fistful of signals, and Sparks got the bullet. We discovered he hadn't done any proper radio work for years and couldn't even read the ship's call-sign, but he was quite cheerful about it all.

'And there was the sub-lieutenant who was a bit of a ladies' man. The first time *Aquamarine* went into Lerwick, in the Shetlands, he arranged a party ashore and decided to smuggle off a bottle of gin by holding it inside his trouser-leg. All went well until we got into the crowded main street, when he lost his grip on the bottle and it went down his leg and smashed in the street. Strong men wept, that's all I know.'

In due course it was decided that *Aquamarine* was to turn over to anti-submarine work, and she went to West Hartlepool for an extensive refit, during which the decks were reinforced, the A/S gear was installed and a new A/S bridge built on.

'After the refit some of the older hands had grave doubts about her stability, and they were proved right in a tragic way. We were off the Faroes, in a gale of hurricane force, the ship yawing and rolling all over the place, when suddenly there was a great crash and she lay right over on her side. The wireless room was partitioned off the messdeck and the water rushed through the vents and flooded it. There was a shout from the deck of "Man overboard!" One of the Kirkwall dancing lads, on lookout on the lower bridge, had gone over the side. He was one of the most popular lads in the ship and a strong swimmer. The ship was put about, but we never had sight or sound of him again. For a long time afterwards there was silence on the messdeck, men just looking at each other and not speaking.

'We could not get the ship upright again and it turned out that our ballast of pig-iron had not been properly secured in the dockyard, and had shifted. So we made for the Faroes, still half on our side. We arrived at Thorshaven and were met by a snipe of a naval officer who hailed us in a loud voice and told us to carry out our repairs and be off as soon as possible, as he had no room for us. He drew some choice remarks from the lads, and I think he'd have gone in the "drink" if they'd got their hands on him.

'*Aquamarine*'s sister ship, the *Kingston Onyx*, had the same conversion and underwent a very similar experience. It was rumoured that her captain went out of his mind and was a mental case for the rest of the war.

'As for our own use as an anti-submarine vessel, early on we got a perfect asdic contact and dropped a pattern of depth-charges, but all we did was nearly to kill the cook. His galley door slammed to and shut him in, the hot water geyser flew off the bulkhead, the galley stove flew to pieces, the galley funnel broke off and filled the place with smoke and steam, the cook was nearly smothered.

'Eventually all our little Kingston ships were deemed unfit for Northern Patrol and were replaced by bigger trawlers.'

The trawler which replaced *Aquamarine* was the former Hull fishing vessel *Lord Austin* – ten years younger and 200 tons bigger, with a crew of around thirty men. As *Lord Austin* steamed from Kirkwall on her first patrol it was the prelude to long months of wearisome work in a sea beaten by severe storms for most of the year, and bitingly cold in the winter.

The monotonous pattern of the Northern Patrol was the worst thing to bear. From the time the copper spire of Kirkwall's ancient cathedral faded from sight, it was two days at full speed out to the patrol line, then more than a week steaming back and forth at slow speed, until the magic moment when, to everyone's joy, the order was heard 'Full ahead!' – signalling the end of the patrol and a fast two day run back to Kirkwall. The lines of patrol were varied a little for each trip, the most northerly line being near to Iceland and the most southerly only miles from the Orkneys. Each patrol was followed by four days in harbour for coaling from the collier, storing up and repairing defects. After coaling up, *Austin* would go to a buoy where she 'drew fires' so that the boiler tubes could be cleaned, engineers descending on the ship like industrious flies, and there was the ring of hammers and raucous cries. There was also a spot of shore leave to sample the delights of Kirkwall, the gaunt Gaelic city of grey houses and narrow streets; then out again to the next patrol line.

By the book, each trawler should have steamed down to Grimsby for a refit every six months, but in practice this period was often extended to seven or eight months. After the six months was up, every return from patrol became a time of eager anticipation, often to be dashed by the signal to take on 200 tons of coal for another patrol. But if the long-awaited signal was received – 'Proceed to collier and take on 60 tons' – it meant that the destination was 'GY' (Grimsby) and leave, and jubilation would break out all over the ship. A refit meant two weeks leave for each watch, and this was the only home leave available to men of the Northern Patrol.

Most of *Lord Austin*'s crew were Patrol Service men. In addition to the hard core of experienced Scots and English fishermen, and ex-Merchant Navy seamen, there were other strong personalities like Peter, the flame-haired son of a tug-master, who had lived all his life among the Thames barges and had all the Cockney aggressiveness, small, tough and afraid of no one, and 'Guns', who invariably brought the house down with his vivid rendering of 'The little dirty drawers that Maggie wore', sung with great pathos and feeling. Guns had a most curious Yorkshire accent. 'Doo goes and does dis,' he would say, explaining the intricacies of his old four-inch, 'and den doo comes back and does dat.' He provided endless amusement for Sparks, a round-faced and rather balding salesman from Cumberland, who never tired of imitating him. Sparks, like Guns, was a specialist. In fact, as the only wireless operator carried on board he was a key man and a law unto himself. He was never heard to address an officer as 'sir' – 'mister' was as much as he would allow himself in recognition of authority. He was in constant wordy warfare with the signals officer, whom he treated with scant ceremony.

The chief engineman, in his mid-fifties and now fighting his second war in trawlers, hailed from Grimsby; he had a suspicious eye and lived by his grumbles. He was engaged in continual warfare with the wardroom, and some of his replies up the engine room voice-pipe made stirring history. Down in his realm lived men like Paddy, the Irish stoker without parents, relations or friends, who spent his leaves living in Service hostels at one and sixpence a night, the rest of his money going on drink. And a fellow stoker, Bill, an ex-heavyweight boxer who had been round the world in the Merchant Navy and claimed to have possessed women of every nation.

On *Lord Austin* as with all the Northern Patrol trawlers, the rigs worn varied from the weird to the wonderful – seamen's jerseys and bell-bottoms, overalls, windcheaters, oilskins, duffle coats and kapok suits, topped by balaclavas, pom-pom and tea-cosy caps and even trilbies. But still among these, Ordinary Seaman Patrick Bryant was a 'loner' in his awful wreck of a leather coat, tattered and stiffened from salt water, and his battered cap.

Patrick had come over from Rhodesia to join up at the age of twenty-one, and he was both a mystery and a source of continual amusement to the rest of the crew. His pleasant, intelligent face usually sported several days' growth of beard, but in contrast to the variety of dialects on the messdeck he had a public school accent. His manner of speech left the crew flabbergasted, for instead of swearing he would abuse his mockers in long words foreign to their ears. He was, as they summed him up, a 'posh bugger – a broken down toff'. He had dramatic and literary ambitions, too, and these peculiar leanings were enough to earn him the label of 'crackers'.

In spite of – or maybe because of – the jibes that were continuously levelled at him, Patrick was popular on the lower deck. Legends of him persisted long after he had left the ship. His 'mourning' underclothes; his hammock, which he sometimes slung as a change from a bunk, and which he rigged so loosely that, when he was in it, it assumed the shape of a 'V' with his backside swinging about two inches off the deck; Patrick singing lustily, doing a ballet dance round the messdeck after a night ashore, or suddenly bursting into Shakespeare with dramatic intensity. Patrick playing tramcars while on watch on the veranda round the wheelhouse: 'Ting, ting, move along please, room for two more up here, standing room only downstairs, hurry along now, hold tight,' and he would work handles and ring bells vigorously. A man like Patrick was always an asset to the morale on the lower deck. His chief virtue was that he could 'take it'; an enviable gift. He also kept a diary, excerpts from which capture vividly the life of *Lord Austin* on patrol. First, the ever changing, rigorous weathers.

'Today has been rough. The messdeck is pure havoc; coal, tables, benches, gramophone records, boots, kitbags, all in together in anything but fine weather. It would seem that the following sea, from which we flee, is a horde of hearty sea-sprites, bluff creatures of blue-green glass and soda-water bubbles which speed us on our way, not gently, but in good heart, and if the sea should slap us and send spray bridge-high, it is only doing it in a non-malicious, sturdy way. The ship seems to take it all in the spirit of a rough game, and she is a good sport.'

And again: 'The weather is heavy. The bows seem to gouge the waters and shoot monstrous plumes of ice-green spray on either side, spray which gusts against the bridge windows like rain and makes crossing the open deck from the shelter of the bridge to the foc'sle companionway a hazard of skill and daring, if one is to avoid a wetting. Some dash the distance and chance that speed will outwit the weather. Sometimes it does . . . sometimes. Others move Apache-wise from cover to cover, with ever an eye for that momentary lull.'

Below, on the messdeck, there are matters of importance.

'A topic of absorbing interest for the major portion of this week has been Peter Piper's constipation. In these days, trifles become matters of much moment. Day in, day out, all minds have revolved about this singular stoppage of the bowels. So universal has this topic been that echoes of it must have reached the wardroom. In vain were administered the most potent pills and draughts, but today the blockage is broken, amid general and sincere relief.'

Then back to the demon weather. 'It has snowed today, soft, slushy stuff which clings for an instant then melts, and the view from the wheelhouse window was that of an old, scratched and flickering film, with the snow streaming before the wind.' 'A freak hailstorm. It came out of a clear sunlit day; over a black-blue sea it advanced like a light mist and rattled down on to the deck, stinging the face and tickling the ears and filling the pockets. It was over as swiftly as it had begun. The sun is warming again and we can see distant rainfall all about us like crude daubs of purple and off-white.'

The diary begins to record the work of *Lord Austin* on her long patrols.

'A convoy was dispersed last night, whether by the enemy or the weather we did not know, but the merchant stragglers beating it for the place of new rendezvous served as admirable targets for our gun crew while each in her turn was challenged and made satisfactory reply. The scene presented rather the one in which the small boy pursues an elderly gentleman with catapault fully tensed; the old man maintains an unhurried dignity while the boy, for apprehension, will not fire but thinks he frightens. Stragglers passed during most of the day, heavily laden – one bore planes on her decks, perhaps from the States – and all had a bearing of dogged persistence, no, placidity, as they hitched their way home. There is about these cargo vessels an almost ox-like, unhurried gait. A couple of them had an ox-herd, a destroyer, for guidance.'

And on another day: 'Smoke was seen during the "Dogs" and, as is our duty, we set full speed towards it. It proved to be from another patrolling trawler, but as we drew nearer a greater shape loomed up, three-funnelled and very large. We must have seemed very impertinent as we made towards her with gun crew at their station, but she resigned her dignity and hove-to, to be duly challenged and to give satisfaction. She was the *Empress of Russia*.

'Later, horizon-smoke was seen to port and away we went again at speed, gun crew to station and Aldis flashing. This second ship, however, did not answer our flashing nor our pennants, but continued across our beam. George, our valiant gun-layer, was eager, as he always is, to plug first and ask questions afterwards, but he was forced to restrain his blood-lust. This flouting of authoritative questioning brought the inevitable result, the firing of a blank. For a half charge the noise was highly satisfactory, the suspect ship altered course. Far from our expectations the ship did not stop, so again the detonation; still she didn't stop. Instead she sent out an alarm that she was being pursued by a suspicious-looking vessel – us. This is, I think, the only time upon which one of HM ships about her lawful occasion has been announced over the air as "a suspicious-looking vessel". On reflection we must have presented an oddly piebald effect, since we are wildly daubed with red lead, being in the throes of painting (intermittently, in these severe weathers). Small wonder that our warpaint, combined with detonations, struck fear.'

There could, on occasion, be more to the day than the simple challenging of every passing vessel.

'The day began on a note of excitement. During the night we received instructions to rendezvous with another trawler and her suspect, a Finnish merchantman, and it was thought that each patrol vessel would put aboard an armed party. So it was that some of us quickly won George Crosses in imagination. In minutes (in our daydream) we were designated for the armed party; fifteen minutes later we were defending the bridge against hordes of fiendish Finns. . . . But the cancelling of orders made us just seamen again.

'An armed party goes aboard well prepared. It takes its own food – parties have been poisoned before now; and one is warned against seduction by cigarettes or French postcards. One uses the eyes to convey what ignorance of language cannot get across. So it was, until the cancellation of orders, that we practised withering glances lest the Finns should try to fraternise with the dignity of RN personnel.'

'Night watch: Yesterday we had three calls to the gun. One was an Icelandic trawler, the *Eldborg*, of very modern lines. The horizon silhouette was very much like that of a surfaced submarine, and her actual identity disappointed. We got out of our tin-hats and it was Watch-Ho.

'We later made use of our searchlight for the first time, and a dazzling white pen wrought blots of ultramarine on the surface of the sea. Then peace reigned for a little while, but soon the beam was probing the dark waters again, fine on the starboard and along our length. There was not an exploration for some time, then the captain came down and asked had we heard anything scrape alongside, as the sound had been reported by the engine room. He said calmly: "Oh, it was probably a mine." This as simply as he might have said "It's ten to six".'

It took a great deal more than a loose mine to disturb *Lord Austin*'s captain. He was Lieutenant N. P. McLeod, RNR, a ruddy-faced Scot who had been *Aquamarine*'s last captain, and had taken command of *Lord Austin* when she replaced the smaller vessel. McLeod was a master mariner, formerly a first officer in the biggish ships of the Bank Line. He was very pusser navy – very much resented being addressed as 'skipper' – and kept a captain's remoteness from his crew, leaving the ship's routine entirely to his officers.

Stocky and bluff, he was a man of variable moods, gay at times and drily humorous, but often bitingly sarcastic. He liked to hum hymn tunes on the bridge, and 'Deutchland Uber Alles'; hated Lord Haw-Haw and forbade anyone to listen to his broadcasts. He was always in command of his ship and men and stood no nonsense, roaring his orders in powerful voice when needed. One of his favourite sayings was: 'A sailor without a knife is like a woman without a fanny,' and he looked with quizzical eyes on his mixed crew. Once, coming from cabin to bridge, he stopped to stare at Patrick Bryant, leaning in elegant attitude on the wheel, and said: 'And I'll bet he's wearing a wristwatch!" To a crewman who, on pay day, refused to join the Savings Stamps scheme, he declared: 'Och, lad, ye'll wish ye had when ye're swimming about in the water one day!'

The crew, in return, had their own measure of McLeod, including a memory of him brought from *Aquamarine*. The most popular rig with Northern Patrol officers was a white polo-neck pullover worn with uniform trousers, and the fashion was not lost on the Scot. He was sent a beautiful white sweater by his wife, with instructions that when necessary it was to be sent home for washing. One evening McLeod wore it for drinks aboard another ship, and returning to *Aquamarine* late but very happy, decided to climb aboard up the ship's side. That day the crew had been painting the hull – black. Every man wondered what story the captain told his wife.

Pusser navy as he was, McLeod retained a strong belief in the old seamen's superstition that it was unlucky to pack in anticipation of leave. He never would pack, with the inevitable result that the steward and signalman would be summoned half an hour before his train was due to leave, to help him wildly open drawers and wardrobes and tumble everything into his suitcases.

Often, as *Lord Austin* steamed her dreary patrols, McLeod's first words when arriving on the bridge would be: 'They also serve who only stand and wait. . . .' For there was no disguising the sense of futility felt by most officers and men of the Northern Patrol, having to follow, day after day, what seemed to be the most unnecessary operation of the war. While they sailed the northern sea virtually untroubled by the enemy, many of their families at home were being subjected to German bombing. Far out in the ocean, crews would crowd round their radios and listen anxiously to the BBC's announcement that 'a certain Midlands town' had been heavily bombed the night before.

The unreality of the patrol was gently probed by a newcomer to *Lord Austin*'s crew, who asked the officer of the watch just what they would do if they encountered the *Tirpitz*.

'He replied, without hesitation: "Go in and attack her, of course."

'The idea of our trawler, with her single worth-while gun, going in to engage the pride of the German Navy struck me as so ludicrous that I ventured the suggestion that it might be better for all concerned if we sheered off, hoping that we'd not been spotted, and radioed the position of the battleship to headquarters. Number Two drew himself up and withered me.

' "It is not in the tradition of the British Navy to run away."

'But a strategic withdrawal, sir?'

' "Certainly not. What is one trawler and thirty odd men to the chance of getting one hit on the enemy!" '

Some slight relief on patrol was afforded by exploding or sinking floating mines, usually those which had broken adrift from the British minefield laid to the north-east. Bryant's diary:

'In a heavy sea, the day's highlight – a floating mine. She was sighted after tea. The ship slewed round and made circuit about it, while all with the inclination made to sink or explode it by rifle fire. Number One was at the Hotchkiss and I must admit his aim was good. The horned emblem of menace reeled and mounted on the swelling sea. About and about we steamed, and the air fast became bitter with cordite vapours, and ears sang with the detonations of the rifles. The Hotchkiss splashed the waters and an occasional tracer ricocheted off the water and danced high in the air. As the firing progressed and the mine, though hit often and sinking, showed no sign of sinking rapidly, McLeod grew impatient and shouted down to the miniature Bisley on deck: "If you don't get her this time round we'll lower the smallboat, fix bayonets and charge!"'

There were sights at sea very strange to the non-fishermen.

'The night was heavily uncomfortable and eerie with Northern Lights. To see this strange ivory fire in the heavens, raying, peaking and fitfully flickering, is to sense loneliness and desolation; such loneliness and desolation as the ice-deserts of the far north, whose reflection, some say, gives this light.

'We passed a Swedish ship and they heartened our fishing hopes by demonstrating great beating silver cod, freshly drawn from the sea. Barter swiftly followed. We got £5 worth of fish in exchange for half a pound of not-to-be-disposed-of-contrary-to-regulations tobacco. The fishers drew alongside and threw fish, not to us but at us, for some ten minutes. The heavens rained fish, and all we could do was to take cover. When the downpour ceased, the after deck was heavy with haddock and whiting.'

Constant reminders of the true occupation of men in the stormy waters crossed by the patrol were the fishing boats sighted red-sailed in the fitful northern sunlight. They came from the Faroes.

'Unlike the Orkneys, these Danish islands are golden like hay, and the cold air has the sweetness of crisp clipped grass. These are precipitous bays, and their waters Prussian blue. The Faroes spring prominent from the surrounding mist like dragon teeth soldiers. All other land looms slowly; these islands, one just comes upon.'

The Faroes were defended by British coastal batteries which became rather bored and trigger-happy. One day *Lord Austin* was steaming up a fiord when there was a 'wham' from the shore and a heavy shell ricocheted off the water in front of her bow. She hoisted her recognition signals and steamed on. On her next call at the Faroes there was a parcel from the Army awaiting her. Inside was a four-inch shell, beautifully polished and mounted on an oak base, together with a card which read: 'Yours – we believe.' The shell had landed on the opposite side of the fiord, been found, polished and presented to the ship. It was displayed in the wardroom ever afterwards.

The story went that these impetuous shore gunners tried the same stunt on a passing British destroyer. But she promptly retaliated by training all her gun-turrets on the Army camp, which was swiftly evacuated.

But *Lord Austin*'s most memorable visit to the Faroes was when, while on patrol, she experienced serious trouble in the exterior fittings of her asdic dome. It was decided she would have to enter Thorshaven and obtain the services of a diver. Signalman Hooper:

'It was a fine summer's evening and we were secured alongside the wall. Ahead of us was a Tribal destroyer, HMS *Bedouin*, about to leave. It was soon apparent that something was in the air, loads of activity among the locals ashore and the racy-looking Faroese longboats assembling. And then the shindig started. A shoal of whales had been sighted just offshore, and apparently this was one of the great events in the Faroese calendar. All the longboats set off down the fiord and formed a wide circle round the whales. Each boat carried a large stone on a length of rope, which its occupants kept hurling over the side into the water and then drawing it out again. In this way they drove the whales like a flock of sheep up into the shallow water, and then the local lads, armed with knives and harpoons, threw themselves into the water and on to the backs of the whales and started doing battle.

'It was an astonishing sight, with the old *Lord Austin* tied up in the middle of it and the *Bedouin* trying to get under way.

'When all the whales had been despatched and hauled up, most of the locals went off on an almighty bender lasting all night in the village hall. Our lads who could scrounge shore leave were not slow to take advantage of the celebrations, which resulted in some fat heads the next morning. In the midst of all this we awaited the arrival of the base engineer officer and a civilian diver. Eventually they arrived, the RN officer in a towering rage and the Faroese diver so tight he could hardly stand on his feet.

' "Drunk or not, he's damn well going down to do the job!" said the officer, so the old diver was literally levered into his diving suit and down he went. He did a first-class job and then trotted off back to his drinking.

'We discovered that these annual whale hunts were one of the main sources of food for the Faroese. They hung the whale meat up in strips outside their homes to let it be cured by the weather.'

There was another, less happy occasion when *Lord Austin* again had trouble with her asdic. Big trouble. She was on passage from Iceland to Kirkwall and running before one of the worst 'blows' anyone could remember. Finally she sighted the lighthouse on North Ronaldsay, Orkney, and was fast going ashore. Lieutenant McLeod said there was only one thing he could do – turn and steam against the wind, and he told his crew to 'hang on' as the helm was put over. *Lord Austin* shot into the air and came down across a heaving sea. All her asdic gear snapped off and was lost, but she made it to Kirkwall. The 'blow' was a hurricane which had swept across Iceland and demolished most of the army camps.

There followed more repairs and then back on patrol, once more challenging everything in sight. Bryant's diary:

'Mist persisted through the night and into the early morning, at which time we ran upon a convoy silhouetted in the mist, sharp bows and many stacks. A Tribal challenged us and an American destroyer steamed round us. We allowed her to proceed – so says the logbook for each and every occasion on which we contact a ship, be it an Empress liner or the lowly bellying sails of a Faroese fisher. Such is the conceit of the Patrol Service!'

And later: 'A pursuit in the dark. She did not answer our signals at first, a lax watch no doubt, but after an hour the captain was satisfied and we resumed our job. No sooner had we settled down to the heavy roll of head-on winds than we were away again with all speed. Over the air had come an SOS. A torpedoed vessel, one of two which have appealed tonight. The first one had a vessel to aid her almost as soon as she called, it was to the assistance of the second ship that we now sped. And as we steamed before the wind with engines pulsating with urgency, what were the thoughts and words which passed on the messdeck? Not all so humanitarian, I think, as the occasion might have merited. We were anticipating towage – the saving of the ship and the resultant salvage money – and high were the tales told of similar incidents and the sums of money collected, money which would make us comfortable sailors in a matter of days. With the slowing down of the engine beats, our dreams of opulence died. Once again our good intentions had been done to death by another and nearer ship. Thank God that someone was near.'

A rescue attempt on another occasion merited only brief mention in *Lord Austin*'s logbook. But Bryant documented the haunting scene.

'We received orders to go to the assistance of a ship on fire, and set off full belt northwards. It was thought there was a crew of 80, so blankets and food were prepared for that number. We sighted first a thin stream of grey smoke on the horizon, then the mast and funnel became visible. Calamity had given a fine purple cloud-curtain for the drama, against which the flames shone fiercely. All hands were on voluntary lookout as we approached our objective.

'It is a popular conception that a fire at sea is dramatic. Not so, for a burning ship is an abject object of resignation, rather like a woman in great pain; she bears it bravely without show. We steamed past to the windward looking for signs of boat or survivor, but there was none. The fire, which had taken a strong hold aft, "morsed" at us as it moved swiftly forward. More than once we mistook the flame-flickers for distress signalling and turned to look hopefully, but were confounded. So we steamed east in hope of survivors, turning only when the ship had receded to a mere cigarette-glow in the dark depths of the night. Our searchlight probed the darkness but found nothing. The howl of the gathering gale fanned the flames maliciously, seeming to laugh mockingly at our earnestness and our straining eyes. As we returned to steam about the ship her sampson-posts were silhouetted against the light, and an underglow illuminated the sea, the driving cloud and the drooling smoke. We stood by her all night, and at dawn were relieved by an Admiralty tug and an escort vessel, who took over the watch from us.'

Then a rescue attempt that did come off, in part.

'At four o'clock this afternoon we contacted *Northern Chief* and took aboard two British airmen she had rescued from the sea when their Lockheed-Hudson developed engine trouble. The plane blew up as it hit the water. Of the four who had baled out only two survived. The others died, one by drowning, the other by being strangled by his shirt collar and tie, which shrank in the water and choked him. An ugly incident and an odd one.'

So life on patrol continued, relieved only by such melancholy incidents and by shooting at mines, and grappling odd bits of wreckage from the sea.

'The ocean is a voracious creature which tires quickly of its hastily snatched prizes. Witness the small collection we have accumulated during the job – a destroyer's lifebuoy, a raft, lifebelts, a body, spars, planks, logs, drums.' More items were added as the days passed. 'Two rafts were picked up with a man's suspender as evidence of late human tenancy. They were Swedish out of Bergen, by name *Rimfrashe*. The biscuit and water barrels having been investigated, matches, flares and a battery were found. . . . We are rapidly making a name for ourselves as a picker-up of junk, much of which is useless, but it gives the grappling party practice. Planks, a jib-boom and an

AA kite fell to our vigilance today. Four destroyers crossed our bows and stood off to the south, throwing spray over themselves as an elephant throws sand.'

If the monotony of life in *Lord Austin* differed little from that in the other patrol vessels, she was different at least in one comforting respect. As one of her crew discovered when, at Kirkwall, he went over to the *Kingston Agate* to see how a friend was faring.

'His trawler was very similar to ours – except that the messdeck was alive with small red beetles of the cockroach strain. There were tens of thousands of them; they were everywhere, on the deck, the bulkheads, the deckhead, the tables, the bunks and even on the occupants of the messdeck, who seemed supremely indifferent to their presence. The whole place seemed alive with crawling, scurrying insects. They ran over the food on the plates and had to be brushed off before a mouthful was eaten; they dropped on to your hair and shoulders as you sat at the table.

'Good God!' I said. 'How the hell do you put up with this lot?'

'He laughed and replied: "Oh, we're so used to them, we hardly notice them."

'I thanked my stars that *Lord Austin* was free from such infestation and for once was thoroughly glad to get back aboard her!'

Though it was part of the duty of the asdic trawlers to watch for and listen out for U-boats, few U-boats were ever contacted or seen. They must have crossed the British patrol lines on their way to and from the Atlantic, yet if they saw the trawlers they did not waste either shot or torpedo on them. It was said the U-boats fixed their positions on the slowly plodding Northern Patrol trawlers when going out and coming back; certainly it was felt among the trawler crews that there was some sort of gentlemen's agreement that if they did not attack the U-boats, the U-boats would not attack them.

This theory of a strange truce existing between the trawlers and the U-boats was given added strength by the affair of the trawler *Visenda*. While on patrol she contacted a U-boat and depth charged it, bringing back evidence of having at least damaged the German, if not actually sinking it. One Sunday afternoon a few weeks later *Visenda's* aft lookout went into the galley for a warm, and at that precise moment a U-boat surfaced astern. *Visenda's* officer of the watch called the captain, at the same time giving the order 'Hard-a-port!' to bring the forward four-inch to bear. But *Visenda*'s captain, on coming up, unknowingly counter-ordered 'Hard-a-starboard!' (single-screw trawlers turned more easily and quickly to starboard because of the clockwise thrust of the screw). This unfortunate muddle gave the U-boat's crew time to man their gun, loose off about nine rounds at the helpless trawler, and crash dive before she could reply. The shells thudded into *Visenda*, shrapnel filling the galley and entering the bread which was just being baked; they struck the bridge, and the captain was killed by flying glass from the shattered bridge window.

Was it revenge by the U-boat she had attacked? Or, if this had been lost, by one of its fellows? There were many who held strongly to this belief.

There were two direct results of the *Visenda* incident. One was that all the patrol trawlers were eventually fitted with protective triplex-glass bridge windows. The other was that they were sent in turn to the newly opened sea training establishment at Tobermory, on the Island of Mull, for an intensive work-up under the gimlet eye of Commodore Sir Gilbert Stephenson. The already legendary old 'Monkey Brand' himself.

8

The Terror of Tobermory

Tobermory! The order to proceed there for work-up was received with apprehension by all crews and positively dreaded by the officers. Not because of the rigours of the battle school, but because of its fiery Commodore, a heavily bewhiskered vice-admiral brought back from retirement to lick the convoy escorts into shape.

Commodore Gilbert Stephenson was known in more polite terms as 'Monkey Brand' or 'Electric Whiskers', or simply 'the terror of Tobermory'. Even his wife admitted: 'My husband is a very fierce man.' Very fierce, very efficient and, despite his years, very energetic and full of drive, for he was in his middle-sixties. At this age he had broken out of retirement to fly his flag at Tobermory in an old Dutch horse boat, once used to run live horse flesh to Rotterdam. This, his base ship, was renamed HMS *Western Isles*. His battle school commenced in mid-1940 and the tremors of its lively coming reverberated throughout the Fleet.

Soon 'Monkey Brand' had secured the aid of Fleet Air Arm aircraft, submarines, motor launches and speedboats to help reproduce battle conditions for the benefit of new corvettes, frigates and sloops sent to Tobermory fresh from the shipyards; and for the veteran ships sent there for refresher courses, like the Patrol Service trawlers.

'Monkey Brand' achieved splendid results by methods which owed nothing to the naval drill book. He worked by fear, surprise and shock tactics. Thorough to the last degree, he would remove on the spot any officer he considered inefficient, once signalling a trawler's C.O.: 'Suggest I remove all your officers and have replacements sent forthwith.' To his credit this C.O. declined. The Commodore really had no power to remove an officer from his ship, only the Admiralty could do so, except when an officer was guilty of misbehaviour – drunkenness, madness or assault. But the Commodore would whip off an officer he considered not up to scratch, then signal the Admiralty that he had taken Lieutenant X ashore 'for training', and would their Lordships please send a replacement for the ship. . . .

The trawler crews on their work-ups, which lasted from two to three weeks, found themselves on day and night gunnery exercises, mock U-boat hunts with a real live submarine, boat-pulling instruction and even field training on the hillsides. A piratically black-beareded chief petty officer with waxen ends to his moustache would give lurid and bawdy lectures on the duties of lookouts, warning them in spectacular language that the Germans knew exactly when the watches on British ships were changed, and often attacked just after a new, sleepy-eyed watch had taken over.

The trawler men had not undergone such vigorous exercises since their early training, and some not even then. They were not enthusiastic about it.

'Gestapo' parties in smallboats sneaked up on the trawlers to catch out unwary quartermasters. 'Monkey Brand' himself, in a fast motorboat which he used to make sorties round the harbour, delighted in getting aboard ships unobserved by day and night, and if possible removing valuable gear from the wardroom. The morning after one of his night raids some unfortunate ship would receive the dismaying signal: 'I have your sextant in my cabin – come and retrieve it forthwith.'

He had other ploys. He would slip aboard a ship, creep up to a rating and suddenly growl in his ear: 'There's a U-boat on the port bow – do something about it, man, do something!' Occasionally, just occasionally, he met his match. Coming thus aboard *Lord Austin* one day he crept up to two ratings and hissed: 'There's a fire on the messdeck!' To which one of the men calmly replied: 'Oh yes, sir – we always keep a good fire going down there.'

They deserved their small victory, for *Lord Austin*'s arrival on 'Monkey Brand's' territory had been unsettling enough. She had sailed into Tobermory Bay, all four of her officers on the bridge wearing clean collars and ties and a worried look. She picked up her buoy perfectly, a model demonstration, and the officers relaxed – at least they had made a good start. But then came the thunderous signal: 'Why have you gone to the wrong buoy? Proceed to number four buoy forthwith!' They need not have despaired, for 'Monkey Brand', who watched every ship come in and timed them with a stopwatch as they made their buoy, often used to order them to another buoy just to see them go through the whole performance again.

But for *Austin* there was worse to follow. It was 'Monkey Brand's' rule that all men aboard should be able to switch roles and do the jobs of others, which created chaos on exercises with everyone frantically changing posts and seamen going to the stokehold while stokers launched the whalers and manned the guns. On one dreadful occasion when all this was going on during a night shoot, some stokers were on *Austin's* four-inch preparing to fire starshells, when at the critical moment a shell stuck in the barrel. The starshells, being delicate, had a grommet or rope ring round the base to prevent damage, and in the dark the stokers had thrust a shell into the breech without noticing the grommet still on it. The gunner's mate fussed and jittered around trying to dig the shell out with his ramrod. 'Oh dear, oh dear,' he wailed in most un-mate-like language – 'My goodness, what a terrible thing to happen at a time like this – what would the Commodore say?'

Austin was exercising with two other trawlers at the time and the most successful feature of the affair was that nobody hit anybody else. They were luckier than some. Like the trawler *Quadrille*, which achieved notoriety by firing both depth-charge throwers while secured to a buoy with another trawler alongside. The depth-charges were set to 150 feet, and the ensuing explosions, besides causing interior damage to both ships, were felt in the church ashore where the Commodore happened to be reading the lesson. His comments are not recorded.

'Monkey Brand' had a wonderful and unnerving memory for faces. He would suddenly roar to a petrified officer: 'You've been here before, haven't you?' To which there was scarcely any answer. Another characteristic was his rigid distinction between lunch and dinner. Every so often, two or three officers from ships working-up would be invited to eat with him aboard *Western Isles*. As the duty-boat brought them aboard, 'Monkey Brand's' chief steward would be waiting alongside the officer of the watch and the boatswain's mate. If it was dinner, the guests would get drinks and plenty of interesting talk until the early hours of the morning. But if it was lunch – nothing but water. It was eat up and away, with 'Monkey Brand's' parting shot ringing in their ears: 'Well, you'll be anxious to get back to the job!' Fortunately the wine steward always knew who had been asked to lunch, and those guests, when they went to their cabin to wash, always found a couple of drinks with which to fortify themselves before facing up to the Commodore.

One of 'Monkey Brand's' favourite tricks was to speed over to a ship in his motorboat, hustle up the ladder on to the assembled quarter-deck, grab off his gold-braided cap and throw it to the deck, shouting: 'That's a bomb – what are you going to do about it?' The ruse never failed to create momentary panic. Until one day, when he tried it out on a trawler. As he flung his cap down in front of the startled company and made his challenge, a rating stepped smartly forward and kicked the cap overboard. The surprised Commodore gazed unbelievingly at his cap floating away on the water. But he was not beaten. 'Good work,' he said approvingly – 'splendid.' Then pointing to the cap, he roared: 'Quick, that's a survivor who can't swim – save him!'

Among the honoured few who actually did get the better of 'Monkey Brand' was the C.O. of a midget submarine exercising at Tobermory. After suffering the lash of the Commodore's tongue he took his tiny craft alongside the old *Western Isles* and left a dummy limpet bomb with a rude message on it directly below 'Monkey Brand's' porthole. It was said that when the 'bomb' was discovered the voice of the Commodore addressing his unlucky officer of the watch stampeded sheep on a hillside four miles away.

But it was the trawler *Rumba* that won perhaps the most satisfying victory of all. Her number one was Sub-Lieutenant Jim Fowler, RNVR.

'We had been accused by "Monkey" Stephenson of having been boarded during the night and found to have no gangwayman or anybody on watch. I personally was rather incensed about this, so was the coxswain and others; we were quite sure this hadn't happened. So that evening, when our captain was having dinner with the Commodore, four of us took the boat away and went up to cable length from *Western Isles*. Leaving one man in the boat, we boarded the depot ship without being seen. Two of us then got on to the bridge, leaving the other man keeping lookout on the foc'sle head in readiness for a quick getaway. It was pitch dark up on the bridge, and we were just getting the magnetic compass out of the binnacle to take away with us when there was a movement in the corner. It was an armed guard.

'He said, "Can I help you?" We replied: "Yes please, can you give us a hand getting the compass out? We'll hold your rifle for you." Trustingly he gave us his rifle and then we were all set; we took the compass and with the guard in tow, went down to the officer of the watch's cabin, nobody questioning us on the way. We entered the cabin and got the O.O.W. to sign a form – we had the rifle – saying that we'd boarded his ship at such a time and taken away his compass. Then we left hurriedly.

'Next morning we got a signal saying, would we please return the compass? And that was all. We had no more trouble after that.

'Next time I went to Tobermory for working-up I was in command of a trawler, and I wasn't looking forward to it very much. But I had a very easy time indeed, as I was "killed" in the first two minutes of the main exercise and it was left to everybody else to carry on.'

Away from the mock battles of Tobermory the war continued hard for Harry Tate's Navy, more than thirty vessels being lost in the first three months of 1941 and the losses piling up with each succeeding month. During January nearly all the losses were from mines. Many other trawlers were damaged, and some, like the former Hull fisher *Bernard Shaw*, had the narrowest of escapes. Her newly promoted commander was Skipper William Thorpe. 'One night while sweeping the Barrow Deep we nearly met our end. It was raining hard and a nice breeze, so I told the gun crew to get under the whaleback for shelter as we were approaching number four Barrow buoy. I heard a plane fly overhead, and trying to spot him with the binoculars saw a parachute mine being dropped. I caught sight of it just under our starboard crosstree, ordered "Hard-a-port!" and the parachute slid over the foredeck into the water. Three more feet to port and that would have been the finish of us.'

Another minesweeper, the old *Stella Rigel*, had swept all day long off the Essex coast without getting a single mine. She went on working through the moonless night. Skipper T. Spall, RNR, kept a wary lookout as he passed each buoy, knowing that an E-boat might be hiding in its shadow. He continued sweeping till the end of the middle-watch, then told the tired hands to pipe down for a few hours rest.

He left the bridge for the first time since *Stella Rigel* had put to sea, but did not go down below to his cabin, remaining on deck near the ready-loaded Oerlikon mounted aft. Suddenly hearing aircraft engines he ran to the gun, and as a searching plane zoomed over low he fired. He did not order action-stations which would have brought the crew from their bunks, for to do that, as he explained afterwards: 'I would have had to run to the bridge to sound the bell, and by the time the hands had closed up, the Heinkel might have been back in Germany.' So he tipped the Oerlikon skywards and kept up rapid fire. The Heinkel lost height and moments later blew up in the sea half a mile ahead. The action had lasted a matter of seconds, but now the hands were astir. Skipper Spall went for'ard and shouted down the companionway leading to the foc'sle: 'Just come up and have a look at this, lads!' They tumbled up on deck to watch the Heinkel blazing in the sea.

That's how Skipper Spall won his DSC.

In the Channel the trawler *Syringa*, commanded by Skipper W. Ritchie, RNR, was sweeping in company with another trawler when they sighted a Junkers 87 flying in at about 300 feet. *Syringa*'s sister ship challenged and was answered by a burst of machine-gun fire. She opened with her 12-pounder and Lewis gun as the plane crossed her quarter and dropped a salvo of bombs on either side.

Then it was the turn of *Syringa*. The plane sprayed her bridge and deck with machine-gun bullets, and dropped two more salvoes, one narrowly missing to starboard, the other to port. The plane then went back to attack the other trawler, injuring her skipper, after which it returned again to *Syringa*. Seaman-Gunner Colyer, at *Syringa*'s Lewis gun, was killed by a burst from the German rear-gunner as the plane passed over, and a bomb pierced the engine room casing. It crashed down on to the platform on the fore side of the engine but failed to explode.

The Junkers circled and returned for a third attack on *Syringa*, but it seemed to be losing height and dropped down within range of the trawler's 12-pounder. Two well placed shots sent the German crashing into the sea a mile away.

Skipper Ritchie, a braw Scot, went down to the engine room, where, despite the presence of the unexploded bomb, Stoker Petty Officer G. Wood had remained at his post. With the help of Chief Engineman E. Clinton the skipper carried the heavy bomb on deck and threw it derisively over the side. That was how Skipper Ritchie earned his DSC and the other two men the DSM.

Skipper Ritchie was indeed a man to be reckoned with. 'It

was on *Syringa*,' a member of her crew recalls, 'that we had a skate of a Welshman, an AB, who was always dodging work, usually by pretending to be sick. One morning he asked to see the skipper, and being at sea he did so on the bridge. I was at the wheel, and down the voice-pipe I got this end to the conversation by the skipper – "Now you go away to your hammock, sonny, and turn in. It takes a man just fifteen minutes to die – if ye aren't dead in fifteen minutes, get back on this bloody deck!"'

As ever, the drifter *Fisher Boy* was in the thick of it. Early January 1941 found her helping in the rescue work off Clacton when the motorship *Strathearn* went down to a mine. Sixteen men were picked up alive out of *Strathearn*'s crew of thirty-four.

Later the same month *Fisher Boy* was on patrol out of Brightlingsea when she anchored in thick weather. All hands turned in with the exception of Signalman Bev Smith and Seaman Cyril Paine. Signalman Smith:

'We heard quite a noise going on out at sea and assumed that a passing convoy was being attacked. I left Cyril in the wheelhouse to go down to the galley to make a pot of tea, when there was an almighty roaring sound and a Junkers 88 came in very low, machine-gunned us and dropped several bombs. We both dashed to the Lewis guns and managed to get them going, but after half a dozen shots both our guns jammed. I got my gun released and trained on the aircraft again just in time to see what I thought was a mine floating down on a parachute. I aimed at the mine, hoping to explode it while in the air, but to my surprise it swung its legs apart – it was one of the crew, the pilot. The plane crashed and the pilot landed in the water. By now, with all the noise going on, our crew had turned out in a bit of a hurry and we found we had barely enough steam to get the anchor up. The wind had caught the German pilot's parachute and he was skimming across the water on his way back across the North Sea – it took us some time to catch up with him. Eventually a neatly thrown lead line fouled his parachute rigging and we hauled the frightened fellow aboard. We dried him down, dressed him up in a sailor's suit, and I called ashore on our radio for someone to come and take him off the ship. An Air Sea Rescue launch came out and we put our prisoner aboard dressed as an English matelot. He had got over his fright now and was a bit cocky. But not half as cocky as we felt, having brought the plane down with a few Lewis shots. We celebrated, highly illegally, with neat rum which we kept bottled, and were highly pleased later to hear it announced over the BBC that the drifter *Fisher Boy* had shot down an enemy plane.'

Success of a different kind came to the trawler *Tourmaline* while on convoy escort. Unlike most other trawlers she had never gone fishing in her life, having been bought by the Admiralty as she was built. In late January she had just been refitted and looked more like a yacht, her decks as white as snow and even her brass polished, though this was an error in wartime.

One night *Tourmaline* was at her station on the port side of a convoy when her officer of the watch, Midshipman Allan Waller, was alerted by starshells fired by the destroyers ahead. Looking towards the land he saw a tell-tale splash of foam and rang the alarm bell. The crew ran to action-stations. Suddenly an E-boat was seen approaching on the port bow at high speed and *Tourmaline* let fly with everything she had – her port Lewis gun, the twin point-fives aft, the Savage guns on the welldeck, and her 12-pounder. As the E-boat shot across her bow only 100 yards away *Tourmaline*'s guns kept up a hail of fire from her starboard side. Answering machine-gun bullets from the E-boat peppered her funnel, and one of her own Lewis guns, which had no stop, slewed right round and drilled holes in the break of the foc'sle just below the 12-pounder platform, narrowly missing the gun's crew. During this encounter a second E-boat sped up astern and began firing. *Tourmaline*'s aft point-five gunners emptied their guns at it, scoring repeatedly with their tracer shots. The damaged boat sheered off and attention was focused again on the first one, which after a crippling shell from the trawler's 12-pounder, had swerved hard to port. Now its engine had stopped, and it was awash and covered in foam. *Tourmaline*, still firing, turned to ram it, but had to hold back when a ship of the convoy came into line. The E-boat sank without survivors, a definite 'kill'.

But it had been a very near thing. In his official report *Tourmaline*'s captain commented: 'The success of this short action was entirely due to the fact that the ship was at full action-stations as a result of seeing the starshells fired by the destroyers. If the warning had not been received, the only armaments ready to engage the enemy in the short time available would have been the point-fives. The ship's complement is inadequate to keep continuous watch on the other guns in the severe weather conditions prevailing at this time of year.'

Unhappily *Tourmaline*'s taste of victory was short-lived. Just thirteen days afterwards, on February 5th, she was again on escort duty, almost at the rear of a convoy as it passed Dover. This convoy was enjoying the welcome air cover of four Spitfires. When a Junkers 87B attacked one of the merchant ships *Tourmaline* fired and took the top of its tail off, and away it limped, hotly pursued by all four Spitfires, who finally shot it down. Unwittingly, however, by all chasing after the German, the Spitfires left *Tourmaline* to her fate. Directly above her was high cloud. As the Spitfires vanished, down through a hole in the cloud zoomed a second Junkers 87B, straight for the hapless trawler. After half a dozen rounds *Tourmaline*'s point-fives jammed and she was helpless; down came three bombs, one of which crashed through the engine room casing and exploded, throwing everyone to the deck and blasting the ship's point-fives off their mounting.

Two of her gunners were injured, one being blown over the side of the sinking ship. Three men were killed and others burnt and scalded. One boat was got away, the other men jumped over the side.

Quick revenge for *Tourmaline* came when the low-flying plane continued over another part of the convoy. The Hull trawler *Lady Philomena* wheeled to the fight and Leading-Seaman Alec Dodd let blast with his four-inch, sending the German crashing into the sea. It was an action for which he won the DSM, and his wiry commander, Skipper Albert Robinson, RNR, the DSC.

Philomena picked up some of *Tourmaline*'s survivors, the others being rescued by a tug acting as a balloon ship. One stoker was so badly scalded that he only lived for a few days afterwards. Among the badly injured was Midshipman Waller. When the ship was struck he was hurled to the deck from the point-five zareba and blacked out. On coming dazedly to his senses he staggered for'ard through steam and smoke, his face and hands scarred by steam, and passed out again on the well-deck. He recovered consciousness to find himself in a boat with five of the crew, and suffering badly from facial wounds and scalded wrists. Taken ashore at Sheerness, he went on to Chatham naval hospital and was there for some weeks, being treated by a surgeon who had been a member of Sir Alexander Macindoe's team of plastic surgeons at East Grinstead. Waller was given only morphia and his face felt as if it was being scrubbed with sandpaper – a very painful process. But the treatment was highly successful, and weeks later he was back at Harwich looking for another ship. However, his reputation as a survivor from two sunken trawlers, *Amethyst* and now *Tourmaline*, in little more than two months, besides being in the corvette *Primula* when she was rammed and badly damaged, had preceded him, and he was almost thrown off two trawlers he visited, being dubbed as 'The Jonah of Parkeston Quay'.

Waller's unfortunate record was not unique. With more than 160 Patrol Service vessels now sent to the bottom there were many other survivors like him. And the ship casualties continued to rise steeply in the early months of 1941, reaching a peak in May of one vessel lost every two days, this chiefly as a result of enemy bombing. There were, in the midst of it, some memorable escapes and none so weird as that of the small and very old Lowestoft drifter *Young Mun*. Her engineman was Walter Walker.

'We were detailed to accompany a group of trawlers steaming out to clear some mines which had been laid near Folkestone, and were only two miles out of Dover when two German bombers swooped down on our small fleet of ten ships. All the vessels opened fire, the trawlers with their anti-aircraft guns, the drifters with their double-barrelled machine-guns. I was at my post at *Young Mun*'s engines when suddenly there was a terrific crash and water poured down through the engine room skylight. I stopped engines and ran up on deck to take a look. It was a fantastic mess. A Junkers 88 had crashed down on our deck, bringing down the mast and covering the ship with wreckage. Two of its crew had been flung out and one hung on a small derrick, the other on the ship's quarter, both bodies with their legs missing. We were ordered to return to Dover, which we did after dropping all the gruesome parts in the water. As we were about to enter harbour we were stopped by the suspicious officer on the mole – because our mast was down we were unable to run up any identification signals. It was only after taking a good look at the evidence piled up on the deck that he allowed us in, much to the amusement of the crew.'

The losses from enemy bombing continued, among them three vessels which went down off Lowestoft, almost within sight of the Patrol Service depot, in as many weeks. These were the trawlers *Ben Gairn* and *King Henry*, and the drifter *Uberty*, which was blown to pieces just outside the harbour. They were joined by the drifter *Thistle*, wrecked by a mine.

June was a shattering month, every lost vessel but one falling a victim to the attacks of enemy planes. But it did not stop the convoys. On the Channel convoys, Portsmouth to Southend, usually five trawlers swept abreast, followed by a destroyer and then the merchant ships, mostly coastal colliers bringing coal from South Wales to the power stations on the Thames; for the railways could not cope with the coal traffic and it had to come by sea, even through the Straits of Dover. When the convoy reached the Straits the trawlers broke formation and two continued to sweep with shortened depths. The three others became additional escorts on the flanks of the convoy, and eventually all five were purely escorts as they approached Southend.

The trawlers spent a night in the Medway and began their return voyage the following night, again passing through the Straits in the dark. Invariably they were shelled from the French coast on the westbound trip, while passing through at about 10 p.m., but on coming east, between 2 a.m. and 3 a.m., they were allowed a peaceful passage by the enemy gunners. It appeared that even the Germans liked their sleep.

Time and again the phlegmatic quality of the trawler skippers showed itself in the most heated moments. There was the occasion when a trawler patrolling five miles out of Grimsby, watching for minelaying aircraft, was attacked by a Heinkel. The ship disappeared in bomb splashes but reappeared seemingly unharmed. However, she made no response to signals from the shore station, so a boat was sent out to investigate. They could see no sign of life on board and the quiet scene had all the eeriness of a *Marie Celeste* mystery; until on the vessel's other side were discovered smallboats with almost the entire ship's company in them busily picking up dead fish.

The trawlers continued to play a large part in rescue work in E-boat Alley and many merchant sailors had cause to bless them. Like Fireman Joseph Willis of the SS *Westbourne*, which was dive-bombed in a convoy passing north of Flamborough Head.

'I had just come off watch at midnight and everyone was in the galley, thinking they were safe at last, when it happened. I was on the poop deck aft with two shipmates, holding a mug of coffee in my hand. The blast of the bombs blew us all overboard. Next thing I remembered was coming to my senses in the cold sea. I swam about in the dark till I got hold of some old hatch-board, which I clung on to and managed to stay afloat. A destroyer raced past, a voice shouting through a megaphone that he would send help.

'Everyone amidships in the *Westbourne* had been blown to pieces. As I hung on to my float in the dark I could see her burning and hear the ammunition exploding. I must have been in the water for six or seven hours, for it had turned daylight, when out of the blue came a Patrol Service trawler and her sailors fished me out of the sea. "God blow me, Geordie," said one, "couldn't you find a better time than this to take a bloody bath!" They plied me with Craven A cigarettes and plenty of rum.

'We could see the *Westbourne* miles away, still on fire and her ammunition going off. Next day at Hartlepool, where I went into hospital, I saw her after she'd been brought in by tugs. Her bridge, funnel, boats, everything was completely gone; she was just like a flat-iron. They found a charred body which they thought was the skipper's, and another body, that of the wireless operator. Others had gone down to Davy Jones, and if it hadn't been for Harry Tate's men he'd have got me too.'

Many Patrol Service men were sent straight from Lowestoft to the trawler base at Belfast. Here, trawlers were employed both on Atlantic convoys and on minesweeping. Within weeks of joining the old Dutch trawler *Friesland*, Seaman Robert Thomas was involved in the tragedy of a sister ship.

'It was a Sunday, and we were duty ship. At about 2 p.m. the quayside telephone started ringing. The sentry who should have been on the quay was on the messdeck, and the rest of the seamen were in their bunks. An argument started between them and the sentry as to who should answer the phone, which kept on ringing. Eventually a young Scotsman with more imagination than the rest said it might be important and dashed up on deck to answer it. He returned with a message that there had been an explosion down Belfast Lough. As duty ship we steamed out to investigate, but when we reached the scene all that remained on the surface was some floating wreckage and a lifebelt bearing the name of the drifter *Jewel*, an inshore minesweeper. She had gone up on a mine. In among the wreckage was the body of her young sub-lieutenant; we found no survivors. Ironically, one of *Jewel*'s Patrol Service crew had only just joined her; he'd been sent to recuperate at a quiet base after a harassing time minesweeping at Dover.

'Soon after we returned to harbour the quayside phone rang again and this time I answered. A woman's voice asked if she could speak to Sub-Lieutenant ——, of one of our minesweepers. I told her that his ship was at sea, which was true enough. The *Jewel* would never return, and Sub-Lieutenant —— was lying on our deck, his broken body covered with a blanket.'

In the North Sea, typical of the small trawler minesweepers was the *Contender*. She operated with three others in a group of four, carrying out regular Oropesa (moored mine) sweeping duties from Lowestoft to Sheringham Shoal. Her signalman was Colin Brown.

'Though we were never actually involved in any skirmishes with the enemy on the water we frequently heard their engines and witnessed the night engagements with the convoys, which were always just astern of us, doing a little better than our sweeping speed of about six knots. With our World War 1 vintage 12-pounder and two single Lewis guns on their bridge mountings, I, for one, was always relieved when we left the swept channel at either end of our stint.

'There was always the floating mine, particularly after a spell of easterly gales, and rifles were handed out with armour-piercing ball ammunition for our "marksmen" to have a bash. Most of these floating mines were ours, washed away from the East Coast minefield, and most were set safe and had to be punctured a number of times before they would consent to sink.

'Our main bugbear at this time were the Junkers 88s which sneaked across the North Sea in periods of poor visibility. Often their real targets were on the East Coast, but they could make our lives miserable, shooting us up with their cannon and machine guns. Lots of our little ships had small steel boxes with peepholes set up behind the bridge, in which the skipper could shelter during an attack and continue to con his ship.'

Nogi, the senior vessel of *Contender*'s group, fell victim of a near miss by a bomb one evening as they were nearing the end of the sweep off Cromer. She started to founder by the head. *Contender* and *Solon* went alongside and with bow and stern ropes secured, steamed all out for the shoreline to drag the wreck off the swept channel. They just managed to do this before the respective skippers had to give the order to chop the hawsers.

Contender's own brush with the enemy had a happier result. It occurred when a Heinkel attacked the group as they were sweeping. 'He made a dummy run, circled and pointed towards the last in line – us. Swooping down he dropped two big bombs at masthead height, and both were travelling almost horizontally when one crashed on to the 12-pounder gun platform and shot off into the sea beyond, where it exploded. The tail of the bomb was sheered off and wedged under the gun mounting, effectively putting the gun out of commission. The bomb must have been a 1,000 pounder, for it so damaged the gun mounting and platform that we were in dock for a fortnight while the plates were straightened out. Had it gone off on impact instead of in the sea, I would not have been able to tell the tale. I was standing on the wing of the bridge at the crucial time with a jammed and useless Lewis gun in my hand, when a fire bucket dislodged by the impact sent sand shooting across the foredeck and over the bridge. I very nearly collapsed with fright, but was able to put on a brave face with the rest when we were congratulated on our return to harbour. We'd had a miraculous escape, and for some reason which I am not able to explain we were treated like heroes, which we were very far from being.'

Another member of the foursome, the *Force*, was not as fortunate. 'We were anchored off the mouth of the river at Great Yarmouth when she caught a packet. Visibility was extremely poor and we had a couple of shackles out waiting for the mist to clear. Unfortunately *Force* did not have a shackle on deck ready to slip in an emergency, and when a Jerry plane loomed up and dropped a stick of bombs across her bows the steampipe to her windlass was fractured and she was unable to pick up her anchor and beach herself. Despite frantic attempts to run out more cable and knock out the next shackle pin she slid to the bottom in about twenty minutes. It was Harry Tate's Navy after all, wasn't it?'

Higher up the East Coast, at North Shields, the 8th Minesweeping Flotilla was based. It consisted of eight paddle steamers with names nostalgic of an idle peacetime: *Laguna Belle*, *Thames Queen*, *Glengower*, *Glen Avon*, *Glen Usk*, *Southsea*, *Snaefell* and *Medway Queen*. Gunner officer of *Thames Queen* was Lieutenant James Reeve, RNVR.

'The paddlers were especially well suited for conversion to Oropesa minesweepers because of their shallow draught, which was up to about seven feet, and their extensive decks, which allowed them to be fitted with powerful steam winches from which sweeps could be streamed on either quarter, and with protective armament – if available! This same extensive deck, however, offered an unpleasantly large target to hostile aircraft, and if the deck was wooden and well scrubbed to please a zealous first lieutenant, it made the ship a conspicuous target on a moonlit night.

'The usual armament of these old paddlers was a 12-pounder on the foredeck, two or more Lewis guns on or near the bridge, a couple of Brens if they had been able to "win" them from the grateful soldiery at Dunkirk or elsewhere, half a dozen rifles for sinking mines, and half a dozen depth-charges. Towards the end of 1941 we carried balloons when sweeping, and there was one other piece of defensive equipment that was unique, the Holman projector, used also by the trawlers. This was the most frightening thing I ever had to handle during the war. It fired a Mills bomb into the air to deter and destroy aircraft engaged on a low-level attack. It consisted of a length of steel piping forming a six-foot barrel which could be swung about freely. The firing power was either compressed air from a steel bottle, or a steam supply from the boilers. Experience was to show that the compressed air was sometimes only powerful enough to spit out the bomb so close to the ship that it broke the lavatory basins, and that the engine room staff objected to their steam being continually leaked away when the projector was in a state of readiness. After one night air attack I was approached by the old "Stripey" who had charge of this infernal machine, with the confession that he had put in a bomb upside down and it was still there after the projector had been simmering away all night. The junior engineer and I got it out and back in its tin, and away into the deep without delay; and when I came to leave *Thames Queen* the Holman projector had ceased to be regarded as an effective weapon.

'*Southsea* had the distinction of shooting down an attacking aircraft, but alas, was blown up just outside Tyne harbour after completing a search-sweep, the victim of an acoustic mine.'

A few months later *Snaefell* met her end, bombed by enemy planes off the Tyne, while down at Harwich the paddlers *Marmion* and *Lorna Doone* were constant targets for enemy cannon shells and machine-guns, suffering damage almost every time they poked their noses out of harbour. *Marmion* finished up a total wreck from enemy bombs. Later, and sensibly, all the surviving paddlers were to be stripped of much of their sweeping gear, fitted with extra guns and converted to anti-aircraft vessels.

In the heat of action collisions were inevitable, and the terse official description of 'Lost by collision' formed an unfair epitaph for some unlucky trawlers which had fought bravely through other hazards. Like the bomb-scarred *Marconi*. Petty Officer Robert Muir:

'Our flotilla sailed from Harwich in the evening as usual for the night's sweeping. At midnight, when we had anchored to a buoy, out came the Ipswich patrol ships at full speed. It was a pitch black night, you could hardly see a hand in front of you. Suddenly the Ipswich vessels were attacked by enemy planes and the noise of battle was terrific. There was a resounding crash and *Marconi* heeled over. We dashed on deck just in time to see one of the Ipswich patrol ships drawing her bows out of our boiler room. The skipper, giving orders to get the lifeboat and raft ready, hurried down to see the damage but was met by the chief engineer coming out of the engine room. "It's no good, skipper," he said, "she's sinking – the engine room's half full already." Out went the order to abandon ship and the boat and raft were launched. The enemy planes must have seen our lights flashing – we were using torches to see and get everything away – and one dropped a stick of three bombs just alongside us. The ship shuddered – it was the finishing touch. The skipper told me to see if there was anyone left down on the messdeck. I shot down and sure enough there was Horace, one of the stokers, fast asleep! I pulled him out of his bunk, dragged him up on deck and pushed him into the raft – poor devil, he didn't know what was going on and was petrified. I then scrambled into the boat with the rest of the crew and the skipper told the rating standing by the bow painter to let go and climb in. He did so, but let the painter trail along the deck and it caught up on one of the dan buoy anchors. *Marconi* was going down fast. The skipper quickly seized an axe and chopped us free, or she would have dragged us down with her – as we tried to row away, the suction of her was so great that I broke an oar in half with the strain. But we got clear at last, and after rowing for over an hour were picked up by a small tug.'

Such was the dismal end of *Marconi*, veteran of two wars; launched 1916, lost 1941.

One of the most bitter collision disasters struck on a North Sea convoy in July.

On the night of the 19th, the brand-new submarine HMS *Umpire* was making her first sea voyage northwards from Chatham, bound for trials on the Clyde. She sailed on the surface in a convoy of merchant ships escorted by trawlers and motor launches. About nightfall *Umpire* developed engine trouble which caused her to drop astern of the convoy, and a motor launch dropped back to act as her escort until she was able to catch up again.

The convoy was due to pass a southbound convoy at midnight

somewhere off the Wash. It was a calm night, very dark, but no lights could be shown because of the ever roaming E-boats. *Umpire* and her guardian motor launch lost touch, and when the two convoys met up, the submarine was some miles astern, alone and almost invisible to other ships even at close range.

By international rule ships in a channel-way should keep to the starboard side and pass port-to-port, but on this night the two convoys passed each other on the wrong side: that is, starboard-to-starboard. Consequently *Umpire*'s surprised captain found the oncoming convoy approaching him head on. He altered course a few degrees to port and the first six ships of the convoy passed safely down his starboard side. But one of the trawler escorts, the *Peter Hendriks*, keeping station on the flank of the convoy, suddenly loomed up almost dead ahead. *Umpire*'s captain took the only action possible to him and ordered hard-a-port. Unfortunately just as the submarine began to turn, the trawler saw her low, dark shape ahead and naturally swung to starboard, making a collision inevitable.

Peter Hendriks struck *Umpire* heavily near the starboard bow. For seconds the two vessels stayed locked together, then the trawler fell away and within 30 seconds *Umpire* sank, taking down all but two officers and two lookouts with her. Thanks to good use of the Davis escape apparatus, many of her company were saved, but two officers and twenty men were lost.

No blame could attach to the *Peter Hendriks*, but that was small consolation to her horrified crew.

In the following month of August a handful of Northern Patrol trawlers played a major part in one of the most remarkable incidents yet in the war at sea, when a U-boat surrendered in the Atlantic to an aircraft of Coastal Command.

On the furiously blowing morning of August 27th the surprised pilot of a Lockheed-Hudson flying on anti-submarine patrol from Iceland saw a big U-boat surface almost directly beneath him. Diving immediately almost to wavetop height the Hudson dropped four depth-charges, which rocked and damaged the U-boat before it could crash-dive, then quickly returned to spray it with gunfire, so preventing its crew from getting to their deck guns. The officers and crew packed the conning tower, and as the Hudson came down on its fourth pass the U-boat's commander held aloft a large white-painted board in token of surrender.

The victorious Hudson wirelessed Western Approaches, and

soon British sea and air forces were converging upon the tossing speck in the ocean. The trawler *Northern Chief* was on patrol only a hundred miles away when her commander, Lieutenant N. L. Knight, RNR, picked up the Admiralty's instructions that the U-boat was to be prevented from scuttling by any means. While he pushed his ship hard through a westerly gale a Catalina aircraft, together with a reinforcement of Hudsons, kept watch on the U-boat, ready to attack again should it attempt to escape.

Northern Chief arrived just before midnight, picking out in the darkness the faint yellow distinguishing light which the planes had ordered the U-boat to show all night. In the rough seas it was impossible for the trawler to launch a boat, so Lieutenant Knight ordered his signalman to warn the German commander not to scuttle; that if he did, his crew would not be picked up. Knight was really bluffing as the trawler would not have left her enemies to drown, but back came the plaintive reply from the U-boat: 'I cannot scuttle or abandon. Save us tomorrow, please.' However, it was not going to be as easy as all that.

Knight switched on a searchlight, playing the beam along the length of the heaving U-boat. It was one of the enemy's new ocean-going boats, more than 100 tons bigger than his own ship. Shortly after midnight the trawler *Kingston Agate* arrived to help in the rescue operation, but then undersea tapping was heard from the German, and the trawlers were instantly on the alert for the presence of another, rescuing U-boat. The tapping then stopped.

Dawn brought another two trawlers, *Wastwater* and *Windermere*, to the scene, also two destroyers. The six ships now ranged close to the U-boat, their asdics still probing for any warning of an enemy rescue attempt. But when danger did come it was not from the enemy but from an Allied aircraft from Iceland; the Norwegian pilot of a Northrop, suddenly breaking from the clouds and seeing the U-boat, thought it was poised to attack a convoy and immediately dived low on it, scoring very near misses with two bombs. The pilot gave no reply to recognition signals made by the trawlers so *Northern Chief* opened fire – until they saw the plane's marking as it vanished into the clouds. Meanwhile, in the heavy seas with half a gale blowing, the U-boat was dipping her bows deeper and deeper. The senior destroyer ordered the German commander to blow ballast and pump oil, and when there was no reply to this repeated order, fired a burst over the conning tower until the Germans obeyed and the trim of the sluggishly riding U-boat improved.

Skipper-Lieutenant Mawer of the *Windermere* now tried to drift a Carley float down to the enemy, but the waves overturned the float and tossed it back. Another attempt made with a fog buoy was similarly unsuccessful and oil poured on the water also had no effect, while a line fired by rocket simply vanished into the sea.

So the six ships withdrew beyond collision distance to await a lull in the gale. When it came, *Kingston Agate*, skippered by Lieutenant H. L'Estrange – his first command – took a hand. Jock Campbell, *Agate's* first lieutenant, was convinced he could now get across to the U-boat in a Carley float and asked for two volunteers from the messdeck to go with him. A line was shot from the *Agate* to the U-boat and Campbell and the two ratings got aboard the float. In no time they were making the crossing – one minute in sight of *Agate's* crew, tensely lining the deck, the next hidden by the towering sea. They completed their hair-raising journey without mishap and hauled over a heavy tow rope from *Agate*.

For nearly five hours Campbell and his men were busy aboard the U-boat. When Campbell forced its crew to come on deck and lend a hand they seemed reluctant to do so, but eventually the tow was secured, though twice Campbell was nearly swept overboard by the heavy seas when crawling along the vessel's narrow deck.

The Germans were then ferried over to *Agate*, but when it came to the turn of the U-boat commander and his two officers, he refused to step into the float – perhaps with some desperate idea of being able to effect a last-minute scuttling. Campbell signalled this refusal to *Agate*, at which L'Estrange bluntly instructed his signalman: 'Tell them there's a four-inch gun here that says he gets into that boat pretty damned quick!' The commander and his officers took the hint and got into the float, Lieutenant Campbell being the last to leave the U-boat. This was at 6 p.m., just thirty hours after U-570's surrender to the Hudson.

When the sea had calmed *Northern Chief*, being the bigger and senior trawler, took over the tow, while *Kingston Agate* made off at full speed with her prisoners. Throughout that night and the next day *Northern Chief* and her escorts struggled northwards against the boisterous weather, finally reaching the shores of Iceland. There the big U-boat was towed in and beached to cheers from the other watching ships. The greatest naval prize of the war had been successfully brought in by one of His Majesty's 'minor war vessels'.

U-570 was soon declared seaworthy again; the Germans appeared to have panicked unnecessarily, for the interior damage was comparatively slight. The boat returned to the sea war, though this time on the side of the Allies and renamed HMS *Graph* – the only U-boat in naval history to sail under the White Ensign.

Meanwhile an even more astonishing encounter took place in the seas off Gibraltar when a U-boat was humbled by a lone trawler, the redoubtable *Lady Shirley*.

9

The Triumph of 'Lady Shirley'

There was nothing to single out *Lady Shirley* from the other converted fishing vessels based at Gibraltar. Nothing whatever. A Hull trawler built in the mid-1930s and taken over by the Admiralty as war loomed, her 470 tons was typical of other ships of Harry Tate's Navy. She berthed quietly with her sister trawlers at the northern end of the Rock.

Lady Shirley's earlier war service had been sound if unspectacular, though she had once come through a fierce attack by enemy aircraft while on patrol, and her name was on the honours board at Sparrow's Nest.

Then had come her orders to proceed to Gibraltar. After a work-up at Tobermory she had reached the Rock in the early months of 1941 and settled to a routine of convoy escort and anti-submarine patrol duties.

Lady Shirley was constantly at sea, which was no real hardship for her crew. Several were from the pre-war fishing grounds and all except one of the twenty-six were Patrol Service men from the Nest.

Their captain was a thirty-six-year-old Australian, Lieutenant-Commander Arthur Callaway, RANVR; quiet, thoughtful and full-bearded. At the outbreak of war Callaway had been managing-director of a bedding factory in Sydney, and an active member of the local RANVR unit. The young number one was Sub-Lieutenant Frederick French, RNR, with neat pointed beard. Just 24, he was an alert and determined officer from Kent, whose war had begun early with service in an armed merchant cruiser.

Another Australian, Lieutenant Ian Boucaut, RANVR, a Sydney solicitor, was second officer; and the third and junior officer, now a Patrol Service veteran but still looking considerably younger than his twenty years, was Acting Sub-Lieutenant Allan Waller, the 'Jonah of Parkeston Quay'.

Shirley's capabilities – and handicaps – were much the same as the majority of her sisters, including a full speed of only ten knots. The crew used to keep their own 'rattle schedule' which graphically informed them of their ship's passage. As one crew member describes:

'We always knew when we were at our full speed of ten knots because the bridge windows began to rattle. Nine knots was when the bridge flag locker shook; eight knots down to five produced minor shakes in the bridge ladder. An extra burst of speed needed in an emergency shook the whole bridge works in harmony.'

But for all her limitations *Shirley* was a highly efficient ship. She carried out a full set of drills every day, wherever she was, and practised her gunnery. A .303 rifle was fixed on the four-inch gun to provide firing practice at barrels and other floating objects in the sea. Many of her crew were highly competent at other jobs besides their own; 'doubling' on the asdic, for instance.

It was this extra 'edge' that was to win the trawler a proud place in naval history.

Lady Shirley did a lot of her work from Gibraltar in company with the trawlers *Erin* and *Lady Hogarth*. Poor *Hogarth* at this time had become popularly known as *Mrs* Hogarth, having been 'demoted' by the senior officer, Gibraltar Escort Force, for the cardinal sin of making too much smoke in a convoy. Frequently *Erin* and *Shirley* were sent out to escort tankers coming in; they brought in the tanker *Denbydale*, later mined by Italian frogmen in Gibraltar harbour.

In early September 1941 the two ladies, *Hogarth* and *Shirley*, went out to find another tanker – and *Shirley* broke down with engine trouble. *Hogarth* was obliged to tow her into neutral Madeira for repairs. Aboard *Shirley* then was Signalman Neville Wilson.

'In the harbour we were at once surrounded by local natives in small boats offering us all the products of Paradise. "Anything for buy?" they chanted, and if not for buy, then for flog. So over the side began to go at first items of personal equipment, and then certain pieces of ship's gear. Before long there were few messdeck blankets left and pillows were a scarcity, as were old suits, trousers, leather boots, rope and hawser. The captain, of course, knew nothing of this; he was to learn of it safely afterwards, when some suitable punishments were meted out.

'It seemed it would only be a matter of time before the four-inch gun went over the side, along with the point-fives and two Hotchkiss guns. One wag pinned a placard on the four-inch: "Useful fowling piece for flog or buy. Needs some attention but could be put in working order. Apply Stoker I/C Govt. Surplus Disposal, aft." Fortunately there were no takers, though at one time it seemed that if things were allowed to continue, a price for the whole ship as a going concern might be worked out.

'On the credit side, *Shirley* was bedecked with flower garlands and bowers of fruit such as might have put the hanging gardens of Babylon to shame. No lady ever looked more ladylike, and all at Government expense. You had to duck along the decks to avoid the net bags of swinging onions, whole vine branches of grapes and tastefully arranged swags of pineapple, figs and oranges. Naturally we very quickly had to get back to naval trim, and after the first rush most of the native boats were kept off by the Portuguese Navy.

'On our second day in harbour a funeral procession filed slowly past the ship on the far side of the quay. Little did we know we were being thoroughly scrutinised, for we learned afterwards that it was a fake ceremony organised by the local Nazi gauleiter. Really, the exercise was pretty pointless as we were moored inside the mole and not far from the road which ran round Funchal Bay.'

Shirley's captain was told by the resident British naval liaison officer that a U-boat was suspected to be operating to the north, off the little island of Porto Santo, and arrangements were made for a system of warning flares between ship and shore in case of trouble. *Shirley* then sailed away at dusk on the third day, anxious fingers on the triggers and butterflies in the stomachs of her crew until she cleared the Porto Santo area. But she saw no sign of the U-boat she was deliberately seeking, and so steamed uneventfully back to Gibraltar.

Shirley and *Erin* were next ordered to escort the 6,000-ton ocean-boarding vessel *Maron* to the Canary Isles. *Shirley* took along with her on this trip two Royal Engineers corporals, to give them a welcome change from tunnelling in the rock. They were not deadweight passengers, for in action they could serve as additional lookouts and gun-loaders.

It was a pleasant job for the two trawlers, steaming along with the plum-coloured *Maron* with her six-inch guns – and in the comforting knowledge that she was the bigger target. They left *Maron* south of the Canaries to look for the Allied tanker *La Carriere* coming from Barbados, which they were to escort to

Gibraltar. But then *Shirley* was detached to patrol in the vicinity of Teneriffe, because of an anticipated breakout by three enemy tankers harboured there.

For two days *Shirley* conducted a lone patrol south of the Canaries. Signalman Wilson had now left the ship but he recalls those waters.

'It could blow hard and bring up a heavy swell, but more usual was a boundless placidity of ocean, the sort of weather met with in the holiday brochures. When a convoy or a patrol was ended and you were released from worries about mass U-boat attacks and could contemplate the pleasant run back home, you were tempted to idealise about life and became a brochure advertisement yourself, lolling about the sunbaked decks, the engine room casing, the gun decks, and even the bridge top, in holidays-abroad atmosphere and without a care in the world. Providing of course you were not on watch, when naturally you did jump to it a little more. There did, however, always lurk at the back of one's mind the nagging reflection that this same calm weather was a U-boat's high delight. In it, a torpedo ran magnificently straight and untroubled towards your hull, and the end could be sudden, quick and total, and thus the end of your holiday.'

While *Shirley* continued her lone patrol a holiday atmosphere could not be indulged, so the early morning of October 4 1941 found her keenly alert. The weather was fine and calm, and the visibility very good, as her great drama began.

The lookout in the crow's nest spotted something that looked like a ship's funnel and reported it to Sub-Lieutenant French, who was officer of the watch. French went up to see for himself, and as he was studying the object it disappeared. It could have been either the funnel of a ship or the conning tower of a U-boat refracted over the horizon. *Shirley*'s captain immediately altered course towards the position.

Sub-Lieutenant Waller, the young signals and navigation officer, had taken middle-watch, and was just about to turn out again.

'At four minutes past ten the alarm bells went. I grabbed my lifebelt and tin-hat and went off to my U-boat action station aft at the depth-charges. I then went up to the bridge to see what was happening and was told we had made a firm contact at about 1800 yards. We were going for it at top speed.

'We had been having trouble with the asdic and had managed to mend it so that we could "ping", but the recorder part of it on the bridge was useless, which meant that distances of echoes had to be measured by a stopwatch, and it was by this means that we went into the attack.

'I ran back aft and waited for the signal to fire the depth-charges, and when it came we dropped a pattern of five. While we were preparing to reload I made my way round to the port side to see how the loading was going on there – and got the most tremendous shock of my life. About four hundred yards astern, amid the disturbed explosions slightly off the port quarter, there appeared first the grey bow of a U-boat, then the periscope, and then, very slowly, up came the conning tower. It was a huge ocean-going U-boat, fully twice the size of our little ship. It was a nightmarish experience – I felt like a small boy caught robbing an orchard.

'Our drill quickly switched from undersea to surface action stations, and being action officer of the watch I had to be on the bridge. When I scrambled up there the captain hadn't got over the shock either, he was just ordering hard-a-port, to give us a chance of bringing our four-inch to bear and also to ram the U-boat if we could get there. Before leaving the twin point-fives aft I had told the gun's crew to open fire on the conning tower in short bursts as soon as they could get a range on it, and this they did as *Shirley* came round hard, steaming flat out.

'We saw that the U-boat had a large gun up for'ard, about the size of a four-inch, and a gun like a Bofors abaft the conning tower, also a cannon-like Oerlikon on the conning tower itself. When our point-fives opened fire this cannon answered with a stream of shells.

'Our only other guns besides the point-fives and the four-inch were a Hotchkiss .303 each side of the bridge. When our four-inch could bear it opened fire, but the first round was a near miss. The U-boat opened up at the same time and there was a flash of tracers all over the place. This burst mortally wounded our gun layer, Seaman Leslie Pizzey, who was hit by a cannon shell. Calling out "They've got me!" he staggered back, collapsed and died at the back of the gun platform. The gun's crew quickly changed round and another seaman ducked under the gun and took over as layer. They opened up again at the U-boat, firing shells in quick succession, a mixture of semi-armour piercing and shrapnel. Our Hotchkiss gunners also kept up a constant fire.

'We could not understand why the U-boat hadn't opened fire at us with its big gun. We could see several members of this gun's crew scattered around it and we had soon killed or wounded most of them without suffering a single shell in reply. It was mystifying. But we took a real hammering from their conning tower cannon. Our bridge was riddled and a steampipe up for'ard was punctured, sending clouds of steam flying about the deck. I had been quickly working out *Shirley*'s position and the captain told me to take the signal down to the wireless cabin, also to yell down to the engine-room to get the steam turned off smartly so that we could see what we were doing.

'The wireless cabin was behind the wheelhouse, but when I tried to leave the bridge by the back door I found it obstructed by one of our two signalmen, who had been hit in the thigh by a cannon shell – one of the Army corporals was trying to patch him up. I dashed back into the bridge, got out through the front window and slid down the ladder at the front. There was a fresh stream of fire from the U-boat as I went down and I felt a shell narrowly miss me. I reached the wireless cabin to find Sparks there all ready to send, but coolly leaning out of the scuttle taking photographs. I gave him the signal and he whipped it off straight away. Just as I was leaving the cabin I heard our helmsman, Leading-Seaman Blowers, give a loud cheer and shout: "The bastards have finished, I think."

'I flew back to the bridge and found that both our Hotchkiss gunners, Billy Windsor and Sydney Halcrow, had been hit in the legs by cannon shells. Halcrow, in spite of his pain, asked me, "Will you reload the gun, sir?" I grabbed hold of the gun and – so they told me afterwards – yelled, "Get off that bloody gun and let me have a go!" I had just reloaded when we were treated to the extraordinary sight of the U-boat's crew all abandoning ship. They jumped into the sea, groups of them, all keeping together in perfect drill, until there seemed to be hundreds of them in the water waving their arms and shouting. We had seen two wounded men still lying forward of the U-boat's big gun, which although we were now only about 100 yards off had surprisingly been trained away from us. All very puzzling – I thought something must have gone wrong with its firing mechanism.

'The end for the U-boat came very quickly, her bow rose up and she just slipped away – at which all her crew in the water gave three cheers! But I was sure we had sunk her, rather than some of her crew opening seacocks. Our depth-charges had forced her to the surface – they must have split her aft, as she never got her stern out of the water. Besides, she had taken at least nine direct hits from our four-inch; she was finished all right.'

And so U-111 took her 740 tons to the depths. The time now was 10.27. The action had lasted just twenty-three minutes from start to finish.

'Everybody lined the ship's side with whatever arms they'd got – rifles, revolvers – as we hauled the Germans aboard one at a time. It was the first time we realised they *were* Germans; we'd thought them to be Italians as they were all so dark, but instead they were just deeply sunburned. We kept pulling them in, dozens of them, until at last there were only two men left in the water. One of these was very badly wounded with a leg shot away at the knee, the other was his comrade.

'Some of the Germans wore Davis escape apparatus, others simply lifebelts, and all were clad in shorts or drill trousers. On counting them up we found we had forty-five prisoners as against less than thirty of us – and four of these wounded and out of action. Eight of the U-boat's company had been lost, either killed or drowned, including the captain, whom we never saw.

'There were two officers among the prisoners. One turned out to be a commander who was learning the job. He was a nasty bit of work and had an injury to his forehead. The other, the U-boat's engineer officer, seemed more amenable. Some other prisoners were injured but the only very serious casualty besides the man who had lost a leg was another with a bad leg wound. We put them down in the ward room, all except the legless man. There wasn't much room there but it was the safest place for us to lock them up, heavily outnumbering us as they did.

'That afternoon we held a funeral service for Seaman Pizzey, who had been a very popular member of the crew. Tragically, by rights he should never have been with us. He'd hurt his leg playing football and ended up in hospital, but had been so keen to get back to *Shirley* that when our cook fell ill he came back, his ankle in plaster, to take the cook's place. It was an example of the comradely spirit of everyone who served in *Shirley*. The captain read the service and we then stopped engines to put poor Pizzey over the side.

'We had kept the legless German on deck and tried to make him comfortable, but he never really recovered consciousness and died that evening. As we didn't like to stop the ship at night the captain held a second burial service the next morning.

We allowed six prisoners on deck for this, and they were very impressed and pleased that their colleague should be given a proper burial. We put him over under a black flag, the captain apologising for the fact that we hadn't a German ensign to drape him in.

'We were four days out of Gibraltar at our ten knots and didn't know if anybody had heard our signals. We naturally didn't like to make too much fuss about the action for fear of drawing enemy attention. It was only afterwards that we discovered that another U-boat had in fact seen everything and sent frantic signals back to the U-boat base at Lorient, not daring to sink us because of the many prisoners we carried.

'So we steamed on, the blood mopped up from the bridge, and several small fires started by the U-boat's incendiaries safely put out, but with the ship full of holes. Our smallboat was holed and there was an ominous hole in a depth-charge which had been struck by a cannon shell; we carefully dumped the charge overboard first chance we had. Fortunately we had no trouble with our prisoners, though we were all ready for it. We discovered afterwards that one or two Nazis among them had tried to dig through the floor of the wardroom, which was over some of the ship's tanks, but it wouldn't have got them far as we'd already thought of that one and stationed a man down there with a Hotchkiss gun unshipped from the bridge. In addition the officer of watch always carried a couple of Mills bombs, and we kept two or three men on deck similarly armed.

'The Germans were dumbfounded and bamboozled by our victory over them and wanted to know "where all the guns had come from". However, it was not the number of our guns which had beaten them, it was the speed and efficiency of our drill. It was at this point we discovered why we had not been shelled by their own four-inch: the German gunners had acted so hastily that they forgot to take the tompion out of the gun; they fired their first shot with it still in and blew up the barrel.

'Their engineer officer, Gunther Wolf, was most co-operative. He noted down in meticulous fashion a list of the U-boat's company – names, numbers, addresses, the lot. He had been to Birmingham University and his English was perfect. We got on very well with him. One of our enginemen who could speak German also managed to get a lot of information out of the prisoners.

'Lieutenant Boucaut, though actually a solicitor, had had three years' medical training, and he and the Royal Engineers corporal who was skilled in first-aid looked after the casualties supremely well, so we did not have anyone else die on us.

'About two days out of Gibraltar, when it grew dark, we sent off another signal; the Vichy French were none too friendly and we had to steam past Casablanca. But we finally got a reply saying we would be met by the destroyer *Lance*. She duly came along, put her doctor aboard us and escorted us the rest of the way.'

Here was *Shirley*'s big moment. Instead of sailing unnoticed to her usual berth at the trawler base end of the Rock, she went straight alongside the nearest mole to be boarded by Vice-Admiral Sir George Edward-Collins, Vice-Admiral Commanding North Atlantic. Everyone knew she was coming. Every ship in harbour loudly tooted a victorious welcome.

'We had half the Gibraltar army on the quay to take the prisoners off. The Admiral came aboard with the base surgeon commander. The surgeon, who spoke good German, told the wounded prisoners where they were going, but they refused to believe him – they'd heard that Gibraltar had fallen long ago to the Germans and so were absolutely lost.

'We said our goodbyes to Gunther Wolf, all *Shirley*'s officers shaking hands with him, a gesture which appeared to upset the waiting soldiers. Once clear of prisoners we went up to the trawler base, cheered by all the trawlers in the pens. Later we had to take *Shirley* down to the other end of the dockyard for a refit and much needed repairs. As we went past, Force H was in harbour and we were cheered by all the ships, including the *Ark Royal*. We were forgivably pleased about that.'

Winston Churchill cabled his personal congratulations to *Shirley*. Lieutenant-Commander Callaway was awarded an immediate DSO – 'For daring and skill in a brilliant action against a U-boat in which the Enemy was sunk and surrendered to HM trawler *Lady Shirley*....' In fact his award came just short of being a VC. Other awards followed. Sub-Lieutenant French and Lieutenant Boucaut each received the DSC; only the junior officer went undecorated, and this for the simple reason that *Shirley* ran out of her quota of medals. No fewer than six of the crew were awarded the DSM, while for Seaman-Gunner Halcrow there was a special award of the Conspicuous Gallantry Medal. In the words of the citation: 'Although so badly wounded that he was ordered to go below, he stood to his gun until the action was over.' Five Mentions in Despatches completed *Shirley*'s honours and one of these was for the Army corporal who had helped so ably with the wounded – a most unusual honour for a soldier, for it entitled him to wear the Atlantic Star.

But after all this, red tape still won the day. Sub-Lieutenant Waller:

'We had to account for all the depth-charges we'd used, and to produce the keys used for setting the depths at which they were to explode. We were one key short. This had been in the depth-charge holed by a German cannon shell, and which we had hurriedly dumped over the side. We had to put in a full report as to why we hadn't first removed the key....'

After her great glory *Lady Shirley* settled once more to the humdrum routine work of one of His Majesty's trawlers. But sadly her final drama was only weeks away.

Early December found her with largely the same victorious crew, except for the wounded and one or two other crew replacements. There had been one change among her officers. Sub-Lieutenant Waller had entered hospital for further treatment of an injury received when one of his earlier trawlers sank, and on coming out found himself swiftly drafted on to Admiral Edward-Collins' shore staff. 'The Admiral was very short-staffed, so they grabbed me. My first duty was to look after the harbour defence asdics; then I became responsible for the U-boat plot.'

And so Allan Waller, his place in *Shirley* taken by a Polish officer, escaped the fate that now awaited his former colleagues, yet by reason of his position at headquarters was to be made grimly aware of it as it occurred.

'There had been some U-boat activity in the Straits, so four trawlers were detailed off to do an asdic sweep. *Shirley* was one of them and another was the *St Nectan*, whose Lieutenant Osborne, an Australian, was a friend of Lieutenant-Commander Callaway.

'The trawlers were carrying out this sweep on the night of December 11 1941. At 3.45 a.m. Lieutenant Osborne came on watch in *St Nectan* and looked across at *Lady Shirley*. She was about a mile off, perfectly in station. Then a sudden rain squall descended on the ships. When it cleared away at about 4.10 a.m. Lieutenant Osborne looked across again at *Lady Shirley*. But she was not there. At some time during those twenty-five minutes she had vanished.'

Nothing more was heard from *Shirley*, but at 5.10 a.m. there came news of a casualty in the area when the armed yacht *Sayonara* wirelessed Gibraltar: '*Cable Enterprise* blown up, have eleven survivors on board.' *Cable Enterprise* was a mercantile cable ship taken over by the navy. Not long after this signal came another one, somewhat obscure, saying that the armed yacht *Rosabelle*, patrolling in the same area, had been blown up and sunk. Both these signals were intercepted by the trawler *Arctic Ranger*. Intercepted, in fact, by *Shirley*'s former signalman, Signalman Neville Wilson.

'I had heard some dull explosions and then came these two signals about *Cable Enterprise* and *Rosabelle*. Not until 9 a.m. were we informed that *Lady Shirley* had vanished. It was a very confused situation. *Arctic Ranger* had been helping another trawler to shadow a French convoy; at 10.30 a.m. we completed this support duty and went off to join in the hunt for the missing *Shirley*. We carried out an extensive search east of Gibraltar but there was no trace of her.

'We could hardly conclude that she had been torpedoed, since there was not even the smallest trace of wreckage, or of the many loose items scattered about her decks which I knew from experience would have floated off had she been tin-fished. There was nothing at all to explain her mysterious disappearance.'

Some wreckage was found by other searching ships, but not *Shirley*'s. It was Sub-Lieutenant Waller's unhappy task to verify this when the wreckage was brought in.

'*Rosabelle*'s captain and I went to identify the bits and pieces retrieved from the sea. *Rosabelle* was a poor little yacht about 40 or 50 years old. I knew her captain well. He had complained bitterly about the condition of his ship and been temporarily relieved of his command as a result; and so she had sailed without him.

'He easily identified some bits of *Rosabelle* among the wreckage, but I couldn't recognise anything from *Shirley*. This was very strange. In particular, on top of *Shirley*'s bridge we had kept two small rafts which rested loosely on a splinter mat and were held in place by vertical brackets; if she had been torpedoed and sunk, these rafts would have floated right off; yet there was no sign of them or of anything else.

'We knew that at least two U-boats had gone through the Straits at the time and the old *Rosabelle*'s end was perhaps inevitable, but the double mystery about *Shirley* was why, if the victim of a U-boat, she should have been so instantly overwhelmed; and secondly, if she had been torpedoed, why – in those waters – there was not a single item of wreckage to tell the tale.

'Another thing. If, as was suggested, the Germans had smarted under little *Shirley*'s defeat of a U-boat and sought revenge upon her, why hadn't they jumped to announce the glad news of her sinking? In my position on the U-boat plot, information came to hand from all kinds of quarters and it was part of my job to read up all the U-boat reports; but the Germans made no claims about *Shirley* – none whatsoever.'

A possible pointer to what could have happened to *Lady Shirley* came at Gibraltar only a few weeks later, in January 1942. Sub-Lieutenant Waller:

'I was then living in a mess just outside the dockyard and working in the tower, the flag officer's headquarters. I was getting ready to go on watch when at 6 p.m., there was a terrific explosion in the dockyard and a huge smoke ring drifted right up over the Rock, a remarkable sight. I dashed out to see that a big fire had broken out in a corner of the dockyard just astern of the aircraft carrier *Argus* – her officer of watch was killed in the explosion. It was a shocking sight in the dockyard, where three trawlers had been tied up. The middle trawler, the *Erin*, had blown up and sunk instantly, while the one on the outside, the little *Honjo*, was fiercely ablaze from stern to stem, another total loss. The inside trawler of the three, the *Imperialist*, was on fire aft and her first lieutenant called to me to help him with the magazine stopcocks – I knew their whereabouts as I had served in *Imperialist* for a few days at Harwich. We managed to do this job although she was really going up fast, and luckily they were able to save her, though badly damaged.

'The explosion was believed to have been caused by a time bomb placed in one of *Erin*'s depth-charges by a Spanish agent for the Germans. And this, to my mind, is the most likely explanation for what happened to *Lady Shirley*. A bomb was placed in one of her depth-charges and she blew up at sea and sank immediately. This would explain everything, including the absence of any wreckage.'

Captured enemy documents at the end of the war ascribed the sinking of *Lady Shirley* to a torpedo from U-374. But as this U-boat was itself sunk by a British submarine only a month later there are no details to support this claim; and as has been seen, two other ships were torpedoed in the area at around the same time. U-boats generally had little opportunity to check their victims; all the British anti-submarine trawlers looked more or less alike, and in the near darkness no one would have known which ship was sunk.

The mysterious sudden fate of the fighting *Lady Shirley* and her four officers and twenty-nine men, remains unsatisfactorily explained.

10

'Don't Hang Your Bloody Heads'

By late 1941 the 'efficient madhouse' of Sparrow's Nest had changed considerably from its early days. It was busier, more efficient, and in some respects even more mad.

The rapid expansion of the Patrol Service had seen its ranks thrown open almost entirely to a new type of recruit. Gone to war were most of the fishermen, tugmen and bargemen, and the weekend sailors with a smattering of what it was all about. Now in came civilians from all walks of life, many of whom had not the slightest idea what the Royal Naval Patrol Service stood for. A popular belief was that it was a force of naval police; other ideas varied from flotillas of motor torpedo boats and gunboats to a special fleet of patrolling destroyers.

When the type of ship they were to serve in was unceremoniously revealed to the trainees it was in many cases a severe shock. They would be led past the sleek, rakish motor torpedo boats in one dock to the rusty, battered, ponderous fishing trawlers tied up in another, and be told by a brisk, no-nonsense instructor: 'Them's *your* ships, lads. Not much to look at but fine sea boats. Not speedy but sturdy.' And, ignoring the obvious dismay of his audience, he would continue: 'I know you're all eager to go to sea – I wish I could go with you, but they won't let me now.' His tone belied his words.

New entries were streaming into Lowestoft at the rate of hundreds a week. Naval lorries met the trains as they arrived and ran the newcomers to the Nest. There they were mustered in batches on the stage and names and details taken by the Regulating Chief Petty Officer. Much harassed, but always commanding, this majestic personage did much to allay the doubts caused on arrival by the curious sight at the gates of the two sentries lounging with cigarettes in their mouths, or sparring playfully at one another with their bayonets. A strange introduction to a naval training establishment.

Signed in and told to report back at 0800 hours next morning

('And do not, repeat NOT, be adrift first morning!'), the new entries were marshalled outside the concert hall to join a big queue awaiting transport to billets. Returning lorries were filled to capacity and roared off to town, weaving in and out of roads branching off the main street and stopping at different houses.

A rating would leap down, knock on each door and call out: 'How many, Ma?'

'I'll take two, son,' would come the reply, and the two men nearest the back of the truck would be ordered down and into the billet.

So it went on until the lorry was emptied and went speeding back to the Nest for more. Billets were entirely a matter of chance and on the luck of the draw would depend either misery or comfort for the newly-joined men. Some billets were little better than doss-houses, others were homes-from home. All depended on the character of the 'Ma's', as the landladies were universally known. Some greedy, avaricious women saw the war as an opportunity to make as much money as possible and give as little as possible in return. They would squeeze the maximum number of men into their small boarding houses, cram together beds, tables and chairs, give as meagre rations as they dared, and make handsome profits out of the plight of the poor ratings. Some would bunk two, or even three, men in a bed together, though this was against strict naval regulations; they banked on the new entries being too green to complain.

Again, some billets might be filthy, with one lavatory to eighteen men, and infested with fleas which waxed fat on human blood. Rooms were unswept, meals had to be staggered for want of space, and the second sitting might not even have time to finish. Some landladies and their families lived and cooked below ground in the basement, and plates of food came up at the end of an apparently disembodied hand. By these means, unscrupulous landladies ended up with fur coats and their own cars.

Many were the men's complaints about fleas, but they had to learn to live with them or find their own remedies, which was hard on those particularly susceptible to the insects, like Ordinary Seaman Paul Lund. By bitter experience he found that the only way to catch fleas successfully was to dab them with a piece of wet soap; they stuck to the soap and you'd got them. For many nights it was a common sight to see Lund standing over his bed, a candle in one hand and a piece of soap poised in the other. To the amusement of his room mates, who seemed to escape the attentions of the fleas entirely.

And there were more vivid experiences, like that which befell Rupert Garratt, bundled into a billet in Nelson Street. 'On our side of the street there were few houses standing and my billet hadn't a whole window – there was oilcloth or something similar for glass, and a cracked and broken front door. All the "livestock" from the bombed houses sought the human warmth of those that were occupied, so my first night was a nightmare. The next night I used a packet of Keatings which I shook liberally over the sheet on which I lay, and although later in the night I applied a more liberal covering, they still got me. The last impression I wished to give was that I was "soft", but after some days my wrists were so swollen that I could not button my cuffs and my bootlaces were well stretched to go round my swollen ankles, so I reported to the Sick Bay with a request that I be moved to another billet. The MO was young, supercilious and probably unsure of himself, or he would not have asked "How do you know they are not gnats?" "Sir," I replied, "gnats do not bite at that time of day, at this time of year, late September, under bedclothes." I got my move and the old billets were closed.'

The majority of men, however, were stuck with the billet in which they had landed. Billets of awful meals and gross overcrowding, where in the morning miracles had to be performed by twenty men in the use of one bathroom and lavatory at more or less the same time – a nightmarish version of the small boarding house in Blackpool at the height of the season. Billets like that of the coalman's terrace house, where every evening the carthorse was led through the hall from the front to the back of the house for stabling. And like the one where the poor, long-suffering trainees pushed a piece of gristle masquerading as liver into the parrot's cage. Whether it was this tasty morsel which choked the bird or the whisky which the frantic landlady poured down its throat to revive it they didn't know, but they did take the precaution of burying the creature to prevent, as one man suggested, having it served up as chicken at dinner the next day.

At first, in all billets, there was no dinner at all on one day a week, for on that day the landladies had to go to the Nest and queue up for their pay. Later they were paid by postal orders sent through the post.

In theory all the billets provided by nearly a thousand landladies were supposed to be inspected regularly by billeting officers from the Nest, but at this period of intensive call-up of civilian personnel there was little time for such niceties; and the newly-joined rating, expecting to endure all kinds of hardships, was not likely to make an official complaint at the start of his naval career. The bad landladies banked on this and generally won.

Those landladies of goodwill and real patriotic spirit were fortunately in the majority and they made the utmost sacrifices for their billetees. By limiting their numbers, providing clean, comfortable quarters and as much good food as their naval allowances would provide, they made real homes for their sailors without profit for themselves.

Many, after all, had sons of their own. Like one 'Ma', who had lost her husband at sea in World War I and now had a son in the Army in India. She looked after every one of her lodgers like her own. She fed them like fighting cocks and was not above slipping any hard-up Jack the price of a night at the pictures. She even did their washing; no light task considering she took in seven or eight men at a time.

Other good 'Ma's' saw hope in the young men they cared for in their own private grief. Like one whose youngest son was killed with others in a depth-charge explosion on his trawler. The pieces of his body were sent to Lowestoft, where he was buried, but as she knew, they may well not have been him, or only partly him. Then his kit was sent back to her, and turned out to be another man's. Such bereaved women cared for the hundreds of men who passed through their homes as their own sons.

The names of the good landladies would be passed from mouth to mouth so that on their next return to the Nest the unfortunates could change their luck. The drill was to go to the landlady before reporting at the Nest, and if she was willing to take them, to tell the RPO on the stage that they had already fixed up a billet. *Fait accompli*.

It must be said that it was not all honey for the landladies, who had to put up with many varying types of men. Here again there were unfortunates, as instanced by the curious but necessary institution of the Wet-Bed Book, kept by the Pay Office at the Nest. The combination of East Coast air and the amount of beer drunk had a potent effect on the ratings' bladders. Beds were wetted every night, rising to a grand climax on pay nights, when many more pints of beer were drunk The landladies naturally complained, hence the Wet-Bed Book. Landladies reported men who had wet their beds and 2s 6d was deducted from their pay. There was quite a harvest in these 'fines'.

With the trainees and other men waiting for ships, together with a procession of survivors from vessels that had been lost, there were as many as six thousand men attending the Nest at one time. As the town billets could not cope, many had to spend a fortnight or so sleeping on the floor of the concert hall with a gas mask for a pillow, nowhere to wash, and eating their meals at the NAAFI set up in the Nest's confines. Some, no doubt, would have welcomed the use of any billet, fleas and all.

Each new intake of trainees attended the first morning's Divisions, a motley crowd in rig ranging from smart lounge suits to open shirts and patched trousers. The Chief Petty Officer barked his welcome.

'After Divisions the Commodore will inspect you. He'll ask you a few questions. And remember this, he likes a man to look him straight in the face, so don't hang your bloody heads as if you've done something to be ashamed of. Even if you have, the police won't get you here!'

And so the new men had their first meeting with Commodore Daniel de Pass. There would be nearly two hundred of them, but he would exchange a few words with every man. De Pass was short and broad, with a pair of brown eyes in which lurked much good humour. He left a rating with the feeling that he knew exactly what sort of a man he was – his strengths and weaknesses, his virtues and faults. Even the biggest 'skates' liked and respected the Commodore. He had the pleasantest and yet the most telling way of delivering a 'bottle' to a man, and he had an amazing memory for faces.

De Pass took over HMS *Europa* in April 1941. Till then he had captained the *Cossack* as Divisional leader in a flotilla of the famous Tribal-class destroyers. His life was the Navy. He had joined it as staggeringly long ago as 1905 and served in Admiral Beatty's Battle Cruiser Fleet throughout World War 1. Between the wars he had devoted himself to training cadets and young ratings. He took over the Nest at a time when the fishermen's navy had to be brought into line with the Royal Navy, though still retaining its strong independence. A lesser man might have fallen down on the task. By being too lenient he could have let the ever-present slackness and un-pusser-like conduct continue;

by being too harsh he could have had half the inhabitants of the Nest doing punishment. But De Pass had a deep understanding of men and of the peculiar composition of the Patrol Service, and he steered a wise middle course to make a grand success of the job.

After the initial words with the Commodore there followed days of getting kitted out. Then the start to six weeks' training: square-bashing and rifle-drill at the Oval; classes in seamanship, gunnery, depth-charges, signals and semaphore, minesweeping and asdics. The instructor at the Oval might be a very young-looking Newfoundlander.

'If you play the game with me, lads (some of the trainees were old enough to have been his father) then I'll play the game with you. But if any of you think you can get the better of me, then you'd better think again. You'll never do ut! No, you'll never do ut! When I tell you to do a thing, I just want you to do ut, that's all.'

This was not easy, as the Newfoundland fishermen, though first-class seamen, were not usually good at explaining things to others. They were essentially doers, not teachers. There were a great many of them passing through the Nest at this time and a number could not, or would not, read and write, though they were no worse sailors for that. They could steer a ship perfectly, but could not box a compass. They were the most happy-go-lucky crowd one could imagine, and on pay nights went on a glorious bust which left them broke for the rest of the fortnight. On that night they would treat anyone within range, for they were recklessly generous. One seaman went on leave to Edinburgh and spent forty pounds; in those days a small fortune.

The Newfoundlanders' speech, like a mixture of Manx and Irish, was equally fascinating. They invariably began a sentence with 'Jeez' or 'Jeez hell', and seemed to have difficulty in pronouncing 'th'. 'Jeez hell, we've got to do ut at tree-tirty!'

Earlier, when a large contingent of these Newfoundlanders arrived in England to join the Patrol Service there was no immediate room for them at the Nest and they were put on forestry work in Scotland. After some months had passed they organised a lie-in strike and refused to leave their beds. They had come over to join the Navy, they said, not to cut down trees. The strike had the desired effect for they very quickly found themselves at Lowestoft.

Gunnery was taught by instructors who were a race apart

and had a staccato language all their own.

'When the bullet leaves the barrel – or-right? – the gasses escape through here – or-right? – and take up against the piston – or-right? – forcing it to the rear – or-right? – thus bringing the breech-block and moving parts to the rear – or-right? – and then the sear – or-right? – takes up against the cutaway portion – or-right?'

Gun drill was an endless repetition of numbering, doubling, falling over each other, clangs, thumps and yelling. Men confused the four-inch with the 12-pounder, and the 12-pounder with the point-five. According to the instructors they were 'solid'.

Semaphore was taught by a three-badge AB nicknamed Donald Duck. He spent ten minutes of each period teaching semaphore and the remainder telling the trainees of his past experience and warning them of the fate in store for them. Pointing dramatically out to sea as in the painting 'Boyhood of Raleigh' he would thunder ominously: 'I've been out there – I know what it's like. I was out there last war, but I'm finished with it now. But you lot are going out there to get bombed, mined and torpedoed – and you won't enjoy it. And if you don't *pay attention* to what I tells you, you'll like it a bloody sight less!'

Less dramatic but more to the point was the instructor who used to tell his class: 'When the action bells ring you don't walk and you don't run, you just fly – your feet never seem to touch the deck.' Thousands of men who wondered at his words later found themselves doing just that.

There had to be some practical training in seamanship, so to be taught helm orders and steering, recruits went to sea in a vessel called the *Umbriel*. She had been intended as an upriver steamer somewhere in Africa, and was rather slow in the tides of Lowestoft. Later, because of the constant enemy raids, it was decided that helm training should be done in the harbour, and sea trips were confined to going out in smallboats and trying, mostly unsuccessfully, not to be seasick.

Those who were to become ship's cooks were taken to a school of domestic science in Lowestoft which, up to the outbreak of war, had been used to teach little girls cookery. There they patiently took tuition from young women teachers. Some men had not even boiled an egg in their lives before, but there were also former employees of large hotels and restaurants; chefs, head waiters, hotel managers. They stood it very well, starting right from the bottom by learning how to wash up, wipe the galley deck and peel potatoes. They were also taught how to cook some very dainty dishes and four-course lunches, though these for four persons, not for a whole ship's company. And they were not told that the galley would, in some cases, be no larger than the average bathroom, and that they would be lucky if they had sufficient cooking utensils to do a decent job. Nor were they told of the agonies of getting meals in a full gale, with pots and pans breaking loose and the cook sliding about and hanging on like grim death to galley supports; or that the crew would demand as good a dinner when a trawler was bucking like a broncho as when she was alongside the harbour wall.

All instructors struggled with and heaped curses on the trainees, each intake according to them being more hopeless than the one before. 'If you don't bloody well pass out, you'll bloody well stay at the bleeding Oval and do another bleeding six weeks!' This threat hung over them constantly like a thunder cloud. In the event they found that 'passing out' was a myth and a mirage. There was a slight formality of some squad and rifle drill under the eyes of the training commander, and a written test on depth-charges, the answers to which were told them beforehand by a kindly petty officer. And that was all. It was impossible *not* to pass out.

For relief for all, there were stage shows of outstanding quality at the Nest, which was not surprising considering that Petty Officer (later Sub-Lieutenant) Eric Barker, supported by his wife, produced and starred in them. And there was also Trevor Little and the Blue Mariners dance band, which included in its players a number of ex-members of famous dance bands, and gave regular BBC broadcasts. They gave the same show on several nights so that all would have a chance to see it. There was Russ Conway, who also occasionally entertained on the piano of The First And Last pub, and there were concert parties and Ensa shows. Tickets for these entertainments were limited, and at the Oval they had their own way of making 'fair distribution' of them.

'Married men with more than five children – prove it. Right, here's your tickets. Single men with more than five children? You don't get 'em for being careless! Single men who should have had more than five children but haven't? Right, you get 'em for putting the latch to safe in the proper manner! Men who've been to jail – prove it! Right, you've done your time – come and take 'em. Men who ought to have been in jail? OK that's being honest. Men with two wives – and I mean real wives – come on, don't be shy, this isn't the Law! But you don't get tickets – you've had enough entertainment already!'

And so on. It was original and it caused a laugh; and more to the point, it wasted a lot of training time and was a buckshee stand-easy.

Novel local 'entertainment', especially for the Wrens on staff at the Nest, was provided by a boatman who delighted in rowing parties along the coast to neighbouring Pakefield, where cliff erosion was causing the whole of a row of cottages to topple one by one into the sea. Falling over the cliff, too, was part of Pakefield Churchyard. The old boatman landed there and went round picking up old bones and skulls expelled from burst coffins and showing them to his horrified passengers. The Wrens themselves were popular for even more than the usual reasons; sailors could only visit the Church Army canteen if escorted by one, which led to the not uncommon sight of a Wren doing her patriotic duty by taking six or more Jacks in tow for a cuppa and a sandwich.

When men had finished their training and passed out they were incorporated in the guard at the Nest until drafted to sea. The guard, when not on watch, slept 'booted and spurred' on the concert hall floor. They spent many weary hours praying for a ship while standing with a bayonet at the gates of the Nest, or at the mail office or the fishnet store. At one time there was a craze for trying to catch the sentries out. This culminated in a certain Chief receiving a bayonet thrust through his forearm while crawling in the bushes, which caused the sport to become less popular. On another occasion, having ordered the sentry to open the gate and receiving no reply, a lieutenant-commander going his rounds called out: 'If you don't open this gate I'm going to throw a grenade over at you.' Back came a sleepy voice: 'If you're going to fuck about like that, I'm going home!'

The guards did have their small triumphs. There was the day Commodore De Pass approached the gate in plain clothes. The petty officer in charge challenged him. 'You know me,' said De Pass, 'I'm the Commodore.' But the petty officer, not to be outwitted, threatened him with his bayonet and said: 'I don't care if you're the King of England, you're not coming in here till you *prove* who you are!' Seven days later, on 'the lawn', the approving Commodore presented the petty officer with his long serving medal.

Men discovered that a simple way to escape from the general misery of the guard, and the duties of sweeping up leaves and scrubbing floors, was to go to the Regulating Office and say they had been an office worker in civilian life. As the Nest was always chronically short of staff they were quickly snapped up as extra clerks. Within ten minutes of asking, Ordinary Seaman Lund found himself installed as an office boy in the Pay Office under a benevolent old Chief who seemed to have a specially soft spot for bank clerks turned seamen. From there, Lund, still waiting for a ship, was switched to more exacting work in the Divisional Office, which gave a green newcomer an insight into the wiles and dodges and cunning of the 'skates', as well as the problems of the honest matelot.

Daily a long procession of request-men, defaulters, men who had lost their kit, and prospective CW candidates (ratings recommended for a commission course) passed by the windows of the small hut. The two lieutenant-commanders who ran the office, named Wheeler and Jordan, had a window each and shared the work. They were complete opposites in temperament. Jordan was gruff, brusque, ruddy-complexioned and short-tempered, and could be frightening to the timid request-man; Wheeler was quiet, calm, soft-voiced, judicial, and possessed of a dry humour.

They did not always see eye to eye, these two dispensers of justice. Wheeler's calm would irritate the choleric Jordan and they would dispute freely. But then, the people they had to deal with were often enough to try the patience of a saint.

The perpetual request-man used a carefully planned technique. Having had enough of the oceans and wanting to spend the rest of his naval career in a shore billet, his method was to put in a request from, say, seaman to stoker. All requests had to receive due consideration, and by the time a request had been round the interested departments and been finally rejected, some considerable time had elapsed – and while a man had a request in being he would not be available for draft. After each rejection the request-man would immediately put in a new request, and when all possible variations had been used up and he actually found himself on draft, his masterpiece of strategy would appear in the shape of Loss of Kit. A man could not be sent on draft without his kit, so while the routine inquiries were being made to railway departments and the like, another man would have to take his place in the draft. And so it went on.

There was 'Lord Haw-Haw', whose accent equalled that of

his infamous name-sake. It was said that when he joined the Patrol Service he arrived with a Bentley, a blonde, two spaniels, a check suit of plus-fours and a silver-topped stick. He had become a CW candidate, done his sea-time, gone the way of all flesh to King Alfred, the officers' training college, and there 'dipped'. He entered the hut one morning, very hurt about it all. There had been a mistake. King Alfred were getting in touch with the Commodore, and the Commodore was seeing him about it. The error would soon be put right. In the meantime he simply desired a good billet and a decent job.

Next day he was listed on the drafting board, and appeared at the Divisional Office more hurt than before. It was ridiculous! Monstrous! Impossible! There had been a mistake. It was . . .

'You will have to take that draft,' said the voice of authority.

Lord Haw Haw drew himself up with supreme dignity.

'Ai shall not take it. Ai could not pawsibly go back to sea on the lower deck.'

'You realise the consequences of refusing to obey a lawful command?'

'Ai do, sir.'

'Very well, you will be given three hours in which to reconsider your decision.'

At the end of three hours he was unchanged. He refused to go. He was taken up on the stage, a warrant was read, and he spent the next week in the cells. What happened to him after that no one quite knew.

One day a man was brought in who boasted that he had done 362 days of cells or detention since joining the Service. He had no kit, was heavily in debt, and said that if drafted he would simply steal another man's kit.

Lieutenant-Commander Wheeler threw out his arms. 'What can you do with a man like that? You can't send him back to civvy street, but he's no damn good at all in the Navy.' The real bad-hats were a problem to the authorities.

Requests, defaulters, advancements, compassionate drafts, CWs, losses of kit; the queue was unending.

'I'll tell you this,' the Regulating Chief PO would emphatically declare, 'we've forgotten what we're here for – we've forgotten what it's all about!'

Amid the tangle of administration it seemed he was right. The pantomime went on at all levels. Two pay sub-lieutenants joined the Pay Office and were there for at least a year before it was discovered they were not in the Navy at all; they had obtained uniforms and faked draft-chits to join.

For a long time the simple business of drafting men had produced its own muddle. The early stages at the Nest were the worst, both through misunderstanding and deliberate switching by ratings. Men awaiting a train at Lowestoft to join a certain ship would find a friend going to a different ship, and swap with another man in order to accompany him, the result being that the wrong men were on the right ships, with wrong pay and allotments, and their letters wrongly directed. The most serious aspect of this was in the event of casualties occurring; a true relative might know nothing, while someone else would mourn a loved one who months afterwards would walk through the front door on leave. It took time before every ship could make a correct return of her crew and their next-of-kin.

Another aspect was the wait for a draft. Men were given their station cards on joining and had to report every day until ships were found for them. There was no other record of them inside the Nest, so some men found that if they went home for a long weekend leave no one would miss them. The weekends stretched to weeks and even fortnights at a time, till the numbers at the Nest each day were so noticeably diminished that the racket was exposed and a new card system installed. Even then, many were the tales of men getting drafted to the ship or trawler base they preferred by slipping a bribe to one of the drafting clerks. Some cases, undoubtedly, were true. In the quick expansion of the Patrol Service almost anything was bound to happen, and did. Starting with 6,000 men and 600 vessels, the RNPS grew to 66,000 men and 6,000 vessels of one sort and another. Besides trawlers, drifters and whalers, it also took in other craft ranging from fuel carriers, motor launches and seaplane tenders to dinghies on reservoirs, these being employed to row about the reservoirs and break up the smooth surface of the water to reduce its effectiveness as a guide to enemy aircraft.

But the drafting system settled down eventually with Wrens sharing the work. And a firm step was taken to prevent liaison between drafting staff and men awaiting ships. This was the opening in Lowestoft of the Drafting Office Club, membership of which was exclusive to the drafting staff, giving them somewhere to gather for music and dancing without mixing with the rest of the depot. It was highly successful in its purpose, though when moved to new quarters above a store it was very nearly a disaster. The Commodore and his wife attended to open the club on its first night, but so did the enemy. In a fierce air raid on the town it appeared possible that at any moment the entire drafting staff of more than a hundred might be missing, which would have caused chaos in the depot. However, the danger passed, though Lord Haw-Haw, in one of his 'Jairmany calling' broadcasts, gave dire warning that 'We haven't forgotten the sparrows in the Nest at Lowestoft . . . .'

Air raids remained a part of the Nest's daily life as Lowestoft went on to earn the unenviable record of the town to receive the third highest number of alerts. In addition to the normal air raid warning Lowestoft operated a 'crash' signal, 'the cuckoo,' to warn of the straffing planes which continually ran in low to pepper the coast. The town suffered much damage, but in spite of Haw-Haw's threat no bomb fell on the Nest, nor was the old lighthouse adjacent to it, set in its unusual position high on the town's main street, damaged beyond having two of its windows blown out. The wags said that the lighthouse, which signalled the Lowestoft channel, was a good landmark for the German raiders so they probably wanted to keep it intact.

A man awaiting draft expected at worst to be sent up on the Northern Patrol, if not to one of the home trawler bases at Belfast, Scapa, Swansea, Brightlingsea, Plymouth, Milford Haven, Portland or Hvalfiord (Iceland). He rarely expected to be put on foreign draft, and many of those who were, complained bitterly, on the grounds that the Patrol Service didn't go abroad but was responsible only for coastal patrol and minesweeping.

However, abroad they went. Some, like a particular batch at the end of 1941, to Tobruk.

11

From Tobruk to the USA

The first stage of the journey to Tobruk was by train from Lowestoft to Glasgow, a slow, endless crawl most of the way. There were a few desertions en route, especially at Glasgow station, where it was easy to slip away unseen. Then on to the troopship *Cameronia*, with more desertions when the ship was held up for a week, anchored at Tail of the Bank, off Greenock. Some Army, Navy and RAF personnel who went ashore with working parties were not seen again.

This was not surprising, for conditions for the luckless 5,000 aboard the *Cameronia* were appalling. With fresh water available for fifteen minutes night and morning, and twelve wash basins to serve 350 men, the only way many could wash was by using the sea water in the urinals. Food was dished out quite haphazardly, the doler-out himself often not knowing what was in the food containers till they were opened for the meal queues, so that anything might turn up. Every man was issued with a hammock but there was no space to sling them, so they had to try to sleep in them laid flat on the deck. Sleeping out on the upper deck was forbidden, but because of the gross overcrowding below many men were driven to do so.

Smoking on deck was strictly forbidden too, but one Patrol Service man at least found a modicum of comfort. 'I had several Hurricane pipes with me, which showed no glow at all, so I was able to enjoy my smokes, though they caused much mystification and annoyance to the naval police, who could smell the smoke but couldn't find the culprit.'

The *Cameronia's* voyage to Durban took four weeks, and as she reached the heat of the tropics the overcrowding became unbearable; three men committed suicide, there was a near mutiny and a riot below decks had to be quelled by force. The only temporary relief for her miserable passengers was when the *Cameronia*, or the 'Altmark' as they nicknamed her, after the German hellship, put in calls at Freetown and Capetown.

Possibly the only man actually to enjoy the voyage was the soldier barber who cut men's hair at sixpence a time all day and every day, and landed at Durban with a small fortune to carry happily to the bank.

After a few days' respite at Durban all were re-embarked in the *Mauretania* for a further grim voyage up the east coast of Africa to Suez, which took another week. From Suez the naval men went by train through the cold night desert air in old, spartan carriages to Sidi-Bish transit camp, just a tram ride out of Alexandria. Here it was the now usual business of 'Fall in, RN ratings on the left, RNPS on the right.' This was an unfortunate arrangement which never failed to cause friction and animosity among the seamen; it was as if they were fighting two different wars. Separation of the divisions was inevitable for the purposes of pay, records and drafting, but such open segregation, the apparent weeding out from the RN ranks of lesser men, the Harry Tates, only served to magnify the differences between them. It was still remembered at Sidi-Bish how, earlier in the war, the *Ajax* had put in at Suez after the Battle of the River Plate, her captain needing fifty men to make up for those killed and wounded in action. He had picked his replacements from an RNPS contingent in transit, but on discovering they were Patrol Service men had turned them down.

So at Sidi-Bish in February 1942 the Patrol Service men who had come out with the *Cameronia* kicked their heels until sent off to various small ships. The ship chosen for one group of men was the old naval trawler *Moy*, a veteran of World War 1. She was an Oropesa sweeper with a maximum speed of only seven knots, and had been run by the RN in peacetime, and in the opening years of the war, in a variety of jobs including boom defence and store carrying.

Moy steamed off to Tobruk to sweep the harbour approaches. Tobruk had been under siege by German-Italian forces for eight solid months of the previous year, and during this time many Patrol Service manned ships, in addition to minesweeping and patrolling, had also ferried thousands of prisoners and carried stores and armaments. Under constant enemy attacks the ships' own casualty list had grown. Those lost included the whaler *Southern Floe* and trawler *Ouse*, both mined, and four other vessels sunk by enemy bombers: the whalers *Thorbryn* and *Skudd*, the drifter *Aurora II* and trawler *Sindonis*.

Moy arrived at Tobruk to find the whole place not surprisingly, 'bomb-happy'. She berthed alongside an abandoned merchant ship, the *Urania*, which had been put out of action by the enemy months ago; she had been hit for'ard by bombs, and *Moy's* crew had to go through the hole in her side to get ashore, each time stepping gingerly over an unexploded 500-pound bomb.

The frequent Stuka raids made the crane on the jetty spin round with each explosion like the dummy on a swivel at bayonet practice. Ships were regularly shelled by a German big gun known as 'Bardia Bill', driving them all to another part of the harbour, whereupon the Stukas came over and strafed them there. When a hospital ship came into harbour one day the Stukas concentrated all their attacks on her. Seething with anger, every ship fired everything she had at the planes. One loader, instead of dropping clips of ammunition into his gun, pushed them in as hard as he could and kept pushing, so that his gun got a terrific rate of fire. Even so the hospital ship was straddled again and again, but escaped a direct hit. One damaged Stuka flew off so near to the cliffs that soldiers jumped cursing out of their slit trenches to throw helmets, boots and shell-cases at it.

There was a Bofors gun on a hillock manned by the Army. In return for rum from *Moy's* crew, they agreed to fire at any Stukas coming for the trawler – a new kind of 'protection racket'. The Stukas came over regularly every day at 2 p.m. and 5 p.m. except Wednesday, which was the British naval men's 'make-and-mend', and presumably the enemy's.

One of *Moy's* crew: 'Food was very short so we pinched what we could from stores left on the jetty. We would take the whaler in below the jetty level and pull the sacks of food down into it. One day we were nearly caught. The guards noticed the sacks disappearing and came to investigate, but we all hid under the jetty and they saw only an unmanned boat. We also acquired some extra guns to augment our meagre armament. Our cook brought aboard a Lewis gun which he said he'd found in a gunpit and which "nobody seemed to want". This made our armament up to five Lewis guns, on one of which was a plate which said "Made in Belgium, 1914".'

But *Moy's* greatest capture was a Breda gun – the Italian equivalent of the Oerlikon. Some of *Moy's* crew 'won' this prize from an Italian outpost in the desert near Tobruk, after the outpost had been abandoned. Having installed the gun they nonchalantly went back and retrieved the ammunition for it.

'If troops on patrol came across Italians in the desert the Italians generally fled, so salvage was easily obtained. By this time the Italian soldiers' morale was very low and the Germans had taken over the war. The Italian prisoners at Tobruk were allowed to work or go about practically unattended, as there was nowhere for them to escape to except the desert.

'The Breda gun was an excellent gun, better than the Oerlikon, having twice the range, and it placed its empties back into the tray instead of all over the deck. We set it up nicely on *Moy's* deck over the galley, the only snag being that every time it was fired, the cook and the cooking got covered in soot.'

Moy spent nearly forty weeks at bomb-happy Tobruk, which had its certain effects. 'One of our crew went to visit a pal on a trawler just arrived from Alex., got filled up with rum and started to walk back to *Moy* on the sea. He said that as Jesus Christ had done it, he didn't see why he couldn't. Naturally he didn't get far.'

Moy finally went off for a refit in Alexandria, and remained there to sweep the approaches to Port Said. At this time Alexandria was expected to fall imminently, and to guard against frogman attack, standing orders instructed all trawlers and other small craft to lay alongside the valuable RN warships at dusk each night to provide some sort of buffer against one-man torpedoes. One night a dirty old trawler dutifully lay up against a destroyer, but the sight of the warship's beautiful new fenders was too much for Harry Tate's men, who could get no sea stores at all. In the quiet of night it was no trouble for the trawler's middle-watch quartermaster to swap over adjacent knots on the rails and exchange the trawler's filthy fenders for the destroyer's magnificent white ones. When the destroyer left at dawn, eyes popped and men stood aghast. A short, sharp signal from her RN commander caused the position to be righted forthwith.

Then there was the case of the trawler with the Crumpled Funnel. Funnel stay-wires were always left slack when the funnel was cold, for when it heated up the wires went tight. A zealous ordinary seaman, seeing the slack wires, decided it was his duty to tighten them, with the result that when the funnel got hot either wires or funnel had to give – and it was the funnel which gave and crumpled.

At Port Said ships flew small barrage balloons during the day to give them added protection against diving Stukas, the balloons having an explosive charge fixed to the wire. Each evening the balloons were taken back to an RAF compound, to be brought aboard again the following morning. The drill was to harness a balloon to an aircraftman, who then made his way with it to the harbour in a series of hops. One man was bringing a balloon back to *Moy* when, as he hopped round the harbour corner, a gust of wind blew him into the water to be towed at high speed across the harbour all the way to Port Fuad on the other side; he had to pay his own ferry fare back to Port Said. It was the first known example of water-skiing.

Also into *Moy's* unwritten log went the episode of the oil drums. She was alongside the jetty and had to take aboard some oil drums from another ship, but some buoys obstructed the passage between the two vessels. A wire was rigged to heave the drums across and over the buoys on to *Moy's* deck, but unfortunately the winchman took up the slack of the wire too suddenly. It went taut and sprung a coil round the door-handle of the captain's lavatory, pulled the door clean off and revealed the captain sitting on his throne to the gaze of a bevy of Maltese Wrens in the office alongside.

That was a trawler's life at Port Said; bombs and shells, madness and monotony, as they went out on sweep carrying an assortment of pets from dogs and cats to ducks, and even trusting doves that made their nests in the mast. And each man with his ready-money kept in a blown-up Durex, so that if the ship went down and he with it, someone at least might benefit.

Among other Harry Tate craft working in the Mediterranean, few were so defiantly debonair as the minesweeping yacht *Calamara*, which was furnished with a grand piano. As she sailed along, the first lieutenant played the piano while the skipper accompanied him on the violin. This skipper was very single-minded about his fresh cup of cocoa, which he would refuse unless it had the requisite circle of bubbles spinning round in the middle. His steward grew so tired of having to carry the rejected cup back to the galley that thereafter, just before delivering the cocoa, he would spit lightly into it to achieve the desired effect.

In pure comedy vein was the performance aboard a whaler bringing a very high-ranking, self-important Italian officer prisoner-of-war from Tobruk. He was confined to the captain's day cabin for most of the day, but allowed exercise under guard. He came aboard the whaler with a mass of trunks and other luggage which astonished both officers and crew. The voyage to Alexandria took longer than usual, owing to the whaler being detached for a time to hunt a U-boat. One day the Italian demanded to see the captain, protesting volubly and quoting the Geneva Convention, complaining that he had been robbed of all his decorations and orders. He got little change from the captain and was finally put ashore at Alexandria, in charge of the Redcaps, still protesting loudly as he flounced down the gangway. Three weeks later, with the watch on deck scrubbing down at 5 a.m., a petty officer was roused by gales of laughter. 'Dashing up to see what was going on, and to stop it before it woke the captain, I found our tiniest AB and biggest comedian scrubbing down decks with his overalls turned up to his knees, bare-footed, but with a full dress plumed cocked hat sideways on his head, a marvellous blue silk sash carrying a dagger across his chest, and half a dozen orders and decorations pinned to his overalls. I don't think I ever laughed so much in my life.'

The trawler *Cumbrae* also acquired a singular passenger. She was escorting a convoy from Cyprus to Port Said when, near midnight, the Commodore ship signalled that she had heard 'voices in the water'. *Cumbrae* was leading escort at the time but she reversed course and eventually traced the 'voices'. It turned out there was only one voice, that of the captain survivor of a sunken Greek coaster. Seaman John Paterson:

'As well as having a Kisbee lifebelt round himself he had lashed himself to a lot of wooden deck-housing. We got him alongside, hacked him clear of the deck-housing and heaved him aboard. He told us in broken English that an enemy submarine had surfaced and shelled his ship until she sank and he was the only survivor. This would have been his third night in the water, and "No save tonight, tomorrow we fineesh!" He had lost the use of his legs so we carried him for'ard and took him down to the messdeck. While we were easing him down the ladder his arm hit the rail and he called out, very upset, "Mind arm – smash watch!" A chance in a million of being picked up, and that was his chief worry! He had some banknotes packed in his oilskins, and the first lieutenant told me to take them into the galley and dry them out. I spread the money round the galley, it came to fifty Egyptian pound notes. The first lieutenant came and asked me how much there was and I told him, "Fifty pounds, sir." "That's right," he said, "the captain told me." I thought, that captain is a very long way from being "fineesh!" '

When the Fleet evacuated Alexandria and most ships went to Haifa, *Cumbrae* and a sister ship, *Islay*, went on patrol out of

Haifa nightly, returning at daybreak. But one day at noon they received the unusual order to sail immediately. *Cumbrae* had trouble at her buoy, so *Islay* was through the boom before her. It seemed she was hardly through before she was dropping depth-charges, and in no time at all she had brought up an Italian submarine, close enough to encourage the shore batteries to join in the fight. When *Cumbrae* caught up *Islay* was doing nicely. Two destroyers came and finished off the badly damaged Italian, but it was *Islay's* 'kill'; she had used up all her depth-charges in the battle. Three days later the Palestine police brought in three bodies from the sunken submarine, which had been carrying one-man submarines on its deck.

Another trawler to put paid to an Italian submarine was the *Lord Nuffield*. This was off Algiers, shortly after the Allied landings in North Africa. *Lord Nuffield* made an underwater contact and was preparing to lay a pattern of depth-charges when the submarine, the *Emo*, came up to periscope depth almost underneath her. *Emo* crash-dived but took a hammering from *Lord Nuffield's* depth-charges as it did so. The trawler ran in for a second attack, lost contact but dropped a single depth-charge, and the submarine panicked and came to the surface again. Unable to start his diesels and pull fast away from the trawler, the Italian commander ordered his men to the guns, but *Lord Nuffield*, captained by Lieutenant D. S. Mair, RN, was far too quick for him. Her four-inch, Oerlikon and machine-guns raked the submarine and smashed the conning-tower, effectively stopping all enemy resistance, and with most of his crew already in the water *Emo's* commander gave orders to scuttle and abandon ship. Eleven Italians died in the battle, the remainder being rescued and taken to Algiers.

Over at Malta in the meantime, the trawler *Beryl* had become the Navy's lone bulwark in the long and bitter siege of the island. *Beryl* was an old hand at work in the Mediterranean. She had been bought by the Admiralty in the mid-1930s and sent out on the Abyssinian Patrol. The outbreak of war found her at Malta under the command of a warrant officer of the Royal Navy, Boatswain Victor Rhind. As the island came under siege both of *Beryl's* sister ships, *Jade* and *Coral*, were wrecked early in 1942 by the enemy bombers which raked the island, but *Beryl* went on to weather the siege and win the same sort of reputation and undying admiration of the islanders as the three aircraft which were all the local defence available at one time. The islanders called her 'the flagship of Malta', for she flew the flag of the Flag Officer, Malta, when there was no other naval ship afloat.

Beryl's first big exploit involved a merchant ship which she found bombed and on fire. Despite continued attacks by enemy planes, *Beryl* rescued the crew and stood by, trying to put out the flames, but the blaze had taken too big a hold. Nevertheless she fought the fire until it was too dangerous to stay near.

She next took part with minesweepers in bringing the heavily damaged and blazing tanker *Ohio* into harbour. Though attacked by aircraft for four days, the crippled *Ohio*, making hardly any speed and looking all the time as though she would crack in half, was finally brought into harbour. The *Ohio*, after her epic run, was a total loss.

One of *Beryl's* trickiest jobs at the height of the siege was as mark-ship for a minelaying cruiser which used to dash for Malta to run in supplies; the trawler would wait for the cruiser at a buoy to lead her in. One night while *Beryl* waited, five E-boats spurted out of the dark to attack her. Cannon shells splintered her bridge and wheelhouse, but she evaded all the enemy torpedoes and came back strongly with her limited armament – her strongest gun was a three-inch for'ard. She sank one of the enemy boats and damaged at least one other, and the rest turned tail. Because of this enemy activity Boatswain Rhind decided to lead the cruiser into harbour by the inshore route, even though there was a danger of mines. It was remarkable foresight and good luck on his part, for in the morning they found that enemy mines had been strewn down the other, 'swept' channel and the cruiser would have been a certain victim. *Beryl* also met and guided in British submarines which sneaked into Malta to land vital supplies of oil and food, patrolling watchfully for U-boats and E-boats while they were discharging.

When an ammunition ship was bombed and set ablaze in the harbour *Beryl* attempted to save her. Braving repeated attacks by enemy planes she went alongside and tried to fight the fire, but the decks of the stricken ship were red-hot and burned through all the hoses that were put aboard her. Finally a lieutenant went aboard her and carried out scuttling work to ensure that she sank without blowing up, an exceedingly dangerous task for which he earned the George Cross.

As the only warship to serve day and night throughout the siege of Malta, *Beryl* had many narrow escapes. Just one instance of her charmed life was when an aircraft carrier was in harbour and the naval authorities foxed the enemy by moving the carrier to a new anchorage. Unluckily for *Beryl* her berth for the night was near that previously occupied by the carrier, and when the enemy swooped over to the attack she found herself the centre of a hailstorm of bombs; but miraculously she escaped with her stern riddled with bomb splinters.

When Malta was relieved *Beryl's* work was still not ended. She laid the buoy which guided the small landing craft to shore on their invasion of Sicily. Later this buoy, at the end of the Malta swept channel, was used for the rendezvous with the Italian Fleet which surrendered and was laid up in St Paul's Bay, Malta; *Beryl* met the ships and led them to the anchorage.

She also helped on experimental work with two-man submarines in a bay at Malta, 'pinging' the bay with her asdic while the miniature subs tried to get in and stick a mine on her. Exercises completed, she would hoist the two-man craft on to her deck and ferry it home to base. Yet another duty found her as a survey ship when the various harbour and approach hazards were plotted by the hydrographical officers of Malta. Towards the quieter days in the Mediterranean she took on convoy work up to Italy.

Though she had many changes of first lieutenant, Boatswain Rhind remained her captain. He was dedicated to his ship and must have spent more hours on the bridge than any other commanding officer in the Navy, for on *Beryl*, with only two officers, it was always, at best, watch-and-watch; and in action, watch-on and stay-on. Rhind, who was awarded the DSO, was a quiet man who seldom mixed much when ashore, although he had friends in the dockyard whom he visited. He was very proud of his position, and of his ship and her record, but he never spoke of his exploits, which accounts for *Beryl* never having received her due, though her logbook showed her to have been in everything, and sometimes as the leading light. She was in commission in the Mediterranean longer than any other ship in the Navy.

Early in 1942 twenty-four anti-submarine trawlers each equipped for the first time with an early type of radar, steamed from Britain across the Atlantic to America, on loan to the U.S. Navy. In charge of Commander Rex English, RN, they went to help the Americans, who, having recently entered the war, were sorely in need of anti-submarine vessels to help them in their struggle against the U-boats now rampaging among shipping off the US east coast. Among the half a dozen Northern trawlers, fine, sturdy sea-boats all, which formed part of the fleet to make the journey was the *Northern Princess*, commanded by Lieutenant Dryden Phillipson, RNR. Like the other commanders, Phillipson did not know his destination until his ship put out to sea from Londonderry and he opened his sealed orders, yet he had been particularly anxious to see his wife before he sailed, which unhappily could not be managed. It was almost as if he had some premonition of his ship's fate.

Among *Northern Princess*'s crew was an eighteen-year-old seaman fresh from Sparrow's Nest, young Alex Macleod. Alec, a very likeable lad, had come over from Shanghai to join up, and was expecting his parents to follow him over. He was a member of the raw bunch from Lowestoft, including Ordinary Seaman Paul Lund, who to their dismay had been sent up to Kirkwall to join trawlers of the Northern Patrol. 'Well, never mind,' young Alec had grinned, 'it's only for three months, and then we'll be back in Brighton to get our gold stripes.'

Poor Alec, to be drafted to *Northern Princess*, for he never received the call to do his commission course – never survived the three months.

On March 6 1942 *Northern Princess* was steaming across the Atlantic to St John's, Newfoundland, in company with her sister trawlers including *Northern Chief*, *Northern Isles*, *Northern Dawn* and *St Cathan*. On the Grand Banks, the fishing ground a few hundred miles from Newfoundland, they ran into patches of fog. Next morning at dawn, *Northern Princess* had disappeared. The other trawlers immediately searched the area but not a trace of her could be found; no wreckage, nothing. It was a complete mystery. The sea was oily calm, there had been no explosion, no radio call-up; *Northern Princess* had simply vanished in the night. The only possible explanation was that she had been torpedoed and blown apart or sent to the bottom within seconds, yet no U-boat ever claimed her. So she joined seven other ships of Harry Tate's Navy which had already vanished without trace, their ghosts now ranging over waters from the Barents Sea to the far Atlantic.

All the other twenty-three trawlers made the crossing safely. They were fitted out American fashion with such sophisticated equipment as air-conditioning, iced water fountains, coding machines and typewriters, and based at New York, Boston and Charleston, South Carolina. From Charleston *Northern Dawn* went twenty miles up the Cape Fear River to Wilmington, North Carolina, where she was given an enthusiastic reception as the first vessel within living memory to visit the place flying the White Ensign.

The Britishers escorted convoys from Boston down the eastern seaboard to Key West in Florida, making calls at New York, Norfolk (Virginia), Wilmington and Charleston. For a long time the only assistance given them by the US Navy was provided by four old American destroyers and some assorted motor patrol boats. There were no blackout restrictions on land and at night the coastal lights silhouetted all the ships to the further advantage of the enemy. In the first mass slaughter by the U-boats many oil tankers were torpedoed and frequently it was impossible for the trawlers to rescue survivors because of the blazing oil on the surface of the water from the dying ships. But the knowhow of the British vessels was invaluable to the hard-pressed US Navy, and one trawler, *Le Tiger*, achieved a triumphant victory in sinking a U-boat. Against this, Harry Tate's men lost five vessels. The *Bedfordshire* was sunk by a U-boat south of Cape Lookout, North Carolina, two months after her arrival; *Kingston Ceylonite* was sunk by a mine off Chesapeake Bay. The others were lost through collisions: *St Cathan* after being hit by a merchant vessel off New York, the *Pentland Firth* also off New York, and the *Senateur Duhamel*, a huge 900-ton French vessel acquired after Dunkirk, plunged to the bottom after a collision off Wilmington.

During their stay in America the trawler men were treated exceptionally well, enjoying all the facilities of the USO with free tickets for Broadway shows, concerts and operas. As an instance of the generosity of some American citizens, while *Cape Warwick* was in Charleston three members of her crew on shore leave were treated to a six-day holiday in Greenville, North Carolina, at the expense of one of the residents, with first-class hotel accommodation and spending money. Even the shops in Greenville refused to accept payment for anything they wanted to buy.

The shades of Harry Tate, however, followed the trawlers even to the US. Followed, at least, *Northern Dawn*, when Leading-Coder David Willing, together with the signals officer, Lieutenant R. B. Belas, RNVR, was summoned to a Court of Enquiry convened aboard a British destroyer in the Charleston Navy Yard, there to answer for a priceless incident that happened aboard *Northern Dawn* just before she left Londonderry. Leading Coder Willing:

'At the time we thought we were going to North Russia, not

the States, so there was gloom in the bunkhouse. We had instructions from NOIC Londonderry that certain of our secret signal books were to be handed in at the naval base. These included most of our code books and some special codes used in conjunction with RAF aircraft. Lieutenant Belas and myself were ordered by the captain (Lieutenant J.O. Williams, RNR) to get all the books ready and mustered in his day-cabin. We worked most of one afternoon and evening getting this done.

'The captain was ashore so we had the run of his quarters, putting all the books into the usual heavy canvas bags full of eyeleted holes for quick sinking in an emergency. We decided to leave the bags in the cabin overnight and take them ashore first thing next morning. Belas would go ashore to get transport, and when he reappeared on the quay he would wave – and I, with the help of one or two of the hands, would start lugging the bags ashore.

'The next morning happened to be Friday the 13th, a date we were both to remember. At 7.15 a.m. Lieutenant Belas appeared and waved. I nipped down to the bunkhouse and shook Sparks, Bunts and one or two others to come and give me a hand, but was told fiercely to "get bloody lost". I dashed on deck again to see Belas getting very agitated at the delay, so decided to try to heave the first two bags ashore unaided. Some of the books were quite big, with leaden covers, so the bags were pretty heavy, but I managed to get them down to the main deck then heave them up on to the ship's side. A USN minesweeper lay between us and the quay, and we were linked to her by a hefty plank, on to which I now dragged the bags. Needless to say, on that cold winter's morning there wasn't a quartermaster to be seen.

'Suddenly I lost my balance on the plank and dropped the two bags between *Northern Dawn* and the sweeper. Down they went in a mighty splash, almost taking me with them. When Lieutenant Belas realised what had happened there was great excitement. I was slapped under close arrest in the hands of the coxswain while Belas rushed off ashore to summon the captain. The captain appeared, closely followed by none other than the NOIC himself. Things really began to happen. I was called to the wardroom and in the presence of the coxswain, first lieutenant, sub-lieutenant and captain, I was questioned by the NOIC.

'*Northern Dawn* was then shifted and other ships around us moved, and a diving operation begun. This went on throughout Saturday and Sunday, our crews having to take it in turns on the pump taking air down to the diver – I wasn't at all popular. To the best of my knowledge the bags were never found, and because of their loss new codes and cyphers were brought into force for the whole of the RN and RAF operating in Western Approaches.'

In America, *Northern Dawn* and her sister trawlers remained with the US Navy for several months until the autumn of 1942, when they had to be withdrawn and sent over to South African waters, where a fresh burst of U-boat activity was worrying the South Atlantic convoys. But other Patrol Service men crossed to America at this time to crew the new British Yard Minesweepers, or BYMS, being built over there for the Royal Navy under the Lease-Lend agreement. The BYMS were sturdy wooden ships – the wood to protect them against magnetic mines – with a top speed of about 15 knots, and their main armament a three-inch gun. Many of these little ships steamed thousands of miles to their stations, crossing the Atlantic quite alone. Petty Officer Robert Muir was among a squad sent out to bring the brand new BYMS 51 over to the UK.

'We went by train from Halifax, Nova Scotia, to the US, finally landing up in a little holiday resort in New Jersey called Asbury Park, where we were billeted in two lovely hotels. Here we were split into two watches and given various duties. At first I was put in charge of a working party to help clean and alter another big hotel being converted into a White Ensign Club for the boys, and in charge of this place was the famous tennis player Miss Betty Nuttal; of course, she loved us all and gave us a very good time. We also used to go up to New York at weekends.

'I got collared two or three times for the town patrol and had to take four men down to the local police station, where we did an hourly routine patrol then waited in the station in case of trouble in any of the bars. When an alarm came, the cops rushed us to the spot in the "Hurry Up" wagon and we'd go in with pick handles flying and bring out our own boys – they took care of their own men. One noted joint was Fox's Bar, which was guaranteed to produce a couple of calls a night.

'After three months we were sent down to Portsmouth, Virginia, and billeted in the US naval base. The food was marvellous and there was a beautiful canteen in which we spent our evenings, but twice our matelots got fed up with the American "bull" and had a sort-out, smashing the place to pieces. You couldn't really blame them as some of the Americans plainly hated us.

'We were finally sent on to the US Navy camp at Charleston. Here we were treated very well, but in Charleston some of us came up against the racial thing. After having a few drinks, a pal and I got on a bus to return to the docks, and of course the buses were divided into two sections, one for whites and one for coloureds. The white section was full so we went into the black section. Up came the conductress to tell us "You're not allowed to sit here". We said we didn't mind where we sat and that we weren't going to stand, so she immediately stopped the bus and said: "All right, bud, you can walk." And the driver chucked us off two miles from the docks.

'We eventually took over BYMS 51. She was a little motor minesweeper about 135 feet long, but nicely accommodated and fitted with every type of sweep. After doing two months' trials out of Charleston we at last received our orders for home. We came right up the east coast to Staten Island, spent a night in New York, then on through Long Island Sound and the Cape Cod Canal, on to Boston and finally to St John's, Newfoundland, where we waited three weeks for good weather. We took a full load of diesel oil and also fifty 50-gallon drums on deck to get our little ship across the Atlantic. As we used the drums we lashed them round the ship's side to act as buoyancy tanks. We made the crossing in six and a half days with a gale of wind up our stern, and berthed at Londonderry. A stop of one day here, then across the Irish Sea, through the Caledonian Canal and down the east coast to Great Yarmouth, where we arrived nearly a year after leaving Britain. We were given ten days' leave and on returning received orders to sail to Milford Haven, take on a full load of oil at Milford and join a convoy to the Azores, which was to be our operational base. We arrived at Milford, and just as we were coming into the fuelling wharf the skipper rang full-astern, but instead of going astern she went full-ahead and hit the quay at 16 knots. She smashed all her bow and was starting to sink alongside the quay, but they managed to tow us into Milford Haven and put us on the slip before she went. And that, after thousands of miles, was that. Back to the Nest we all went.'

The flow of British Yard Minesweepers continued by the hundreds. Chief Petty Officer William Davies, RNR, went out to commission BYMS 2188 at Brooklyn Navy Yard.

'We were at Staten Island, Coney Beach and Iona Island for about five months, during which we experienced the usual epidemic of brawls. In "Pop's Bar" on Staten Island the old 'un who ran the place would climb on the bar and wield a baseball bat at whoever came within range. Once, as we were going along the main "drag", the sounds of catchy music attracted our attention and we all piled into this hall for the local hop. There were some red faces when we were stopped in the foyer by a coloured man who told us: "I'm sure sorry, boys, but you can't go in dere – it's de house of de Lord, and I don't reckon as how you're looking for him right now." Well, Negro spirituals always did sound gay and lively.

'From New York we called at Boston, where we were involved in what became known as "The Battle of the Silver Dollar". That's where it started, over a girl of course, at the Silver Dollar in Scully Square. From there into the street and down the subway the fight raged with US Marines. The police and the USN Patrol rushed along, but an officer yelled: "Let the stupid bastards fight it out down there – we'll clean up later!" Which they did, and a sorry looking lot were bailed out of the "cungee hole" in order to sail BYMS 2188 out of Boston – all under stoppage of leave and pay.

'En route for the UK we were held up by the Royal Canadian Navy at Halifax, Nova Scotia. U-boats had laid a minefield outside the harbour, blocking the entrance to Bedford Basin; the Canadians didn't know how to deal with the situation so our flotilla, the 170th, was attached to the RCN to do the job for them. We cleared eighteen mines. No sooner had we done this than the Germans laid another minefield outside St John's, Newfoundland, so away we had to go and sweep up that little lot. We blew up sixteen mines, and were iced in, but finally returned to Canada.

'Eventually we sailed home via the Azores. On calling in there for three days we were honestly shocked to find a chap bringing his "good lady" down to the jetty wearing only a Burberry, his price for her services being just one woollen sweater, of which we had plenty. None of our crew availed himself of this service. We still had some pride.'

12

'Tally-Ho, Drive On!'

In home waters early in 1942 *Fisher Boy* was helping the old 'Smokey Joes' of the 14th Minesweeping Flotilla, led by the elderly naval minesweeping sloop *Fitzroy*.

Mines laid between the Thames estuary and Great Yarmouth were causing the sweepers a great deal of trouble, their wire cutters were getting caught and not managing to cut through the mooring wires.

To try to overcome this, boffins at HMS *Vernon* invented an explosive wire cutter – a small charge snapped its cutting edges together – and *Fisher Boy*'s job was to steam up and down behind the Smokey Joes, retrieve mines that were cut loose and tow them to the beach intact. It was hoped the explosive cutter would also clamp on to the lower part of the mooring wire, so that the wire could be hauled in together with the all-important mine sinker; but unfortunately the charge not only blasted the wire apart, it also blasted the sweep cutter and everything else.

This operation saw the death of the old *Fitzroy*, when she struck a mine just off Yarmouth. *Fisher Boy* hurriedly steamed out to find the sloop rolled over on her side and men struggling to keep afloat in the water. She was successful in saving most of the crew. Signalman Smith:

'One old Stripey we picked up caused us great amusement. He was in his mid-fifties and seemed quite elderly to me, but after we had given him hot rum and a mug of tea he was quite lively. He told us that when *Fitzroy* rolled over he got on to the hull, quietly looked round and assessed the situation. He decided *Fitzroy* was going to sink and that the best thing to do was to get the hell away from her. So he dived into the water and swam like fury for half an hour, after which something hit him in the back of the neck. He looked round and saw it was the keel of *Fitzroy*. He'd been swimming in the wind, and it had brought the capsized ship hard up behind him. But he was a brave old boy and could see the funny side of it.'

In a further effort to recover one of these same troublesome mines, *Fisher Boy* moved to Harwich and picked up a diving crew from HMS *Vernon*.

'The diver was "Pincher" Martin, a little fellow who, in his diving kit, was virtually lost and quite helpless until we lifted him over the side. Working with the yacht *Bystander* we swept with a single wire off Orfordness for a couple of days and finally did come fast with the wire. *Bystander* passed her end to us and we hauled on it till it was taut, then hove-to beside what we hoped was a mine. We had to wait some hours for Pincher to go down and investigate, and this waiting period was heavy with suspense. We'd been given a little fox terrier in London which we had christened Blitz, and during the time we were moored to the mine two of the crew cut up an old sailor's suit and made a smart little rig for the dog; it was one of the odd ways people found to ease their minds in times of tension.

'When slack water came we were able to send Pincher down the wire. Divers had to wait for slack water because the tide in the North Sea ripped along fairly smartly, stirring up the sandy bottom, and according to Pincher it was like a thick fog down there at any other state of the tide than slack water. He got down and we passed a wire down to him which he secured to the mine sinker. We hauled this up, released the mine from the sinker and towed it behind us, rejoicing, to Harwich. Here all this gear was put ashore and specially dealt with, then sent down to *Vernon* for them to devise ways and means of sweeping it. We got our usual reward for a dangerous piece of work: five days' boiler-clean leave – whether or not the boiler needed cleaning.'

Shortly afterwards the minesweepers operating from Grimsby had trouble with a protective device which the enemy began mooring outside their minefields. This was an explosive cutter which blew up the sweeps as the trawlers went in.

'At Grimsby one day Lieutenant Armitage came to *Fisher Boy* and asked me to go up to an office where he'd been allowed some accommodation. One of the sweepers had brought in or towed in a pear-shaped metal canister standing some 3ft 6in. high. Somehow or other Armitage had got it up into the office and he told me he'd been on the phone to Lieutenant Glenny, RN, down in Portsmouth, and Glenny thought he knew how the thing should be taken apart. We had some tools in the office, so Armitage now took instructions over the phone which he passed on to me while I got busy with a screwdriver and spanner. Just then the RN captain of the base came into the office and asked what we were doing. When he heard, he almost exploded, telling Armitage where to go and how to get there. I suppose it must have been somewhat upsetting for the old boy as his office could quite easily have gone up in smoke.

'After this, Armitage sent me home for a couple of days. On getting out of the train at Peterborough I saw a porter helping Armitage with his luggage. The porter was carrying a wooden box on his shoulder, something like a 3 ft 6in. coffin, which contained the works of this small mine, together with a potato sack containing the casing. I doubt very much whether he had any idea what he was lugging across Peterborough station.'

A little later, with her mine recovery officer away at *Vernon*, *Fisher Boy* was quietly lying up in her favourite corner in the Royal Dock, Grimsby, when a damaged fishing trawler was towed into the fish dock.

'She had been skim-bombed by an aircraft coming in low over the water. The bomb had smashed through the hull into the living accommodation aft and the crew had promptly abandoned ship, though the bomb hadn't gone off. Someone had heroically towed the trawler in, and she was moored on her own away from the other ships. The base maintenance commander, faced with the problem of what to do with the trawler and the bomb, sent for an Army bomb disposal lorry. This came and parked alongside the trawler, but the bomb being on the ship it was argued that naval personnel must remove it. The maintenance commander, remembering that the mine recovery vessel *Fisher Boy* was in harbour, decided we were just the people to handle it. We really knew nothing about the technicalities of handling mines and bombs, all this work being done by our officers. However, together with the skipper, about six of us went over to the trawler and found this 500 lb. bomb down in the after cabin. Trying to get it up the ladder out of the cabin was quite a task; we were all scared to death and hadn't a clue what to do.

'At last we got it up the ladder and on to the concrete quay, and gingerly carried it to the tailboard of the lorry. As we lowered it on to the tailboard someone pulled his hands away quickly because his fingers were being trapped. The bomb started to fall and we all ran like hell and got down flat. The bomb, fortunately, just lay there, a lump of useless metal on the quay. After a while, the thing not having gone off, we got up, hoisted it back on to the lorry, wedged it so that it couldn't roll about, and wished the Army driver a fond farewell.'

Down at Portland the small and very old Lowestoft trawler

Thrifty was working with her port sister ship, *Kindred Star*. They had as consorts two French diesels, *Cap Ferrat* and *Pierre Gustave*, together with an ancient wooden tub of a drifter, BTB, which had been pulled off the beach inside Lowestoft harbour to go seafaring again. Commanding *Thrifty* after his long spell with the paddlesweepers was Lieutenant James Reeve.

'Our motley group would sail at dawn from Portland harbour searching the approach channels southwards of the Bill and eastwards to St Alban's Head, for enemy mines. Of the five ships *Pierre Gustave* was always the smartest – and the least used. BTB leaked and was likely to sink from sheer old age, while *Thrifty* and *Kindred Star* had old boilers which, conveniently for us, had to be cleaned every three months if we were to reach our ten knots.

'*Thrifty* and her flotilla each carried at the bow an enormous bracket and bucket containing the noisy automatic hammer designed to trigger off acoustic mines. Astern, to counter the magnetics, we streamed almost a mile of two heavy rubber-covered copper cables which pulsed electricity into the sea. This unwieldy tow wrapped itself round the propeller when I put the ship slow-astern to help the crew manhandle it inboard after my first trip in command. *Kindred Star* towed us home, and there a diver cut us free. Experts found that the cable had been pierced in many places by some reluctant, seasick conscript, who would commit sabotage rather than sail in HMT *Thrifty*.

'Navigating with our cumbersome gear between the Shambles and Portland Bill, where the race at spring tides ran faster than our own speed, caused more anxiety than the hazards of war. Sometimes these anxieties came from an unexpected quarter. In the middle of Weymouth Bay, *Thrifty* and *Kindred Star* were surprised and straddled by a double fall of shot coming from a shore battery doing a practice shoot. Then there was the torpedo, again a blank practice shot, which sped straight for a motor torpedo boat but stopped when it got alongside *Thrifty*'s well-worn plates.

'Returning to harbour in line ahead, *Thrifty* could put up quite a bow wave, but sweeping against a head sea made her old engines squeak and splutter. Her venerable engineer, Chief Petty Officer Brown, who knew her from her fishing days, nursed her jealously and well. Anxiously sounding the siren in thick fog, I received via the voice-pipe the message: "If the Old Man doesn't stop blowing that bloody whistle we shan't have enough steam to get home tonight!"'

At Dover, eight former fishing trawlers from Hull, Grimsby and Fleetwood, together with a dozen assorted drifters, comprised the Dover Patrol. In the Channel front line, under constant attack from raiding aircraft and shellfire from the big guns of Calais, theirs was an eventful life of minesweeping, escorting convoys, rescuing ship survivors and ditched airmen, besides undertaking peculiar duties like releasing pigeons in mid-Channel at fixed times; where the birds went to they never discovered.

Easter Sunday 1942 found the men of the Dover Patrol marching through the town on church parade to Dover Priory, whose old pile, though damaged by bombs, was still usable. After the hymns came the sermon. The parson mounted the pulpit and silence reigned except for the cooing of pigeons in the eaves. The parson announced: 'My sermon today is "Who Moved the Stone?"' At that moment a small stone, no doubt dislodged by the pigeons, fell into the church. In the hush that followed a voice from the back said: ' 'Itler!'

It needed a strong sense of humour to survive the daily pressures. One drifter, the *Ut Prosim*, was sunk by shellfire even as she moored in Dover harbour. There were other losses, but the saddest of all was that of the trawler *Waterfly*. A short time before she went down under the bombs of German aircraft off Dungeness, Leading Seaman J. P. Rampling went to *Waterfly* as a relief gunner from his own trawler, *Yashima*.

'We in *Yashima*, *Adam*, *Wigan* and the other trawlers had our own routine at sea. Leaving harbour for sweeps or escort duties we would load all guns and keep the gun crews closed up ready for action. Only on "out-sweep" and "in-sweep" did they leave the guns to help, and then there was always someone standing by. These precautions were very necessary as it was Jerry's habit to pay us a sudden visit. Pairs of ME 109s would sweep in low over the water, give us a stick of bombs and zoom off again. They seldom came back for a second go, so it was the sudden first attack that mattered. We were always ready to let go with everything we had; it accounted for our scraping through with minor damage. However, not *Waterfly*.

'She was the smartest looking trawler in the Dover Patrol, commanded by a lieutenant-commander who was a real Navy man. His ship was not as the other Harry Tates, she was always spick and span.

'When I was loaned to her as gunner for one trip, as we left harbour I carried out the routine job of loading the guns and closing up the gun crews. After we had been steaming for about ten minutes the Chief Petty Officer came on to the 12-pounder platform and asked why I had the gun crew closed up. I said it was the usual practice in *Yashima*, but he replied: "In this ship everybody is working party – out-sweep, in-sweep, and then part of ship. Action-stations will be sounded on the enemy being sighted." Well, on that day's sweep nothing happened, but I told some of the crew that I didn't like it, and that if she continued in this fashion some day she was bound to "get the works". It seemed she did – that action-stations was sounded, but Jerry was first.

'We heard that *Waterfly* took a direct hit in the magazine and there was only one survivor, the Bunts, who went insane.'

Up in northern waters the fight was more often with the weather. Sub-Lieutenant Dormer graphically logged *Cape Argona*'s experience on Bill Bailey's Bank, between Scotland and Ireland.

'Hove-to at midday, the first of the convoy escort to give up. The next forty hours were memorable. The vicious shriek of the wind, the great ridges of water appearing level with the hounds (the point at which the rigging is attached to the mast), their last ten feet or so as steep as a wall. . . . The lovely green of the crests just as they curl over to break, and the ship climbing, climbing, and the sea piling up, leaping up, like two rugger players jump- for the same ball. Every so often she didn't quite make it and tons of water crashed on board, springing the wooden deck till it leaked like a sieve, carrying away wardroom ventilator and stovepipe, smashing the bridge ladder, buckling the Carley float frame, and throwing a depth-charge clean out of the port thrower, over the galley to the starboard quarter, sending most of the others rolling about the deck, washing away the log and line streamed from the stern, and the collision mat, and a dozen other things. We waded around trying to lash things up. I crawled round the gun platform in my pyjamas to throw away the fused H.E. shells after their rack had gone; the coxswain declared it was too dangerous to send a man, so I left my last dry clothes in the wheelhouse.'

And again in *Hornpipe*, when Dormer was first lieutenant. This naval-built Dance-class trawler left South Shields bound for work-up at Port Edgar.

'Sailed in a terrific gale. My fault . . . NOIC phoned for the CO who was not available, so I took the call. If we liked, our sailing could be postponed in view of the weather. I had never heard of such a thing... we were tough. I said: "Oh, we'll sail – doesn't worry us." Just outside the piers both seaboats started wandering. We had to heave-to and all hands got soaked and were nearly blown overboard while securing them. The ship leaked like a sieve and rolled very badly, often to 40 deg. Everything was flooded out and almost everyone seasick, even the CO. In the afternoon the ship "fell over" on her beam ends. I was on watch. Down in the seamen's mess Johnnie Bentham was thrown against a stanchion and fractured his knee-cap. Simultaneously the paint locker door at the top of the companionway burst open and several hundredweight drums of paint spilt, largely into the seamen's mess, as well as over the deck above.

'Ready-use ammunition lockers, welded on to the superstructure, broke adrift, and great concrete dan-sinkers, weighing two hundredweight if not five, were wandering about, while the whole ship was swept by a continuous storm of cutting spray as cold and painful as powdered ice. There was indescribable chaos below, two or three inches of paint on the deck and everything in the seamen's mess smothered with it. The place was ankle-deep in water, broken crockery, clothes and furnishings. The watch below were being sick over everything while more water poured through the leaky deck, and because of the violent motion and the paint it was impossible to stand up. Poor Johnnie yelled with pain every time his leg moved. We had quite a job to fix it.'

Fog, too, was a great menace. It resulted in another Dance-class trawler, *Sword Dance*, coming to a miserable end off the north-east coast of Scotland. In her life of less than two years *Sword Dance*, employed almost entirely on escort work with coastal convoys, had taken a severe shaking from a bombing Heinkel and been caught up in air raids on Hull, when she lost two ratings. In the early morning of July 5 1942, while senior escort of an eastbound convoy, she was rammed in dense fog by one of the merchant ships. She was holed in the starboard coalbunker and the boiler and engine rooms immediately flooded, taking her down in less than an hour. Another escort rescued her company.

Over at Belfast the trawler *Friesland* led a dull but reasonably safe existence sweeping off Northern Ireland. Until she became a plague ship. One of the crew contacted typhoid, at which she was quarantined in a far corner of the dock. Seaman Robert Thomas:

'We were all innoculated, the ship scrubbed down with disinfectant and a watch kept to see that no one came near us. The skipper blamed the cook, which was unfair, though allegedly he had on one occasion been mistaken for a stoker coming off watch. The crew knew the source of the trouble, however. It was the rats. They were everywhere, infesting the galley and messdeck and nesting in the provision store. The bins containing rice and lentils were obviously contaminated by them, and lentil soup and rice pudding disappeared from my menu. A loaf of bread left on the messdeck table was torn to pieces by the brutes. One night coming off watch I saw two running up and down a man's bedclothes. We tried trapping them, and inside a quarter of an hour there were half a dozen in the cage. A heaving line was attached to it and it was lowered into the sea. Half an hour later the cage was hauled up with one rat still running round. Much as I loathed them I felt there must be a better way of despatching them than this. Finally, fumigation was tried, the crew being turned adrift for twenty-four hours while the operation was on. This seemed to be successful. But the rats had the last laugh, for when the cold weather came and we dug out our overcoats, there wasn't a button to be found on them.'

The *Friesland* captain's suspicions of his cook were probably not entirely without foundation, for a legion of stories grew up around the trawler cooks, perpetually harassed men as they all were. Cooks were notorious and cooks were fiercely individual.

There was the excellent one aboard a motor minesweeper who put on a lunch for the Paymaster Commander at Harwich in order to qualify as leading cook. He was helped by a friendly petty officer who washed up his pots, and fortified by the coxswain's rum bottle. The lunch was perfect, the sweet out of this world; then came the cheese and biscuits and coffee. By now the cook was dangerously well fortified. He pushed up the wardroom hatch and passed the cheese and biscuits to the steward, commenting boldly: 'I dinna make these, and if he doesn't like 'em, he can stick 'em up his fat arse. Never wanted to be a bloody leading cook anyway. . . . '

But of all the ratings aboard the Patrol Service ships the 'asdics' were perhaps the most remarkable. It was generally agreed that they were without exception quite mad. This because of the hours spent with a continuous 'ping' in the ears while on watch, and the special training that they all had to undertake for the job. A prime case was Andy, of the naval trawler *Fir*. For justice Leading-Cook F. J. Scadeng tells Andy's story.

'He was from the North and never went ashore without coming into contact with the police. He was once removed by his shipmates from the middle of a fountain, from whence he was determined to annexe a statue nearly as big as himself. On another occasion he had to appear in court to answer a charge of damage to a weighing machine. Found guilty, he was given time to pay the fine. He always forgot it, and at regular intervals would be seen strolling along the deck saying with great dignity: "I've just had a letter from my solicitors. . . ."

'His great day came when, as we were entering Plymouth, he reported "Something, sir!" and gave the estimated direction and distance. Great excitement was felt when he convinced the skipper that it could be a U-boat. In the galley I had no warning of what was about to happen until a terrific explosion, much heavier than any mine I had experienced, shook the ship and lifted her stern well out of the water. The galley clock started to race, the minute hand whizzing around at the rate of knots. The coal shot out of the bunker and joined pots and pans on the galley deck. I found afterwards that they'd failed to calculate the depth for the depth-charge to go off as against the speed of the ship.

'Undaunted, Andy insisted that he could still hear "echoes", so the skipper ordered a turn round and another run. This time they got it right and the depth-charge waited until we were clear before exploding. After three or four runs and some wonderful depth-charge practice somebody spotted oil on the water and we started to congratulate ourselves. Highly pleased, we turned to continue our way back to Plymouth. The skipper stepped down from the bridge to make his way aft, probably to commend the depth-charge crew on a fine piece of work. He was making his way along the port waist when he saw a stoker lolling against the stokehold hatch. The skipper stopped dead in his tracks. "Have you thrown any oily waste over the side lately?" he demanded suspiciously. "Oh, yes, sir," the stoker replied – "I thought we'd better get rid of it before we entered harbour." The skipper did not finish his journey aft and the depth-charge brigade did not receive their commendation. He went sadly but thoughtfully down to his cabin.'

Further sadness for *Fir*'s skipper came in Plymouth harbour. 'We had to allow another trawler to move out from an inside berth and go to sea. We got out of her way all right, then made to get back again. The sea wall at this point was built at right angles to another, forming a corner, and there were some steps down to the water. Against the steps was tied an old steam picket boat used to take mail and stores to ships in the stream.

'We had to get back against our wall with the stern about thirty feet from the picket boat. The engine room telegraph worked overtime and we went backwards and forwards in a whirl of water that stirred up more muck than a messdeck "buzz". Eventually the skipper forgot to telegraph full-ahead in time to stop his "way" before we went in and sat on that poor little picket boat. Fortunately the boat's crew had foreseen what might happen and scrambled up the steps in time. It was quite a peaceful end. The little boat just folded up with a long "Weeeeeeee . . . " from its boiler and went down without a splash.'

On the small ships the rum was always 'neaters', but once on the trawler *Hazelmere* they started to issue grog (two parts water, one part rum). The only way the men had of voicing their protest was to empty the grog into a bucket, which was then taken by the leading seaman to the first lieutenant. 'The grog, sir,' he reported, and emptied it over the side. After a few days of this the astute coxswain sorted things out. He made the men drink their rum neat, then follow it down with two tots of water. And gradually the water was forgotten.

On the bridge of *Hazelmere*, Lieutenant-Commander Nichols had his regular saying for the day. 'Do you like Hitler?' he would ask. 'No, sir,' his crew would reply. 'Good! Tally-ho, drive on!'

At the other end of the scale to the sometimes stiff-upper-lip command of some trawlers was the jolly lot of the motor minesweepers or 'Mickey Mouses', small ships with a crew of fifteen. Like on one MMS when the skipper and his first lieutenant both got plastered while out sweeping and were beyond bringing their ship back to Parkeston Quay. The leading seaman, a fisherman from Aberdeen, donned the skipper's cap and went on the bridge, while the coxswain, a fisherman first mate from Hull, went on the wheel; and with Bunts making all the correct signals to Shotley Tower they brought the ship into harbour, and no one was any the wiser. But the climax came when the skipper, on sobering up, played merry hell with the leading seaman for getting his cap dirty. You couldn't win with the wardroom!

Unfortunately some officers carried their drinking bouts too far, which resulted in such farcical situations as at Grimsby, when Chief-Skipper Sidney White had to take an officer under arrest for being drunk on duty. 'I was driving him through town when he asked to go to a public lavatory. I agreed and he went down the steps while I and my Wren driver waited outside. After ten minutes I got suspicious and went down to find that he'd ducked out by another entrance. I was in dead trouble for losing him. However, three days later he was brought in. He'd left his false teeth on a ledge in the lavatory, gone back later for them and been caught by waiting police.'

But the most remarkable escapade of all, even including that of the cook who deserted *Foxtrot* and was picked up in Liverpool passing as an admiral's son, concerned the strange disappearance of Sub-Lientenant 'X' of the trawler *Turquoise*.

In very rough weather, *Turquoise* was bound for her base at Harwich with a southbound convoy. One of two lookouts standing the morning watch on the point-five guns aft was William Davies.

'I called the forenoon watchkeepers at one bell, and as I returned to my post Sub-Lieutenant "X" came from the bridge and told us to tighten up the gripes on the lifeboat, saying, "I'm just going to check the log." The lifeboat gripes seemed all right so we returned to the guns, were relieved and went below for breakfast. At 0900 hours word was passed round that Sub-Lieutenant "X" hadn't returned to the bridge, and that his scarf had been found wrapped around the log. A thorough search of the ship was made, even to the chain-locker, while the officers checked their quarters, but there was no sign of him. We got permission from the convoy escort leader, the destroyer *Richmond*, to leave convoy and search the sea. In such rough weather this was difficult and proved fruitless, so we entered harbour with our flag at half-mast, Sub-Lieutenant "X" being presumed lost at sea.

'It was a great puzzle to us all how he had gone overboard, though of course such things could happen. He was a pleasant enough young officer, well liked by the lower deck; he suffered from seasickness but so did thousands more. He was the grandson of the founder of a well-known shipping line, so his family were among the gentry and he himself was the perfect gentleman. His mother came down to the ship and collected his things, spending a little time with the captain, and we all felt sad at her distress.'

Sub-Lieutenant 'X' was officially reported missing, his name appearing under 'Fallen Officers' in *The Times*, which also published, by a correspondent, a full and wistful appreciation of the young man, whose mind, the writer said, 'was always alive with some fresh enterprise.' A memorial service was held at St Paul's, London, with many VIPs attending, besides another held at his parish church.

A month afterwards *Turquoise*, returning from convoy duty, was putting into Parkeston Quay when her crew saw an astonishing sight.

'There on the jetty under close arrest was our Sub-Lieutenant "X". He was court-martialled on the base ship, and I believe as he left the quay and stepped on to the station he was taken by MPs as being eligible for military service. The grapevine said that he had somehow retained his OD's paybook and drafted himself into Devonport Barracks, where he was awaiting draft. How was he discovered? How did he hide? How did he get ashore past the quartermaster? Was he helped by someone? And the biggest question of all – why did he do it and cause so much distress? We never knew. Authority, his family and the newspapers were all silent.'

Turquoise's finer claim to fame came when she sank an E-boat during a big sea-air attack on a convoy off Sheringham, in E-boat Alley. Seaman Davies:

'Each of our convoy trips had its moments of excitement with the usual attacks by aircraft, but this one was really special. Our charge numbered 72 ships, including tankers, the largest convoy to date. It had been a balmy sunny day and the second dog-watch came round with one of those glorious sunsets travel agents speak of, on a calm, oily sea. It all seemed rather unreal, until shortly after my arrival on duty at the twin point-five aft the alarm went, and over on the far side of the convoy the firework display of tracers etched their wonderful pattern in the evening dusk. The time was 6.10 p.m. It wasn't long before we were engaging enemy aircraft, Heinkel 113s, and the sky now seemed full of these roaring, bat-like messengers of death. Our entire ship was shrouded in gunsmoke and the pungent smell of burnt cordite hung in the still air. One lost all sense of time and between the frantic bursts of firing, of near misses, it seemed that an unearthly, ghost-like silence descended over the area of the sea with *Turquoise* appearing motionless. The moon was now shining and suddenly the four-inch crew shouted "E-boat – Green 10, sir!"

'At this time the angle was too acute for us to see the German, but our forward guns were letting fly. In the starboard wing, manning the Lewis gun, was the steward, a Cockney veteran of Word War 1. He was a four-foot-nothing man and had a beer crate to stand on, and we could see him up on his crate blazing away. Now the E-boat was in sight at 80 yards, the whine of bullets was loud in the air and the thud of them finding a home in the padding round the bridge sounded clear above the turmoil. Our little steward raked the German gunners at their guns and, doll-like, they fell over and firing ceased from her. She was now running broadside on to us and our guns methodically raked her, then as she sheered away from us one had the impression that she was finished. But before we had time to collect scattered thoughts a cool voice ordered "Shift target – aircraft bearing Green 90, angle of sight 20 degrees".

'The rest of the night wore on – "Load, open fire, shift target" – until the sun came up over the horizon, bathing the sea with its shimmering yellow light. "Stand down – tea up!" Blessed relief. Now was the time to feel scared. Later the *Richmond* came over and congratulated us on defeating the E-boat, which had sunk some hours after the action. Some of the Germans had been rescued.

'On our return to Harwich we were given twenty-four hours excused duty and a bottle of beer each. Later our CO (Lieutenant C. M. Newns, RNVR) received the DSC, and there were four Mentions in Despatches. One of these was for the steward, who had been more instrumental than anyone in saving casualties among our ship's company. My wife sent me a telegram: "Heard news on wireless – write – worried." The news item she had heard stated that a large-scale air and sea attack on a big East Coast convoy had been repulsed with the loss of only seven ships . . . HMT *Turquoise* pursued and sank an E-boat. "Pursued" be damned with a 7-knot trawler!'

The E-boats had a lean time of it during 1942 as the Patrol Service ships found their measure; only three trawlers went down to their torpedoes. The U-boats were stiffer opponents, destroying twelve trawlers for certain and possibly more among other ships lost by 'cause unknown'. Less than a dozen of the minesweeping trawlers, now more adequately equipped, were sunk by mines, but more than twice that number were overwhelmed by the attacks of enemy bombers. The year's total of more than seventy vessels lost was considerably lower than the previous year, but it still raised the losses of the Patrol Service since war began to well over three hundred vessels.

The last entry on the casualty list for 1942 was dated December 5th. It was a curious one recording the loss of three trawlers at once 'by accidental explosion and fire' at Lagos. Brief accounts of the incredible disaster filtered their way through Harry Tate's Navy, but the full story was never told. Now it can be.

Early on the morning of that fateful December day the trawler *Kelt* tied up to the Nigerian Marine wharf at Apapa after bringing in the motor tanker *Athelvictor*, which she had escorted four hundred miles from Takoradi, in the Gold Coast (Ghana). The *Athelvictor* berthed port side to the jetty at the Shell Company's wharf upstream to discharge her cargo of high octane petrol. Aft of her lay three trawlers in port for refitting, with native workmen busy on each of them. The vessels were the *Canna*, a naval trawler only two years old, and two requisitioned fishers, *Bengali* and the *Spaniard*. *Kelt* lay astern of these three. A handful of her crew had gone ashore on store duties and her captain had also left the ship, leaving her chief officer, 23-year-old Sub-Lieutenant Jim Fowler, in charge.

'During the forenoon a report came round that the tanker had accidentally discharged about 20,000 gallons of petrol into the harbour, and we doused our galley fire and told everybody to stop smoking. We were well aware that there was petrol on the water as the fumes made our eyes sting.

'There were four of us down in the wardroom, myself, two other officers and the steward. We were having coffee. Suddenly there was a rumble as if an oil drum was being rolled down the deck above us, followed by shouting and the noise of running feet. Next thing we knew there were flames coming down into the wardroom. It was immediately clear what was happening – that somehow the petrol had caught alight. In seconds we decided we had better get ashore quickly because of the danger of the ammunition exploding if the ship got properly ablaze.

'It was at the bottom of low tide and the petrol was surrounding the four trawlers. *Kelt*, as did the others, lay with her gunwhale below the level of the hollow quay, and the fierce flames were acting like a giant blowtorch, blowing straight across the ship. The heat was tremendous. Our only gangway and means of escape, having so recently arrived, was a wide plank going up rather steeply from the foredeck on to the quay.

'The other two officers and the steward took it in turns to go up the companionway from the wardroom and out on to the burning deck. Two got ashore but none survived. As they were disappearing into the flames I had a little extra time to think things out and decided it would be wiser to get thoroughly wrapped up in anything I could find. I realised I wouldn't be able to have my eyes open in the flames, so I kept a visual picture in my mind of where the gangway plank would be, and went out on deck quite slowly. The heat was intense, but I found the front end of the plank with my foot, lined myself up by running my foot over the width of it, and then ran up the plank, luckily without falling off. When about twenty yards from the edge of the quay I stopped – it was as close to the ships as one could bear in the fierce heat. Several men, all badly burned, came by me and I shouted to them to run on to the main entrance gate of the dockyard, 400 yards away. My own injuries were slight, just burns along the side of my face and on one hand, and I was standing there waiting to see if anyone else was coming off when the three trawlers ahead of *Kelt* went up into the air. There wasn't a sound, they went up absolutely silently, bits and pieces shooting up into the air in front of me. I think I probably then did the silliest thing of the lot, which was to lie down, because by the time I was flat on the quay everything had gone up and was coming down; stretched out flat I was a bigger target than if I had remained standing. A lot of things bounced around for quite a considerable time, and then, when it was all over, I stood up again, turned round to go to the entrance and see what was happening, and found that the whole of the very big sheds behind me had gone. I still had no injury, I was not blown over or anything, and the only thing I had lost was my hat. What had happened was that I was at the apex of a great piece of the quay which had been carved out by the explosion and all the blast had gone over my head. I had heard no sound because I was in the dead spot of the explosion.

'There was a tremendous amount of damage to the dockyard, the main building 400 yeards away being severely damaged at the entrance, and as for the three trawlers, when I looked back they had vanished completely – they just weren't there. All their depth-charges had blown up, which was astonishing in itself, as depth-charges were never known to explode, only to burn. The explosion had put out the fire on *Kelt* except on the boat deck, but her bow was blown off and the front of the bridge pushed in, while the foredeck had collapsed. Her steam whistle was blowing furiously, an eerie sound in the sudden stillness.'

An RN captain arrived at the main gate and Sub-Lieutenant Fowler told him the three ships had blown up. They went back to *Kelt* and he and Fowler removed the primers from the ship's depth-charges, which were hot. They found one of the native stewards on board who had been blown out of the foc'sle head and was sitting on the remains of the foredeck unhurt. The boy died of fright three days later – he was sure he had died in the explosion and refused to speak to anyone. He was another casualty in a huge death roll.

'About twenty-six of our crew were caught in the fire, and hardly any survived. They had been caught on deck, most of them not even wearing a shirt, and although the majority got to hospital they were so badly burned that despite living in some cases for several days, they eventually died. One or two men never got ashore and their bodies were recovered from the water.'

And so Sub-Lieutenant Fowler had the traumatic experience of being almost the only survivor of the men aboard *Kelt*. A later official account gave the total number of dead in the disaster as sixty-eight, but these figures represented only those people who could be reliably checked.

'The authorities were never really able to take a complete account of the natives who were lost, many of whom jumped into the water. Very few bodies were recovered from the water, so I should think the dead numbered many more. We were told at the time that an estimated 200 people had lost their lives. *Kelt*'s losses were the heaviest among the naval men. The casualties among crews on the other three trawlers were small, as the ratings were living ashore and few were on board at the time, the ships having been taken over by large numbers of West African workers.'

The badly damaged *Kelt* herself survived to steam on to the end of the war and be sold back for use in her rightful occupation of trawling. Also at war's end, in a case which dragged itself through the law courts to determine the liability for damage arising out of the disaster, the cause of the *Athelvictor*'s lethal leakage of sixty tons of petrol into the harbour was established. Three sea valves used to admit water ballast, and to flush the pipeline when cleaning it, had negligently been left open after use, so allowing the petrol to escape when the tanker discharged her cargo.

13

The Grim Run to Russia

Of all the jobs given to the trawlers the most dreaded was the Russian run, helping to escort Allied supply convoys to North Russia.

There was a special horror about working up there on the icy roof of the world which struck at a man's heart. It was an emotion compounded of the sick fear of those dark, desolate waters, which froze a man as he fell into them; fear of the treacherous weathers; fear of the enemy sea and air raiders; and last but not least, a nagging distrust of the almost unknown Russians themselves.

The Russian run undoubtedly was one of the toughest jobs afloat. The slow moving convoys had to fight, besides the enemy, ice-strewn seas and black fogs, and sub-zero weathers unequalled for their gale-torn ferocity. If anything showed the superb seaworthiness of the converted fishing boats it was the Arctic convoys, when ships cleaving their way through the grim Barents Sea in mid-winter threatened to capsize under the weight of quick-frozen ice, listing at 30 degrees and more with their signal halyards thickened like stovepipes.

The trawlers' exposed steampipes on deck constantly froze up and had to be thawed out with burning paraffin rags. Their guns, winches, and all exposed deck gear also became sheeted with ice and had to be thawed in the same way, or by blow-lamp, or by having boiling water poured over them. Their bows had not been strengthened to resist the constant heavy blows from the floating ice, and they were still in the black-and-tan garb of the Northern Patrol, while all other escorts wore Arctic camouflage. They lacked effective anti-aircraft armament, and their slow speed was a bar to U-boat chasing. Even in their additional role of rescue ships they were greatly handicapped, having limited accommodation, no doctor nor sick bay attendants, and no spare crew to look after injured survivors.

Yet in spite of it all, the trawlers earned considerable honours in this, one of the strangest theatres of war.

The convoys to Russia sailed from Hvalfiord, near Reykjavik, and steamed north up the west coast of Iceland, turning eastwards into the Barents Sea, travelling as close as possible to the polar icefield in order to keep the greatest distance between them and the enemy planes which flew out in droves from the North Cape of Norway. The majority of convoys steamed supplies to Murmansk, the only North Russian port which remained ice-free all the year round; other convoys, or sections of them, sailed 400 miles farther on to Archangel, which was clear of ice during the summer.

The famous 'PQ' series of convoys began in late 1941 and carried on all through the black hell of the Arctic winter, when every day was darkness except for a brief period of 'twilight' at noon. Despite increased resistance by the Germans, more than half the battle was fought with the shocking weathers, and by the time PQ 12 sailed, only six merchantmen had been lost through enemy action, though there had been losses among the escorts.

Where possible, four trawlers were employed on a convoy, helping both as anti-submarine vessels and rescue ships. Among the first trawlers to join the Russian run was the *Lord Middleton*. She saw her first enemy action off the North Cape on PQ 14, which sailed at the tail-end of the Arctic winter in April, 1942. *Lord Middleton* was steaming close to the *Empire Howard*, the Commodore ship (leader of the merchantmen), when *Empire Howard* was struck by two torpedoes from a U-boat. Engineman Douglas Finney:

'As I looked across I heard three explosions, saw her shudder, and in three minutes she had gone, taking the Commodore and many others down with her. We managed to pick up fourteen survivors. Among these was a young lad no more than fourteen years old and in a state of shock. He had probably lied about his age to make the voyage. He recovered, but four others died. The night before entering Murmansk we stopped ship in a howling gale to hold a burial service and put them overboard. During the service we heard enemy aircraft overhead, but luckily the storm screened us, and we steamed into Murmansk safely next day.'

In Murmansk *Lord Middleton* was used to ferry some badly frost-bitten British airmen to the cruiser *Edinburgh*, which was to take them back to the UK. To the *Edinburgh*, too, went the survivors of *Empire Howard*, relieved at the thought of safety in a big ship. The transfer was not made without incident. An enemy plane dived on the *Edinburgh* and let loose its bombs, narrowly missing both the cruiser and *Lord Middleton* as she lay alongside.

'We left in convoy again to return to Iceland, and were six days out when a Russian ship lying 13th in line was suddenly torpedoed by a U-boat. We started to pick up survivors immediately. It was intensely cold, I had never encountered anything like it – our hands were so numb that it took four of us to lift one man out of the water. Hearing shouts from starboard I ran across to see a young Russian girl, probably a stewardess, desperately hanging on to a rope in waters that could stop your heart in a minute. I called to our wireless operator to help me drag her in, but our hands were so numb that try as we would, we couldn't do it quickly enough. I'll never forget how she gave one last cry and lost her hold, and we could do nothing as she slipped away. Just then I realised that shells were exploding around us. Three German destroyers were steaming on the convoy. The *Edinburgh* stopped one of these, but was then hit by torpedoes, and the order came to us to get to hell after the rest of the convoy.'

Edinburgh struggled on in tow but was hit again by a torpedo which almost cut her in half, so all aboard her were taken off and a British destroyer sank her with a final torpedo. The *Empire Howard* men saved by *Lord Middleton* were among those taken off *Edinburgh* by minesweepers; shocked men who, aboard the cruiser, had felt themselves to be safe.

Lord Austin, also making her first Russian run should have gone through to Murmansk with *Lord Middleton* on PQ 14. But hers was a woeful tale. Through frequent snowstorms she steamed with the convoy steadily north around the snowbound Icelandic coast, fog and icy winds making it difficult for her crew even to keep their eyes open, and frozen snow having to be scraped regularly from the bridge windows. Iceland behind her she forged on, but on the third morning, daylight broke after a night of particularly vile visibility to reveal herself and six large merchantmen alone in a waste of grey sea. The rest of the convoy had vanished.

The convoy's Vice-Commodore was aboard one of the merchantmen and he signalled all ships to turn about and return to Iceland. So *Lord Austin* took them back, out of stormy seas into a placid fiord in the north of Iceland, at the naval base of Akureyri. She quickly received a 'rocket' from the NOIC Reykjavik. He demanded: 'Why have you become detached? Sail forthwith and rendezvous convoy at position X.'

Austin's captain, Lieutenant E. Leslie Wathen, RNR, saw that this would entail him taking a more northerly route than the rest of the convoy, in an effort to catch up. Two of the merchant ships conveniently developed 'engine trouble', but the other four sailed out with the trawler, and out into drifting ice, with grey masses of snowstorms bearing down on them across the water and blanketing them in a swirling whiteness.

Two more merchantmen returning from the convoy were sighted, one with a gaping hole in her bows where she had run into ice. The undamaged ship turned round and tagged on to *Austin*, flashing the warning signal 'Bad ice ahead'. Later another straggler passed, homeward bound and so disgruntled that she refused even to answer *Austin*'s signals.

It was a filthy night. *Austin* made a violent entry into some ice-floes and in the process her asdic dome was sheered clean off. Rough repairs were made and she pushed on, through intense cold and fog, into a huge field of ice-floes stretching as far as the eye could see. The merchant ships had vanished and she found herself alone in a weird and desolate sea of ice where the only sign of life was the occasional seal scrambling on to an iceblock or bobbing in the water, but she struggled on.

The chief engineer gave the captain high warning not to run the engines in thick ice or they would lose the propeller, so *Austin* took to drifting through the ice-floes, only using her engines in clear patches. Iceblocks banged against the hull day and night, and if a swell had sprung up the trawler would have been crushed like a matchbox, but fortunately the sea remained calm. Lieutenant Wathen was on the bridge for almost every minute of five days, his hair visibly greying under the strain.

At last they reached position X, only to find no trace of the convoy. They steamed on in thin fog in the hopes of finding it, but still no ships were seen, even though a lookout was sent up the crow's nest, a move which added to the tension for it was the first time the nest had been used, and there were fears the ratlines would break. The fog thickened, and suddenly from the hollow depths of it was heard the siren of one of the corvette escorts, giving her pennant numbers. *Lord Austin* urgently replied on her whistle, but because of the dense fog the two ships were unable to make firm contact. The sound of the corvette's siren grew weaker, and was lost.

As a consequence of her battering in the ice, and of being so far north, *Austin*'s magnetic compass was now nearly 40 degrees out. She was eventually forced to turn in the dangerous ice and make for home, frozen up even in the engine room, having a near miss with the cliffs of Iceland on her return.

Lord Austin was defeated, but not disgraced. The Admiralty had placed the edge of the polar icefield, in which she had spent six frustrating days, a hundred miles farther north than it actually was. When Lieutenant Wathen made his report they were 'most surprised' and said they had based their calculations on information received from the weather men. In fact they were calculations that not only led *Lord Austin* astray, but which resulted in no fewer than sixteen of PQ 14's twenty-four merchantmen, and two of the escort ship, having to turn back because of the ice. With the loss of the *Empire Howard* only seven merchantmen had reached Murmansk.

Such Admiralty errors, and the old, outdated and inadequate charts with which they had to work, were by no means the only sufferances of the trawler commanders on the Russian run. For the remoter outposts of war like the Arctic were unfortunately riddled with gin-soaked recalled naval officers who appeared to care nothing for the trawlers' welfare but only for their own comfort and pleasures. When *Lord Austin* called at Seydisfiord to make reports and carry out various duties, her first lieutenant went ashore to see the senior naval officer and ask for shore leave for the crew. He found a doddering old man, recalled from retirement, pacing up and down his 'quarter-deck' – a space on a wooden jetty marked out by two white lines.

'What the hell do you want?' barked the SNO.

'Permission for shore leave for the crew, sir,' replied *Austin*'s number one.

'Certainly not. I'm not letting any more trawler crews ashore here after the way the last lot behaved. They can stay aboard!'

But *Austin*'s captain and his lieutenant resorted to playing by the book and put in a request for the crew to go ashore for 'necessary exercise and recreation'. This time the request went through.

A high-ranking officer afloat at Reykjavik was a classic example of the worst type of senior officer to be found in such circumstances – hard drinking, womanising, bullying his inferiors. He gave *Austin*'s first lieutenant a severe reprimand in front of a bevy of Icelandic girls in his cabin, and bullied a rating into confessing to a crime he had not committed. He was constantly under the influence of alcohol, but his watchful first lieutenant kept him out of trouble. At last some of the disgusted trawler officers caught him drunk without the protection of his watchdog, put him under arrest and took him ashore, where he was finally court-martialled. All this and Russia too.

PQ 15, which sailed early in May, saw *Cape Palliser* join the Arctic run, still in her black-and-tan of the Atlantic patrol, which made her stick out like a sore thumb in the white wilderness. During the night hours the convoy was steaming along in hazy half-light when six enemy torpedo-bombers streaked in low and dropped their 'tinfish'. Three planes were shot down, but three merchantmen received fatal direct hits. Young Leading-Seaman Raymond Smith was aboard *Cape Palliser*.

'Horrified, we saw one of the merchant ships go straight up and disappear in a purple flash. All that was left of her afterwards was a mass of floating debris of deck cargo, all else had gone to the bottom.

'Our four-inch was practically useless as the low-flying planes were on us before we knew it, and it was impossible to bring the gun to bear. As I was strongly built my action-station was on the stripped Lewis gun, a contraption which could be fired from the shoulder, like a rifle, instead of from the usual tripod. Only someone with a bit of weight could fire the monstrosity – if you didn't hold on tight you spun round with it.

'I was on the starboard side of the bridge near the wheelhouse when a low-level bomber swept over us from the port beam. Its rear-gunner was 'hosepipe firing' and I could see him as clear as day working the gun in a figure of eight – and not too bad with his gunnery, either. I was told later that his shot fell just short of the starboard waterline – I don't think I'd time to look. I managed to get off somewhere near a pan-full, gradually spinning round and trying to keep the Lewis somewhere near the target; it was a hell of a thing to use. Our point-fives also got close to the target, but the two twin-Hotchkiss, one each side of the bridge, proved useless.

'The survivors we picked up were mostly lascars, but among them was one Nigerian, whom they seemed to resent and wouldn't have in their presence, until after much trouble we told them they were all in the same boat – and lucky to be in it, too!'

At Murmansk all hands set to and painted the black and brown *Cape Palliser* in Arctic camouflage in double quick time. On her return journey she also brought back some of the crew of the luckless cruiser *Edinburgh*.

The next convoy, PQ16, sailed in the round-the-clock daylight of the Arctic summer. With nothing but intermittent fog to hide it from the enemy, it suffered the heavy losses of seven merchantmen; and the trawlers *St Elstan* and *Lady Madeleine* were loaded to the gunwhales with survivors, some of whom later died from their injuries and were buried at sea. It was on this trip that a third trawler, *Northern Spray*, was given the task of towing back to Reykjavik a damaged American merchantman, the *Carlton*, crippled when an enemy bomber shot down by the escorts crashed in the sea and blew up right beside her. *Northern Spray* hitched herself to the 5,000-ton vessel and successfully brought her home, fighting off another plane which attacked them both. A shell from *Spray*'s four-inch exploded under the German's tail and sent him packing.

Ironically the *Carlton* was saved only to be torpedoed on the next convoy, the disastrous PQ17. She was the first ship to die when the Admiralty ordered the convoy to 'Scatter' because of a believed threat from the immensely powerful battleship *Tirpitz*. *Lord Middleton*, *Lord Austin*, *Northern Gem* and *Ayrshire* were the four escort trawlers and narrowly escaped in that dreadful holocaust which sent twenty-four ships to the bottom.

Again, on PQ18, four trawlers were with the escorts, and prominent among them was the Hull trawler *St Kenan*, and the German-built *Daneman*, a reparation ship. After the bitter lesson of PQ17, this convoy of forty merchant ships had a formidable escort of eighteen destroyers, a cruiser, an aircraft carrier, two anti-aircraft ships and the four trawlers, but still in devastating attacks by the Germans, thirteen vessels were lost. On September 13 two ships were sunk by U-boats, the Russian *Stalingrad* and the American *Oliver Ellsworth*. *St Kenan* rescued the master and three other survivors of the *Oliver Elsworth* from a raft. Later that same day there was a mass attack on the convoy by ninety torpedo-bombers, which produced the fantastic sight of more than one hundred torpedoes racing for the convoy. Eight ships were hit. *Daneman*, steaming at the rear of the convoy, picked up four survivors from one of the stricken ships, the British *Empire Stevenson*. Seaman Gunner G. R. Lunn:

'One of these four seamen couldn't swim and we put it down to his threshing madly about in the sea which kept him afloat and warm enough to survive. Another older man was about to be rescued when the planes attacked again and we had to get under way and leave him to drown. I can still see him, cold in the water, trying to reach one of our sailor's hands to get a grip so that he could be pulled aboard to safety, but we were being attacked by a torpedo-bomber and the skipper rang full-ahead. We had to leave him and watch his bald head and red football jersey vanish behind us; as we were the last ship in the convoy he would never be picked up.'

St Kenan rescued 64 survivors during and after the mass torpedo-bomber attack. These included the entire ship's company of the Panamanian ss *Macbeth*, all picked up from boats and rafts, and survivors from the American ss *Oregonian*. Ten of these were grabbed from the sea in a shocking state from their icy exposure and the oil and water they had swallowed. When rejoining the convoy with her mercy load *St Kenan* was attacked by a twin-engined bomber which hurtled in on a shallow dive, but the trawler's pumping Oerlikon forced the German to release his bombs prematurely and harmlessly, and smoke was seen to break from the plane as it made off. *St Kenan*'s crew then set to caring for their passengers, and in the words of her captain, Lieutenant J. Mackay, RNR: 'Though exhausted by prolonged action-stations many gave up their bunks and hammocks to survivors, and the hardships of feeding and sleeping so many men in cramped quarters was cheerfully accepted. The behaviour of the ship's company as a whole was excellent.'

Still the attack on the convoy by planes and U-boats went on. The American *Mary Luchenbach* went up in a flash and a bang – she was said to be carrying H.E. ammunition and gelignite fuses. Gunner Lunn: 'There was a tremendous explosion and debris showered down on us on *Daneman* like hail. Nothing and no one was left when the smoke cleared.'

For four more days convoy PQ18 fought off its attackers, and then the weather took a hand. As the ships neared the River Dvina leading to Archangel they ran into a fierce gale. Several merchantmen ran aground. *St Kenan* was dangerously unstable and had to heave-to. When caught in the trough of the sea she took an exceptionally heavy roll which carried away her lifeboat and badly bent the davits, but she righted herself and rode out the storm. For *Daneman*, however, the luck ran out. Gunner Lunn:

'When the big gale blew up in the Dvina we were entirely without coal and having to chop up all the woodwork to get some steam on. The skipper ordered a rum for everyone, but it was found that the rum jar had already been broken open and many of the crew were quite drunk. We had a terrible night; tossing about like a cork, no fuel for the engines, and just burning anything that would burn to try to keep the engines going, but we still finished up by running aground on a sandbank. Next morning we abandoned ship, but then went back as she lay on her side. And there we were marooned for days. We made rafts and pulled wood from the shore to get a bit of power up so that we could charge the batteries to listen to the six o'clock news; and that's just about all the listening time we did get, for all our day's toil.'

It was hoped the Russians would pull *Daneman* off the sandbank, but they could not be prevailed upon to do so until two weeks later, by which time *Daneman* had completely run out of food. She then limped home to Belfast with a return convoy, for her damaged plates to be repaired.

PQ18 was the last of the 'PQ' convoys, for the code letters were then changed. It was on the first of the new convoys, which pushed on now in the pitch blackness of the Arctic winter, that the veteran *Northern Gem* played a strong mercy role in the fateful last voyage of the destroyer *Achates*.

In December 1942 convoy JW51 sailed for Russia in two sections. The first, sailing in mid-December, successfully reached the Kola Inlet, leading to Murmansk, on Christmas Day. But the second section, JW51B, which sailed on December 22, was destined to have a more eventful passage.

JW51B consisted of fourteen merchant ships escorted by seven destroyers, two corvettes, a minesweeper and the trawlers *Northern Gem* and *Vizalma*. Other cover was to be provided later by the two cruisers returning from Russia after escorting the first section.

The troubles of convoy JW51B began six days out, when a destroyer had a compass failure and lost the convoy. The same night a severe gale overtook the ships and the *Vizalma* and five merchantmen lost contact. Three of these ships found the convoy again next day, but *Vizalma* and two others never returned, making their own way to Russia miraculously unscathed.

The dark morning of New Year's Eve saw the storm abated and the ice-covered ships of the now depleted convoy pressing on under constant snow squalls. Elsewhere in the darkness, unknown to them, the enemy cruiser *Hipper* and pocket battleship *Lutzow*, together with six destroyers, had sailed out from Norway to the attack. Aboard *Northern Gem*, rear escort on the convoy's starboard quarter, they saw the first gun-flashes in the blackness astern as the enemy destroyers moved in; it was 9.30 a.m. At fast speed the destroyer *Achates* steamed across the convoy laying a protective black smoke screen, but within minutes she was hit, partially flooded and ablaze with several fires. The fires were quickly brought under control and she carried on laying smoke as the escort's senior officer, Captain R. St V. Sherbrooke, in *Onslow*, took the remainder of his destroyer flotilla to meet the enemy.

From *Northern Gem* they could see the faint outlines of the British destroyers and the repeated gun-flashes as they harried the *Hipper*. But the German cruiser scored several hits on *Onslow*, causing considerable damage and casualties and severely wounding Captain Sherbrooke, blinding him in one eye (for this action he was awarded the VC).

The blizzard came down again, but the one-sided battle went on. The minesweeper *Bramble* was sunk, then it was again the turn of *Achates*. *Hipper*'s guns blasted and damaged her severely, a direct hit on the bridge killing her captain. The coxswain and signalman, the only survivors on the bridge, carried on until the ship's second in command, Lieutenant Loftus E. P. Jones, DSC, who had been controlling work against the floodings, returned and took over. He steered the crippled *Achates* on a zig-zag course, still valiantly making smoke to protect the merchantmen. For four hours the battle went on, until the returning British cruisers finally drove off the raiders, sinking one German destroyer.

Achates was now nearing her end. Hit again on the port side, which was like a pepper pot from shrapnel holes, and with more men killed and the boiler room flooded, still she tried to protect the convoy, reducing speed to keep afloat. But her engineers reported that they could not keep speed on her one remaining boiler, so she stopped engines and her wounded signalman flashed to *Northern Gem* to stand by.

But when *Gem* closed the *Achates* it was already too late for many of the destroyer's crew, including some thirty-five badly wounded men gathered in the captain's day-cabin, and cared for by two volunteers who elected to stay to help them when the order was given to abandon ship. Acting-Coxswain Sid Kerslake of *Gem*:

'Suddenly *Achates* rolled over on to her port side. In the darkness we could see the red lights on the lifebelts of the men and the red-tipped cigarettes of some ratings who were even smoking as they clambered over the rail and on to the ship's starboard side, which in a few seconds had become the "deck". Seconds later the ship's bottom started to rise out of the water as the superstructure vanished from view on the side away from us.

'The men began to slide into the water off the ship's bottom, laughing and joking as they did, then to our astonishment someone started singing "Roll Out The Barrel" and soon, even above the noise of the wind and the sea, we heard them all singing as they fought their way over to us. Some men still smoked, or tried to, as they swam in the icy waters, others held up wounded shipmates or dragged them along. *Gem* acted as a kind of lee for them in the heavy sea and our skipper (Skipper-Lieutenant H. C. Aisthorpe, RNR), taking over the wheel, kept giving a touch ahead or astern if he spotted anyone in danger of floating past. In spite of this a few men did drift past, but they must have been dead, either from wounds or from the killing cold of the water; our main concern was for those who were now struggling for their lives.'

Achates sank in three minutes, taking all the wounded in the captain's cabin down with her. Coxswain Kerslake:

'We had dropped our rescue nets over the side. We had no boats to lower, our port boat had been washed away in the gales, while as for our starboard boat, none of its running gear would work – we hadn't been able to get to it to clear it of ice, and everything was frozen solid. In the waist of the ship some of us dropped over the side and hung on to the rescue nets with one hand, pulling and pushing the frozen survivors up to where other willing hands could lift them on deck. As we clung on to the nets we would first be lifted right out of the water as the trawler rolled to starboard, then when she came back we would be plunged up to the neck in the freezing sea, but we managed to come up again each time clinging to a man and pushing him up the ship's side to those above.

'Every member of the crew was at *Gem*'s side. Those not busy in the waist or on the rescue nets stood throwing out heaving lines to men still struggling in the sea. I left the nets and ran to the port quarter to help throw out these lines and tow in the men who caught hold of them. One very young sailor, scarcely more than a boy, began drifting past the stern. We threw him a line which he caught, but as we pulled at the rope it slid through his frozen hands. Again we threw the line, but as he grasped it he panicked and started to cry "Mother, mother!" It was heart-rending. We yelled to him to hold his hand up so that we could get a turn or two of the line round his wrist, but he slid out of sight for ever with the rope still slipping through his fingers and still crying for his mother.

'Our rescue work reached a point where we seemed to have saved all but a number of bodies floating by with no sign of life. At this moment there was a huge underwater explosion as the

Achates' depth-charges went off, certainly killing anyone still left alive and lifting *Gem* almost out of the water. So great was the blast that we thought at first that we had caught an enemy torpedo on our starboard side; pots were smashed to pieces, cupboards blown open, clocks stopped; but she didn't take any water and luckily escaped damage to the hull, so we turned again to helping our survivors. Except for a few who had got over to us in liferafts they were so frozen they could not stand or help themselves in any way; we had to carry them below, strip them and rub them down as dry as possible to help get their blood circulating again. We had to do this very quickly, and possibly did not spend as much time with each man as we should have done, but there were eighty of them, nearly twice as many as us, and some of us had to carry on with the duties of the ship as well as doing battle with the ice rapidly freezing all over the superstructure and threatening *Gem*'s stability. About half an hour after being rubbed down the circulation would come back again to the survivors' shocked and maimed bodies, it was agonising for them and their screams had to be heard to be believed.

'The wounded sat or lay down as they could, shocked and staring into nothing, or groaning with pain; others were seasick, some vomiting fuel oil, which covered them from head to foot. Being only an escort trawler we were not rigged out for dealing with severe casualties. Our crew gave up their bunks and spare clothing and did all they could, but we had no doctor on board and our medical resources were practically nil.

'One lad I helped to strip kept looking over his shoulder, though due possibly to shock or cold he never said a word. Yet as we pulled his jersey over his head almost the whole of his right shoulder came away with the jersey, and we had to separate the wool from the flesh. All we could do for him was to put antiseptic lotion over the wound and bandage the loose flesh back in place. Fortunately one of our crew, Seaman Edward Mayer, a former bank cashier from Rotherham, was able to give some treatment to the wounded; he had learned quite a bit from his wife, who was a nurse.

'I went the rounds with the rum jar both for the survivors and our own men, for we all badly needed a tot, and in the galley I came upon a lad of about twenty sitting on the cook's seat locker. He was shivering with cold even though the galley stove was glowing red and someone had given him their duffelcoat to wear. I gave him a tot and asked if he was okay, and he said his ear hurt. I examined it and saw that sticking out of the bone behind the ear was a piece of shrapnel an inch long. When the surgeon who eventually got aboard us saw it he could do nothing, but when the shrapnel was removed in hospital at Murmansk it was the length of a cigarette packet; it was remarkable that the lad recovered.

'One very young sub-lieutenant who had swum over to us with the strength of an ox rapidly showed signs of weakening. We couldn't make out what was wrong, for there was no sign of a wound, so we put his quietness and pallor down to shock, and tried to make him comfortable in a bunk on the messdeck. When the surgeon examined him later he, too, could do nothing, the unfortunate man had taken the full blast of a shell explosion in the stomach and was smashed up internally. We gave him everything he asked for, but he died soon afterwards and was buried at sea.

'With the *Gem* crowded with the sick and wounded it was a ghastly night. Everything was blacked out, no lights at all allowed on deck. It was like living, or rather existing, in a howling, raging and totally black hell on some other planet; black, that is, except for the snow lizzards and the ice. Not until late morning did the wind and sea drop slightly, and it was then, despite a heavy swell, we managed to get the surgeon aboard from one of the destroyers. During the brief lull in the weather and the slight greying of the darkness at noon, the destroyer went head-on into the wind and sea at a speed just fast enough to give her steerage way and slow enough for us to come up astern of her and place our starboard well-deck alongside her port quarter. With a heavy sea running this was no mean feat by our skipper. As the two vessels closed, our starboard rail was bent inwards when the destroyer's quarter dropped on to us, and as she lifted up again her depth-charges came up smack under our remaining lifeboat. But the eyes of everyone was fixed on the surgeon, who stood poised, waiting his chance, and when the destroyer reared up again and looked dangerously like coming aboard the *Gem*, which was now in the trough of the sea, he jumped feet first and bag in hand, landing safely by the grace of God on to our heaving, pitching, roller-coaster deck and being caught in the waiting arms of some of our crew. It was a fantastic leap under any conditions.

'As the weather rose again there began the grim business of performing what operations we could on the badly wounded. All the time the surgeon was busy *Gem* was blown by gale force winds and tossed by mountainous seas that swept over the entire ship. Everything was frozen, the rigging swollen to four times its normal size and our lifeboat, boatfalls and boatdeck just solid blocks of ice. It was treacherous to move about the deck anywhere. Below, meantime, no fewer than twelve emergency operations were performed on the messdeck table, one after the other. Each time, so that he wouldn't be flung off by the pitching ship, the patient had to be held down on the table by two or three of the crew or the fittest survivors, anaesthetic being administered by Lieutenant Jones of the *Achates*.

'No words of mine can describe the courage and skill of that surgeon. We all thought he deserved a medal. Whether he received one or not I don't know, but I do know that he lost his life a year later on another Russian convoy. On that occasion he was passed to a merchant ship to look after a sick member of the crew, and in the early hours of the next morning the merchantman was torpedoed. His first thought was to get his patient into a lifeboat, and he only just succeeded in doing this before the ship sank with him still on board. A very gallant man.

'For the rest of *Gem*'s voyage through the dark to Murmansk everyone helped each other, sharing sleeping quarters, clothing and cigarettes, and the only moan to be heard was: "When's this bloody wind going to drop!"'

Gem's Skipper-Lieutenant Aisthorpe received the DSC for his trawler's heroic rescue work.

And so the work of the trawlers in the Arctic went on. *Northern Spray*, towing home a second, and bigger crippled ship, the 12,000-ton *Empire Unity*, after she was torpedoed. This mammoth tow was being made at a painfully slow two knots when a U-boat was sighted on the surface. It dived to the attack, but *Spray*, having quickly slipped her tow, steamed hard for the U-boat and rammed it, smashing up her asdic dome as evidence of her bold assault. With the U-boat claimed as a 'possible' she re-engaged the tow and pulled her huge charge home.

And on the trawler *Paynter*, there was a poignant rescue involving none other than that terror of the Nest, Ted the Bastard – Chief Petty Officer Edward Pugh. When a merchantman carrying passengers was torpedoed he dived overboard to save women and children struggling in the icy water. Among those he saved was a child who later died without anyone ever knowing her name; he gave her the same name as his own daughter, and stood by her grave as she was buried at Seydisford.

He received the DSM. And lost his nickname for good.

14

One of Our Ships is Missing

In the Capetown Officers' Club, the skipper-lieutenant of a trawler took a long, cool look at a monocled RAF squadron-leader, and told him in blunt terms that he only needed a monocle in another part of his anatomy and he'd make a 'bloody fine telescope'.

The Harry Tates had arrived. In December 1942 the trawlers loaned to the US Navy were withdrawn to South African waters, to combat growing U-boat activity there. From the American east coast the trawlers steamed down through the Caribbean Sea to Trinidad, then on to the Brazilian port of Pernambuco, where they coaled up for the passage across the South Atlantic. En route to Pernambuco they engaged in a fruitless reconnaissance off the French penal settlement of Devil's Island, French Guiana, where the presence of U-boats had been suspected. Then across from Pernambuco to Freetown, Sierra Leone, and on down the African west coast.

Some interesting, if uncalled for, advice was given to *Lady Elsa*'s first lieutenant by a Belgian pilot taken aboard at Pointe Noire, in the Congo. 'He gave me the "useful" hint that when flogging natives, always string them up in wet canvas, as it left no marks. The advice did not pass unheeded by our asdic operator and signalman, and for some time afterwards my movements were closely watched to see if I intended getting in a little practice on the ship's company.'

And so on to Walvis Bay, German West Africa, down to Capetown and up the east coast to Durban. The trawlers were to remain in South Africa until the war's end, the crews being relieved after a long spell. Joined by a handful of other trawlers to make up for their losses in the US they were employed on asdic patrol and as escorts for convoys from Walvis Bay round the Cape of Good Hope and up to Durban and Mombasa. It was generally wearisome work, though occasionally highly eventful. Like the adventure of *Cape Warwick*.

Captain of this trawler was Lieutenant W. E. 'Paddy' Goggin, an Irishman of great renown among the Harry Tate commanders. There was the time when *Cape Warwick*, working in Icelandic waters, took in tow a merchantman which had grounded on the coast. After losing most of her cables, *Cape Warwick* managed to get the cargo vessel into Reykjavik. On the way into harbour a tug attempted to take over the tow, only desisting when Paddy Goggin vigorously promised to use his four-inch. Paddy lodged a salvage claim and a year later the princely payout was made by the Admiralty. Paddy, as captain, received £10, his other officers £4 each, and the ratings £1.

A jaunty and a strong-hearted ship was *Cape Warwick* – even if it was aboard her that an officer was about to tuck into his lunch when the steward shot into the wardroom and suggested that he skip the soup, as they had just got to the bottom of the pot and found a black sock resting in the remains.

At 4 p.m. on April 2 1943 *Cape Warwick* and *Northern Dawn* set out from Walvis Bay, a known hot-bed of German spies, as escorts to a small convoy of three ships bound for Capetown. Two of these were cargo vessels, one carrying a large quantity of ammunition. The third ship was the 7,000-ton *City of Baroda*, with more than 300 passengers and crew aboard, including ninety European passengers and a hundred lascar seamen in transit. As darkness came a thick fog descended, and the speed of the convoy was reduced. Coder Jack Clegg, of *Cape Warwick*:

'About 9 p.m. a dull thud was heard from what appeared to be a considerable distance. The ships in convoy were not visible owing to the fog. Shortly afterwards a mysterious SOS was received from a ship whose identify was unknown, and whose position given was on dry land! At the first light of dawn, when it was discovered that *City of Baroda* was not in line with the convoy, *Cape Warwick* was ordered to make a search.'

What happened between the time of the 'dull thud' of the night before and 9 a.m. the following morning was told by survivors when *Cape Warwick* found a lifeboat from the liner.

Without warning a torpedo from a U-boat had struck *City of Baroda* on the starboard side, destroying one of her lifeboats. Almost immediately a second torpedo exploded, again on the starboard side. The captain gave the order to abandon ship and six lifeboats were quickly filled and lowered. A seventh boat upended, throwing the occupants into the sea and five people were drowned, including a mother and child. The attacking U-

The POUND in your pocket is worth MORE

with the PEARL

OUR "TEN YEAR SPECIAL" INVESTMENT PLAN can earn for YOU:-

★ Income Tax relief applicable to the premiums.
★ Substantial Reversionary Bonuses each year.
★ A Terminal Bonus related to capital growth.
★ A sizeable tax free profit upon maturity.
★ Life cover for double the sum assured (plus declared bonuses).

Premiums are payable yearly, half-yearly or quarterly.

(Facilities for a Ten Year Plan are also available for as little as Two Pounds monthly through our Industrial Branch)

DON'T MISS YOUR OPPORTUNITIES THROUGH DELAY COMPLETE AND POST THIS CARD TO-DAY

(No postage stamp required)

To PEARL ASSURANCE Co. Ltd., HIGH HOLBORN, LONDON.

I should like, without committing myself in any way, to have full particulars of your new "TEN YEAR SPECIAL" PLAN.

Name ....

Address ....

Date of Birth ....

Face the future with **PEARL** *assurance*

DO NOT AFFIX POSTAGE STAMPS IF POSTED IN
GT. BRITAIN, CHANNEL ISLANDS OR N. IRELAND

BUSINESS REPLY SERVICE
LICENCE No. WC964

PEARL ASSURANCE COMPANY, LTD.,

PUBLICITY SECTION,

HIGH HOLBORN,

LONDON, WC1V 7XE

POSTAGE WILL
BE PAID BY
LICENSEE

boat was never seen. All night the survivors kept afloat in the fog and dark, until five hours after beginning her search, *Cape Warwick* came upon the first lifeboat. Within a few hectic hours she had found other boats and picked up a total of 260 people. Among them were score upon score of lascar seamen, together with European crew and passengers, among them three children and a dozen women, including some Quaker nurses on their way to Burma. Gallantly Paddy Goggin handed over his cabin to the womenfolk.

Paddy and his officers, with fresh visions of salvage in mind, wanted to take the stricken *City of Baroda* in tow, as she appeared to be floating fairly well, but orders came for him to abandon the hulk and proceed to Capetown with the survivors. This was a four-day journey which no one aboard was ever likely to forget. Coder Clegg:

'Conditions on board with 300 souls were terrible, and everything that could possibly be jettisoned went over the side. Every inch of deckspace, chartroom, wireless cabin, officers' quarters, was occupied during waking and sleeping hours. The crew gave up their bunks to survivors and slept on deck, but even here people had to sleep sitting up because there was insufficient room to lie down. The lascars were accommodated in an unused fish hold and the for'ard messdeck, and the scenes here were unbelievable.'

The trawler men distributed all the clothing they could rake up among the survivors, but food was a different problem. It was perilously short and the only way they could give everyone a meagre two meals a day was by using up all the concentrated rations kept in the lifeboats for emergency use. For some of *City of Baroda*'s crew who had been torpedoed before – one man had been sunk nine times since war began – every discomfort was small; even so, there was hearty relief when the grossly overladen *Cape Warwick* reached Capetown. And a pleasant surprise. Coder Clegg:

'While there were supposed to be security restrictions in force, every ship in the harbour sounded their welcoming hooters as we sailed alongside. Even more remarkable was the sight of trestle tables laid out on the quayside laden with food, and more than 300 chairs. The food had been provided by the WVS of South Africa. All 260 survivors, together with our forty crew members, sat down unshaven, unwashed, and in many cases only partly clothed, to enjoy their first real meal for four days. Before leaving, all the survivors expressed their thanks to us by singing

"Auld Lang Syne".'

Captain Paddy Goggin afterwards received a letter of gratitude from the High Commissioner's office in Capetown. It was sent on behalf of the survivors and thanked him for the manner of their rescue and the 'overwhelming kindness and hospitality displayed by his officers and crew'.

Sub-Lieutenant 'Mick' Hargraves: 'A month afterwards we were in Durban and came across a paymaster lieutenant-commander, RNVR, who had been one of the survivors. He was looking a little down in the mouth and quite naturally so, as he told us he had just been landed at Durban after being torpedoed again and losing all his belongings for the second time in a month.'

A final sadness was when the Quaker nurses rescued by *Cape Warwick* joined another ship, only to lose their lives when she also fell victim to a U-boat.

In home waters in 1943 the long struggle against the E-boats continued. In February, after a heavy E-boat attack on a convoy of ten ships off Start Point, Devon, there were jubilant claims by the Germans. A cargo ship hit by a torpedo broke into pieces, a tanker was sent to the bottom, and another freighter was left sinking, the escorts faring just as badly. When a big 900-ton tank landing vessel was hit but did not sink, German sailors boarded her, killed some of the crew with revolvers, took a dozen prisoners and then sank the ship with a torpedo. Another E-boat torpedo sank the minesweeping whaler *Harstad*, leaving only one survivor; another sank the escort trawler *Lord Hailsham* along with eighteen of her crew.

Weeks later another E-boat victim, this time off Lowestoft, was the RDF or radar equipped trawler *Adonis*, based at Ipswich. Among the few survivors who lived to tell her story was young RDF rating T. Roy Sparkes.

'Running out of Ipswich at that time were two flotillas of patrol vessels, each with an RDF-equipped master ship, one of which was *Adonis* and the other the *Norland*. The RDF (early radar) had a range of only six miles, and was a diabolical and misleading thing of false comfort. But our ships were converted French trawlers, possibly the ugliest and without doubt the roughest boats to put out from Ipswich. Many was the time in heaving *Adonis* that I prayed for death as I stared at the green grass in the miniature cathode, trying to distinguish echoes from ground-base waves, writing my log and vomiting profusely into that vital piece of equipment, the bucket.

'Towards the end of March 1943 we entered Immingham Docks for a refit and leave, and sailed again on the ominous date of Friday, April 13 1943. I had a premonition that something was about to happen, the feeling being so strong that I sewed a pocket into my old Mae West lifejacket, bought from a crewmate for a dollar of beer money, and into it stowed my wallet and a few personal photographs.

'On the night of the 14th, after manoeuvring my way across the pitching deck to take over the middle-watch, I had been settled down in the radar caboose astern for about an hour when I became aware of a movement on the screen. There was a blip or two at about 6,000 or 7,000 yards. With the general conditions and the hand-turned radar "aerial" to contend with, the blip was at about 2,000 yards before I could make any really definite report. At 1.15 a.m. I whistled up the old voice-pipe to the bridge to report my suspicions, but they could see nothing. The range then closed to 1,700 yards. From the bridge I heard the muffled order given to fire starshells, a task for our foc's'le gun crew with their pride of weaponry, an old Japanese 14-pounder.

'Then all hell was let loose. Faintly I heard the gun's report, followed almost immediately by a huge explosion – the whole ship appeared to heave her guts and shudder. Up in my radar caboose, on its four spindly angle-iron legs, I was flung violently forward, crashing my nose into the radar tube. All the lights had gone out and I felt the floor beneath me begin to tilt.

'Not having the full picture of what was going on I sat there calmly awaiting instructions, but none were forthcoming. I whistled up and called the bridge again, but my voice was obviously lost on the night – I was cut off. Even then the full truth didn't strike home. Other than blurping, muffled gun reports I had no feeling of life outside, no sound of a voice. I stood up, grasping the voicepipe, and tried again to get some information, though inwardly I knew it was hopeless. Turning and slithering on the now frighteningly sloping iron floor, I tried the cleats on the watertight door; one moved, but the rest seemed to be solid and would not budge. I was trapped in an expensively attired steel coffin. For a brief second I visualised the whole thing at the bottom of the sea and myself waiting for the water to slowly seep in, then nothing. I stood there unemotional, coldly resigned.

'There was a further lurch, the whole cabin tilting even more alarmingly towards the bows. At that moment a quiet voice spoke to me, seemingly out of the air. It insisted that I try the door again. With one mighty sweep of the palm of my hand I clouted each cleat in what seemed one movement. Destiny or luck was with me, the sinking movement carried the heavy door the right way and it swung away, the open space now rising above me. The night sky was lit by tracer flares. With an effort I clambered through the door on to the small cat-platform, but a sudden lurch flung me down. I grabbed a rung of the narrow steel ladder which led to the deck and found myself twisting until I was hanging by one hand underneath the slope of the ladder. I remembered stories of men clinging to guardrails and going down with their ships, absolutely terrified to let go, clinging on as if the cold iron was a life-saving straw, and even though I was considered a strong swimmer I just couldn't let go of that ladder and drop clear into the lapping sea which I had glimpsed beneath me.

'Then a rumbling noise arrested my thoughts and anchored my mounting panic; the depth-charges astern were loose and threatening to roll in my direction. I let go and dropped into the icy North Sea, kicking and threshing, catching my legs and shins on floating wood and wreckage as I tried to make clear of the stricken ship. A large wave caused me to all but give up the ghost there and then, for in spite of the lifejacket in which I had lived, eaten and slept, I was almost a gonner. Then I kicked out strongly and began to make headway through the seething black water, while around me I was aware of lads and men shouting, throwing up their arms and sinking from sight, and large timbers suddenly shooting up from out of the depths like huge rockets. One poor lad was impaled on one such muderous length before being carried down and out of sight.

'I continued swimming. I then heard my first coherent conversation out of the chaos, voices crying out for guidance on freezing rafts or cutting a boat adrift from the fast sinking debris, though icy water, rusty cleats, and rope that had not been disturbed for months, resisted all their attempts. I swam on in no particular direction, not caring so long as I cleared the two halves of *Adonis* which I saw standing starkly, bow and stern to the night sky. The rising moon helped to illuminate the ghastly picture. Away to the stern I was aware of small pockets of stabbing lights and tracers as the E-boats, for that is what the echoes had turned out to be, continued to pump death-dealing lead into the fast disappearing trawler.

'I saw a group of heads bobbing about and recognised one

voice as that of a leading seaman. I struck out in that direction, but then again that "voice" I had heard in the radar cabin spoke to me clearly: "No, no – this way." As if to confirm it someone shouted: "Over this way – the skipper's here!" I changed direction, swam towards the sound and came upon a well-laden Carley float with the second-in-command, Skipper Cyril White, there among the survivors (our commanding officer, Skipper Draper, had been lost in the first few seconds of the action). But there was no more room on the liferaft and I could do no more than grab a loop of rope and continue to dangle in the freezing water.

'After some time it became obvious that I couldn't hold on to the thin line much longer, so with struggling effort and rocking change of position, everyone sitting straddle fashion, a small space was made on the raft and I was lugged aboard, or rather placed in a position of semi-submerged floating, for with eleven souls aboard the raft was well below the surface, in fact we were up to our waists.

'A biting wind seared across the sea and only by grabbing pieces of scrap wood and attempting to keep up a form of useless paddling did we prompt blood to circulate. The moon had fully risen and by its light we did at one stage glimpse a launch silhouetted against the horizon, but despite our shouting and waving it churned away. Singing half-heartedly to try to keep up morale, and encouraged all the time by Skipper White to keep paddling we drifted for the better part of the night. In the early dawn, just as two or three men were beginning to give way to the effects of exposure, we heard again the throb of engines, and into view loomed the craft we had seen before, now about half a mile away. We shouted and waved, at the same time holding aloft a rather dim Carley light on a lanyard. The boat carried on, and for a moment our hearts sank as we felt that our last chance before our energy and will faded had deserted us; then to the amazement of us all she heeled and turned. This time there was no doubt – she was making for us straight as a homing pigeon.

'As she drew near we managed a feeble cheer. She was an RAF rescue launch and we were soon being dragged aboard. The RAF crew were the Samaritans that night, giving us their last smokes and brandy, even their personal and precious stored caches were brought out of hiding. They said they had been almost to Rotterdam seeking a ditched bomber and failed to locate it, but none the less their journey had been necessary –

sentiments we were quick to echo.

'We reached Harwich about 6 a.m., and fixed up with some temporary gear we eventually returned to the base at Ipswich which some of us had given up hope of ever seeing again.

'The loss of *Adonis* was summed up in a communique which my mother heard the next day over the BBC: "One of our ships is missing . . . the Admiralty regret . . ." What was not given was the fact that only eleven of us out of a total crew of 32 had escaped. Some six of those lost were barely eighteen, having joined the Navy about eight weeks before; it was their first trip to sea, and their last.

'Next day, destroyers from the Harwich flotilla took part in a revenge raid on the E-boat pens at Rotterdam, putting the base and craft out of action for many months. Surveying the area of the action, many bodies from *Adonis* were picked up, including the luckless leading seaman and his group of men to which I had originally been swimming.' Such were the victims of the E-boats.

The trawler *Red Gauntlet* was sweeping out of Harwich early one morning when an E-boat attacked her. With her sweeping gear out and so unable to make a quick counter, the fight was short and *Red Gauntlet* went down with heavy casualties. Weeks later the *Franc Tireur*, also sweeping from Harwich, was torpedoed and sunk with half her crew. In this desperate action with the E-boats two trawlers collided, with the result that one of them, the *Donna Nook*, foundered. Yet further losses were the *William Stephen*, torpedoed by an E-boat off Cromer, and the *Avanturine*, sent to the bottom off Beachy Head.

The old minesweeping trawler *General Botha* found herself abruptly removed from these realities of war to take on the surprising role of an enemy ship – unsettling for a veteran trawler which had served through half of World War 1. It was all to do with the documentary film 'For Those In Peril', a story of the Air Sea Rescue units being made by Ealing Studios. *Botha*, based at North Shields, happened to be the first ship of Seaman-Gunner Lionel Gray.

'When I joined her she was already at work in her film role and I was given a German naval suit and hat with the name *Königin Louise* on the hatband; *Botha*'s name had been changed to this for the film. It was a bit embarrassing filming out in the North Sea with a damned great swastika flying from the ship. The film took three months to make and we seemed to be the laughing stock of all the other sweepers and drifters as we sailed from the fish quay in North Shields in our German gear and with this big German flag flying. Once at sea we began to film, firing round after round from the old 12-pounder, running and shouting around the deck. It was a worrying moment one day when we heard a plane overhead, but it went off all right, and for our efforts at film acting each member of the crew received a whole pound note.

'It was not until much later, when I was home on leave and went to the pictures with my future wife, that I found out what the film was all about. It appeared that we were a German armed trawler steaming through thick fog to reach a British bomber crew which had ditched in the Channel, while racing out from the British coast was an RAF rescue boat with the same intentions. They sank us in the film, and there we all were on the *Königin Louise* – "Germans" panicking as we went down. It was an especially comical sight to see one of my pals, Jimmy Bentley, doing his acting bit, running around in his German uniform with the seat of his pants out and his shirt-tail blowing.'

Another unusual role, though a real life one, came the way of the small but fast Aberdeen trawler *Star of Freedom*, working as a store carrier from Longhope, in the Orkneys. She was given the job of taking small mines and arms to Lerwick, in the Shetlands, where members of the Norwegian Resistance, in fast motorboats, ran out from Norway at night to pick them up. The mines were the size of a football, with a grass rope for securing to the seabed; the Resistance fighters laid them in the fiords.

Perhaps the most unexpected duty was that which befell *Cape Portland*. She was an escort trawler with good service in northern waters, and her ship's company consisted of Yorkies from Hull and Geordies from the Tyne, together with a few Scots, East Anglians and Cockneys. Her chief engineman, John Brown, had been with the ship fishing in peacetime and continued to nurse her engines with supreme care. Once, when she refitted at Hull, the owners came aboard for a look at their requisitioned vessel. On seeing the spotless condition of the engine room they presented John Brown with a handsome cheque.

In the summer of 1943 *Cape Portland* was at Liverpool. Her number one was Lieutenant Arthur Miles, RNVR.

'There was great speculation when we were first fitted out

with de-freezing equipment, as though to cope with iced-up conditions in the Arctic. Then came a full issue of tropical uniforms and kit. After one or two false starts we at last set off, and our sealed orders informed us we were bound for the Azores. Before leaving, Burton's of Liverpool had measured every man aboard for a civvy suit, so we had suspected it would be a neutral country – the "buzz" was Turkey. We officers had trilby hats and the ratings cloth caps, but I never saw any of these worn ashore!

'In fact, the true purpose of our voyage was to hand over the *Cape Portland* to the Portuguese Navy.

'The first few days at the Azores port of Ponta Delgada were alarming. A nucleus of Portuguese officers and ratings came aboard and we were required to circle the islands keeping an asdic watch and burning full navigation lights. My opposite number informed me that he had taken the German hydrophone course at Bremerhaven as well as an asdic course with our people, so he had the best from both sides.

'At last we went ashore, leaving only an anti-submarine officer and six key ratings with the ship. They did well, drawing Portuguese pay as well as their own, I believe. The rest of us had three delightful weeks ashore before passage home.'

Cape Portland was one of several escort trawlers handed over to the Portuguese Navy on lease-lend for patrol duties off the Azores, when the Allies were granted the use of bases for air protection of Atlantic convoys.

At this time, in 1943, the trawlers still on Atlantic convoy work began to take on more the roles of additional escorts and rescue ships, as proper naval escorts became more plentiful. Many trawlers were engaged on 'buttoning' and 'unbuttoning' convoys; that is, leading sections of incoming convoys to ports, or taking out groups of merchantmen to the convoy assembly points. These duties were not without incident, but it was in their mercy work with the actual convoys that the trawlers earned eternal gratitude.

In May 1943 *Northern Spray* was involved in a fantastic battle by a US-bound convoy against wolf-packs of some thirty U-boats. In four days of attacks ten ships of the convoy were sunk, the escorts in reply destroying five U-boats, two by ramming, and claiming a further four 'possibles'. As the incredible battle went on, *Northern Spray* steamed among the chaos and carnage saving exhausted and wounded men from the sea, picking them up from boats and rafts, rescuing them as they clung to wreckage or struggled in the oil and debris-strewn sea. As one British merchantman was sunk, *Northern Spray* got a U-boat contact on her asdic and had to steam through the screaming, cursing survivors in the water to drop depth-charges; afterwards she turned back to rescue the men, many of whom had suffered badly from the explosions. One man was unhinged by his ordeal and had to be put in a straitjacket; a lascar fireman who had floated up through the ship's vents as she went down clung to a floating wooden box, unable to grasp lifelines, so he was hooked aboard with a boathook. In one day *Northern Spray* packed 145 survivors aboard, the officers and crew giving up their cabins and bunks and sleeping where they could. The American seamen rescued all volunteered to help clean up the ship and assist in the galley, but the lascars sat around on tables and would not move, drawing knives and threatening to use them. *Spray*'s commander formed an armed party to round them up and lock them in the chain-locker. The trawler then detached from the convoy with her survivors and steamed on to St John's, Newfoundland. Here, in thick weather, an American destroyer challenged and was ready to fire on *Spray*, until her angry captain ordered a huge battle ensign to be flown at the starboard yardarm and the four-inch to be uncovered and manned, at which forceful display the deflated destroyer signalled 'Sorry, buddies' and offered penitent escort to harbour.

Another battle-weary trawler to enter St John's after a long, hard fight against the U-boats was *Northern Foam*, commanded by Lieutenant 'Bryn' Harris, RNVR. *Foam* had set out across the Atlantic as additional escort and rescue ship to one of two convoys sailing separately from the UK. Gales slowed the convoys on the first part of their voyage, and on the evening of their fifth day at sea the battle commenced. An escort destroyer, sighting a U-boat well astern, made several attacks on the enemy vessel but had to retire from the fray after a serious explosion aboard. Next morning it was decided to merge the two convoys and so increase the escort power considerably. By nightfall the convoys were almost together when a U-boat closed in again and torpedoed the destroyer *St Croix*, which instantly blew up. Shortly afterwards the corvette *Polyanthus* was torpedoed and sunk. Then fog closed down and shrouded the harassed ships.

In thick fog next day *Northern Foam* sighted a U-boat running awash only 300 yards off her port beam. She turned immediately to ram, but the U-boat just managed to get across her bow. Quickly opening fire with her four-inch, *Foam* hit the U-boat abaft the conning tower, and was manoeuvring to ram again when the U-boat dived, so close that the trawler passed over the 'flurry' of its diving. Getting a firm asdic contact *Foam* next fired a 10-charge pattern of depth-charges. Hardly had the explosions subsided when the U-boat was heard blowing tanks in order to surface, and shortly afterwards was heard and seen surfaced, making off fast to southward. *Foam* valiantly gave chase, but the U-boat was doing at least 15 knots and was soon lost in the fog. Nevertheless, it had been heavily damaged by gunfire and shaken up badly by the depth-charges, which had forced it to the surface.

Hours later the fog lifted and the convoy tried to form up into some semblance of order, but the result of an alteration in course was an unwieldly formation which exposed a long flank to attack. Sighting another U-boat about 1500 yards off her port quarter, *Northern Foam* again turned to ram, firing a starshell as she did so, but by the time the starshell burst, the U-boat was nearly submerged. *Foam* tenaciously went in and attacked with patterns of depth-charges . . . once, twice, until her charges caught the zig-zagging U-boat on the point of its course. A very loud and prolonged bubbling noise was then heard coming from undersea, and *Foam* stopped engines and turned ship to listen. The bubbling was heard for some time, gradually growing fainter, until at last it faded. A large patch of oil had welled up to the surface and a sample of this was taken, the strong smell of oil hanging over the dark sea. As the convoy was by then several miles ahead *Foam*'s commander decided to leave the scene and regain his station, as the convoy was seriously threatened and he considered the U-boat destroyed.

Foam had only just reached her station when the main enemy attack started and three merchant ships were torpedoed. Immediately the trawler switched to her role of rescue ship, steaming to pick up survivors in the darkness, though she was now totally exposed to the enemy, the heavy depth-charging having put her asdic out of action. First to a raft to rescue the solitary seaman aboard it, then to a large lifeboat carrying 30 survivors of the ss *Fort Jamseg*. This merchantman was still afloat but settling down, and as *Foam* approached, the calls of an injured man still aboard were heard. In the heavy swell running it was too dangerous to go alongside, so *Foam* lowered a boat, and away went Sub-Lieutenant Morgan to board *Fort*

Jamseg and rescue the injured man, Then on to pick up 40 more survivors, mostly Norwegians, from another sunken ship. When *Foam* had finished her part in the mercy work she carried 75 survivors; but the injured man from *Fort Jamseg* died and had to be buried at sea. The rest of that long day consisted of a hard chase to regain the convoy before darkness fell again, and with Chief Engineman Crosland and his men cursing and coaxing the badly shaken engines, she just made it. There followed a night of alarms, the fog closing in again thicker than ever. As *Foam's* commander commented in his official report: 'I look back on the remainder of the voyage as a nightmare. The convoy was very scattered and all the escort vessels in a state of nerves. I think it doubtful whether the U-boats were still around, but many depth-charges were dropped, including three more by us, probably on unsuspecting whales, of which there were many, and which added to our discomfiture. It was with considerable relief that at last the time came for us to leave the convoy, the thick fog following us right up the entrance to St John's harbour.' Lieutenant Harris had then been five and a half days on the bridge of *Northern Foam* and was thankful for some rest.

Unhappily, in their rescue work the Atlantic trawlers frequently had the task of burying at sea numbers of survivors so badly wounded or affected by exposure that they died after rescue. Holding the solemn burial ceremony was one thing, preparing for it was another. Coxswain Sid Kerslake of *Northern Gem*:

'Our asdic operator and myself often found ourselves being the ones who had to stitch up the dead in their canvas shrouds after putting fire-bars at their feet. We used to get a good tot of rum before and afterwards, and it was always badly needed; you never got used to the job and it was worse if it was one of your own crew, as was the case with us on three occasions. Once, when an American we picked up died, we had to use thick sackcloth and found we hadn't a needle strong enough to go through it, so we had to bind the cover round him with twine. I couldn't get it done fast enough, as I had the eerie feeling he would get out of the cracks or vents I'd left in the cloth. This fear was with me for weeks afterwards, and if I had to go on deck during the night, when all was dark, I had the overpowering feeling that he was after me for not giving him a proper shroud.'

The final chapter in the story of the unfortunate Arctic trawler *Daneman*, after her rough grounding in the River

Dvina, began at this time, when, her repairs at Belfast barely completed, she was ordered to a North Atlantic convoy. Her new commander was Lieutenant Stanley Lock, RNVR.

'The ship was recommissioned and we were ordered off to Tobermory for a "crash" work-up. Several civilian shipyard workers were still on board when the time came for sailing and they had to be turned off whether they'd finished their work or not. After work-up we were appointed to a convoy, and I then realised that our bunker capacity would be insufficient to see us across the Atlantic except under the most ideal conditions and by the shortest route, neither of which was likely. We accordingly had to take tons and tons of coal on deck, to be shovelled down as the bunkers emptied. I was also advised by Captain (D), Belfast, to ask one of the merchantmen to give me a tow if I ran short of fuel!

'When the convoy sailed from Londonderry we were given station astern in view of our rescue duties. All went well until about the third or fourth day out, when the chief engineer reported flooding in the engine room. The pumps were kept going but were unable to prevent the water rising. I reported this to the senior officer escort in destroyer *Keppel*, as we were beginning to lose speed and consequently were unable to maintain station.

'As darkness approached it became obvious that the engines would soon be put out of action. We organised a bucket chain of all hands except those on essential duties. Every bucket and can available was passed along a chain of about forty hands from the depths of the engine room along an iron cat-walk and up a steep iron ladder to the deck, and emptied over the side. It was not very effective, but at least it gave our crew something positive to do.

'We had now dropped miles astern of the convoy and with our last flicker of auxiliary power I reported our plight to *Keppel*. It must have been very difficult for him to decide what to do. The convoy had already lost one escort in ourselves, should he weaken the screen still more by detaching another to stand by us? He would probably have been correct had he decided the safe arrival of the convoy to be of more importance, and left us to our fate. However, he detached not one but two escorts to come to our aid. One was the ocean rescue tug *Bulldog*, and the other a Free French corvette.

'We were now in the middle of the ice zone, at the time of year when the ice breaks away from the polar icecap and drifts southwards either as icebergs or small "growlers" which are very difficult to spot if there is any sea running. I counted no fewer than thirty icebergs on the surrounding horizon. Not that there was any fear of collision; I reckoned we would all drift together at the same speed.

'We were listing heavily to starboard when *Bulldog* arrived. She said she would try to lie alongside our port side and pass one of her enormous six-inch pipes down through our skylights into the engine room and get her powerful pumps to work. It was very difficult keeping our two ships alongside, for although there was not a very big sea running it was enough to cause the ships to separate and crash together intermittently. All the fend-offs we could find were ground to pulp. Still, after the heavy silence that had pervaded our ship for the past ten hours it was good to hear the rhythmic throb of *Bulldog*'s pump. We couldn't see where the water was going and the level did not seem to be going down. We soon saw the reason why: after one particularly bad lurch a bight of the pipe was crushed between the ships' sides – and the inside of the pipe was bone dry.

'*Bulldog*'s captain and I then held a megaphone conference, and it was decided they would ship one of their donkey engine pumps aboard *Daneman*, with an operator, and then take us in tow. I also suggested he should take half my crew on board, in case the situation got really difficult for us, but he was unwilling to do this.

'The pump they passed to us was a pretty hefty affair about the size of a lorry engine. *Bulldog* rigged up a derrick to get this over to us, but there were some perilous moments as the thing swung around in the air and a few feet above our heads. Meanwhile we were preparing for tow, and soon had the tug's enormous steel wire hawser led through the fairlead on the stem, twice round the base of the gun platform and aft on to some very stout "bits" amidships, all well padded with chunks of timber at any likely chafing points. Having no power for the windlass we could not follow the correct method of attaching our own cable to the towline as a "spring". All this time the corvette had been lying off, giving us a protective screen, though it was doubtful if a U-boat would have thought it worthwhile to waste a perfectly good torpedo on us.

'The wind increased and the sea got rougher. *Daneman* by this time was half full of water and had a list of 40 degrees; it was really like trying to tow a covered swimming bath through a fairly heavy sea. *Bulldog* cracked on the knots and I was concerned that she was going too fast, for *Daneman* was travelling through the water faster than she had ever done under her own steam.

'After some anxious hours the inevitable happened and the tow parted. It was night, there was a heavy sea running, our list had increased to 45 degrees and the level of water was rising more rapidly as a lot of the sea breaking over the ship was finding its way below. Our whaler, carried on deck amidships, had been stove in by the heavy seas. I seriously considered whether it was worthwhile renewing the tow under these conditions, even if it were practical to do so. How long would she stay afloat? Certainly not long enough to make harbour, even under a reasonable tow. I decided we would have to abandon ship as soon as daylight broke.

'We had one Carley float, and the idea was that this would take its full complement of fifteen men and drift down to the corvette, which would take them aboard. The rest of us would have to jump for it on to *Bulldog*, which would do her best to lie alongside our starboard, windward and "low" side – the starboard rail was well under water by this time. Our confidential books and documents were sunk in their weighted bags, the Carley float party was selected and all the ship's company instructed on the drill for abandoning ship.

'At dawn the Carley float was launched and manned with a junior officer in charge. There was a very big sea running. Although the first lieutenant supervised this operation he could not prevent one of the ratings left on board from suddenly scrambling over the side on to the raft, followed by two or three others. Consequently the raft was seriously overloaded and three men were lost from it, slipping away in the freezing water. Of the others, taken aboard the corvette, one subsequently died from cold and exhaustion.

'*Bulldog* did her best to lie alongside us and tried to keep her bridge-deck aligned with our foc'sle and four-inch gun platform, which were roughly on a level when *Bulldog* was on an even keel. But now she was rolling madly in the heavy seas and both the level and the space between the ships were varying all the time. At times there would be 15 to 20 feet between the hulls, then they would crash together. One had to choose the right moment to jump decisively. If you chose the right *second* you could step over the rail on to *Bulldog*. Some men did this, some hesitated a few seconds then jumped and clung on to the rails of *Bulldog's* bridge-deck, where they were clawed inboard by her crew before the ships crashed together again. Two men jumped at the wrong moment and went down between the ships.

'*Bulldog* had meanwhile been preparing a large net on her towing deck aft. This was held out by about ten of her crew, fire-brigade fashion, and the remainder of our crew jumped into this. This also needed correct timing, but it was easier and safer than before. When my turn came the only other man left aboard *Daneman* was *Bulldog's* pump operator, who had been trying to make up his mind to jump ever since the operation started. I mounted the gun platform, got on to the outside of the rail beside him and told him to jump when I gave the word. As the ships rolled together and the net was about 15 feet immediately below us I bellowed "Jump!" and descended fairly comfortably into the net. I looked back – he was still there! However, he did make it a few minutes later.

'*Bulldog* then sped on while the corvette gave *Daneman* the coup de grace with a few rounds of shell from her four-inch. Rather surprisingly *Daneman* caught fire and finally settled in the water belching smoke and flames. So ended this depressing episode.

'The loss of six lives in this way was particularly tragic. Fortunately the convoy was not attacked, but it seemed incongruous that the rescue ship herself had to be rescued, and that the rescue tug had to desert the convoy to do so. An inquiry was held at St John's on our arrival and the finding was that *Daneman* had sustained damage by floating ice which caused flooding and subsequent loss. I wonder. It was my belief that the repair job down below, following her misadventure in the Arctic, was never really completed. In normal circumstances I would have insisted on a proper survey, but in this most critical period of the Atlantic war you just had to get on with the job and hope for the best.'

Tragedy upon tragedy among the trawlers. And yet, as was the way with men in constant danger, it was often the humorous incidents that registered most. *Quadrille*, returning to the trawler base at Liverpool in thick fog on the Mersey; she took on about ten pilots and they were all on the bridge when she touched bottom and lost her asdic dome. *Lady Madeleine*, complimented by King George VI on her smart appearance when he visited her base; he was not to know that she was painted on one side only – one side of the ship, one side of the funnel, one side of the whaler; simply because there wasn't the manpower to get the full job done in time. And on *Northern Gift*, escorting one of the HX convoys from Newfoundland to Belfast, the priceless moment when her captain was caught with his pants down. Lieutenant Fred Bentley:

'We were, of course, always fully clothed all the time on convoy, and on a beautiful day with a calm Atlantic swell I thought it would be a safe time to take a bath. My number one offered to look after the ship, and I fell to temptation. Halfway through my bath the alarm klaxons went, so hastily putting a towel round my middle and my uniform cap on, I belted up the steel ladders to the bridge. On the last ladder the towel came off and I arrived before the startled signalman in my uniform cap and my birthday suit. It was a false alarm as many were, and it was the laugh of the ship that the Old Man had been caught with his trousers down. However, mine was the last laugh, for when we got to Liverpool I had all their trousers down by ordering an F.F.I. (free from infection).'

The weather, as ever, produced its constant punishments, and one of the most bizarre experiences was that of *Cotillion*, when she rode into the dead centre of a storm. She sailed from Londonderry in December 1943, attached to a Gibraltar-bound convoy and commanded by Lieutenant Jim Fowler, survivor of the Lagos disaster the year before.

'We were routed to about 25 West before turning south and the weather was extremely hard. In the first week, steaming through a series of storms, we got exactly 800 miles, which was very slow going. On the morning of the eighth day the wind was gusting to a hundred miles an hour, quite the worst I ever experienced in the Atlantic. The waves were very far apart but completely flattened out, and we could see little because of the flying spray. It was more or less darkness at that time, eleven in the morning, and the convoy had scattered long before.

'We suddenly came out into brilliant sunshine with a very, very confused sea running, a frightening sea. Visibility was about three miles all round and spiralling helplessly were millions of seabirds, all in a very exhausted state; they had been trapped inside the centre of the storm and couldn't get out – they poured on board the ship in their thousands. After ten minutes, however, we were almost from a flat calm straight back into the full force of the wind, hove-to in a completely different direction, having cut across into another sector of the storm. The contrast from no wind to force 12 again was really remarkable and frightening, and it was during the course of this afternoon that we failed to rise to one of the big seas.

'By this time I had been alone on the bridge for a long time, for the simple reason that anyone who had gone below to the wheelhouse had not been able to come up again, so my only communications were with the people in the wheelhouse, round which all the weatherboards were up. I was standing behind the binnacle, as I had to watch the compass fairly carefully. Visibility again was very bad. We were being blown off as much as 90 degrees and putting our stern right under when we went over the crest of the waves, having to bring her round again in the troughs; so we were going as slowly as possible. Then came this giant wave and we went right underneath it.

'I was just able with all my strength to hold on to the compass platform under the weight of water which came over the top of the bridge. For a second or two the whole bridge was completely filled with water, until it began to drain out down the two companionways. We lost both our boats and the boatdecks with them, the windlass shifted for'ard, part of the four-inch gun platform was bent right back, and all the small ventilators and suchlike simply vanished. For a time it felt that the ship was never going to come up again, she was quite dead under my feet. But at length she did come up. . . . From that point unwards the storm seemed to ease off fairly rapidly. I went down to my cabin to find it under two feet of water, but turned in and just slept.'

In the Mediterranean, 1943 saw increased activity by Patrol Service vessels as patrol and supply ships, especially with the Allied landings and the capitulation of Italy in September. But at the start of the year the picture did not look as favourable. In February. when a group of asdic trawlers including *King Sol* left Milford Haven for Gibraltar they did an anti-U-boat sweep in the Atlantic en route. It was the height of the U-boat war, as was vividly brought home to *King Sol*'s telegraphist, Fred Howson.

'One night a coder passed me a situation report after he had decoded it, and it really showed us for the first time just how serious the position was. The details read something like this: "15 U-boats shadowing X convoy, 20 U-boats shadowing Y convoy, 12 U-boats inward bound Bay of Biscay, 25 outward bound." Yet somehow we got through without seeing a thing.

'*King Sol*'s first trip out of Gibraltar was quite something. We coaled and watered, and steamed out with other escorts to rendezvous a convoy from the US about 250 miles west of the Rock. There was a long, slow swell and one or two of us remarked how little movement there was, especially considering the extra top-weight on either side of the bridge. After twelve hours the asdic packed up and the leading asdic operator had to take a look at the works. These were situated under the messdeck, and as soon as he lifted the trapdoor it became apparent why we were riding through the swell so smoothly – we were flooded to within a few inches of the messdeck.

'Immediately the pumps were started up, but within minutes they too had packed up. The reason was that our entire stock of Naafi cigarettes and chocolate was stored down there and it blocked the pumps. The C.O. decided there was no alternative but to bale out the ship by bucket and hand. For two days and nights it was a case of coming off watch, grabbing a meal, then joining the human bucket-chain from the trap to the deck. The cause of the flooding was discovered: a seacock was found turned to "open", and it was suspected that this had been done by one of the Spaniards aboard while we were coaling. Ever after that there was always a deck guard and a quay guard when we were tied up at Gibraltar.

'But this was not the end of our troubles. The coal we had loaded was of very poor quality, more like black sand, and the convoy was quite fast, about 10 knots. Our daytime station was ahead of the convoy, and our night station at the rear. Everything went well the first night, but next morning, when we had to take up station ahead, it proved almost impossible. We eventually made it, but only after hours of work and sweat by the stokers; it was so hard on them that we were given an extra stoker when we arrived back at the Rock.

'Ships kept leaving the convoy at intervals for various Algerian ports and eventually we sailed into Bone, the Allied base. Here we cleaned out properly below the messdeck and stacked up all our sea-spoiled Naafi stores on deck so that they could be declared unfit by someone from the base, and reimbursed free of charge. This done, we were told to throw them over the side. I could scarcely believe my eyes at what happened next. None of the harbours out there was tidal, the result being they were full of filth and oil scum; but as we threw the stuff overboard the Arabs scooped it out of the water, ate the sweets and chocolate and put the cigarettes on one side to dry out. For the first time in my life I saw the results of extreme hunger and poverty.'

Another trawler which reached the Mediterranean at the same time as *King Sol* was *Foxtrot*. From patrol off Algiers she went as additional escort to a convoy which took a bitter hammering. Her commander was Lieutenant John Bald, RNVR.

'It was a lovely misty morning. We had just secured dawn action-stations and I was arranging myself on the deck of the bridge for a nap, when there were three very loud bangs. A U-boat had slung a handful of torpedoes into the convoy and hit three ships. One, a tanker carrying high-octane, just disappeared in a white flash, and by the time I had leapt to my feet all that was left of her were pieces coming down out of a grey mushroom-shaped cloud. Another of the torpedoed ships was the *Siddi Bel Abbes*, a Frenchman, carrying 1,500 Senegalese troops; she turned on her side and sank in three minutes. The third ship, the American *City of Michigan*, slowly settled by the stern and remained hanging like an unkempt lighthouse before sliding to the bottom fifteen minutes later. The senior officer escort, as he dashed past me on the hunt in his destroyer, signalled me to pick up survivors. With the aid of another ship we managed to rescue 400 men in many stages of mutilation, and these we took to Oran.'

Just two or three weeks before Italy's surrender the trawler *Hornpipe* was on patrol off Bougie, near Algiers. Her number one was Lieutenant Dormer.

'There was an eclipse of the moon, very beautiful and weird, and portending strange events. It was midnight and I was asleep when there was a roar of aircraft, followed by the alarm. I tumbled up on the bridge in bright moonlight to see the sea ablaze. What the hell? My first thought was that a tanker had been hit, but no, it was a Heinkel 111 which, after having a good look at us, had dropped a torpedo fine on the starboard bow about 600 yards away; it splashed twice and ran down the starboard side as the ship went hard-a-starboard. The plane, turning away, somehow crashed into the sea and became a mass of flames from which there was one man shouting as we passed.

'We could not stop and did not think of throwing him anything as there was a second plane about, which shortly came at us. We let fly at him with everything . . . four-inch shrapnel, Oerlikon, twin-Vickers, twin-Brownings, and certainly gave him a damn good fright as he practically looped the loop to get away. He, or another, returned a few minutes later in a rather half-hearted manner, but a burst from all guns quickly drove him away and, after circling out of range, he disappeared for good.

'The authorities ashore jumped to the conclusion that we had shot the plane down and were full of congratulations. It was rather embarrassing for the C.O. to have to explain that it had flown into the sea by itself, without us firing a shot. The officer of the watch rather prided himself as an aircraft recognition expert and had "recognised" the plane, which was in fact Italian, as one of ours, and had allowed it to take a good look and then attack before realising anything was wrong. Luckily he woke up in time to comb the track of the torpedo. The Italian communique announced the loss of two aircraft, so perhaps we did the second one no good.

'The body of one of the Italians was recovered and we inspected it with mixed emotions. A dark little chap, somewhat burned and battered – I wondered who he was. So unnecessary, the Italian surrender was already being arranged.'

The following month found *Hornpipe* at Phillipville, some 120 miles along the coast from Bougie. Lieutenant Dormer's diary:

'Liberty men came back aboard ... an inoffensive little chap is talking quietly on the deck outside my cabin. Suddenly he says in an offhand way: "Excuse me a minute, I'm just going to strangle the C.O." He trots to our door with someone in pursuit warning him: "Now don't do anything you'll regret in the morning." He insists: "But it won't take a minute ... I'm just going to strangle him." He is dragged away, disappointed.'

Later, at Malta. 'Stored up with everything we could get, using our own two pulling-boats which had to row miles and miles. The Sub. was so late that I got worried and borrowed a motorboat from a fleet sweeper, *Clacton*, to look for him. *Clacton*'s officer-of-the-day was very snooty and would hardly speak to me although of the same rank. His ship is not all that much bigger than ours but, because it is a different shape, there is an unbridgeable social gulf.'

Fate knew no such distinctions. Only weeks later *Clacton* was sunk off Corsica, after hitting a mine.

And so late October found *Hornpipe* at Naples. 'Broken down ... no lights, no radio, no hot water. A five o'clock curfew makes the evening gloomy, but we are having mild air-raids which happen just after supper and conveniently fill the time till bed. Everyone blazes away at random, balloons come down in flames, we shoot each others' masts, and there is a terrific din and fireworks display. Any bombs are lost in the uproar. Great fun. There is nothing to do ashore except for the very foolish ... one can get anything for tobacco.'

In November an unusual event took place back at Algiers, where Admiral Sir John Cunningham, the C-in-C Mediterranean, had his headquarters ashore. The Admiral would fly his flag on a warship in harbour, generally a destroyer or cruiser, or something larger, but in an unexpected departure from routine he asked the trawler *Staffa* to fly his flag – a rare distinction. So there followed the unlikely spectacle of the beflagged trawler returning the salutes of warships large and small moving in and out of harbour at all hours of the day. It imposed quite a strain on her company, but the four days of glory was well worth it, and afterwards her commander asked the C-in-C's permission for *Staffa* to keep the flag as a memento, a request which was speedily approved. The Admiral added: 'I would not hesitate to order you to hoist it again should the occasion arise.'

Well, that was the trawlers, always equal to the occasion, big or small. Like the captain at Gibraltar, who, having an appointment with the Admiral, and his trawler being involved in the filthy business of coaling up, donned impeccable white uniform and had himself wrapped up in sheets and carried off the ship down the quay to a safe distance from the flying black dust.

Of the trawler losses in the Mediterranean in 1943 two, the *Jura* and the *Bredon* were sunk by U-boat torpedoes and two more, *Horatio* and *Tervani*, were torpedoed by Italian submarines. Three others were destroyed by mines.

At the year's end the total casualty list of Harry Tate's Navy now stood at more than 350 vessels lost. The last entry was a stark Christmas Day tragedy in home waters. *Kingston Beryl*, on convoy duty off Skerryvore, ran on to some floating mines which had broken loose from a British minefield.

She sank with all hands. British mines were supposed to go 'safe' when they broke loose, but these were not.

15

'Sir, the Wheel's Come Off'

January 1944 and a renewed burst of E-boat activity. The trawler *Wallasea* was escorting a convoy section from the Bristol Channel round to Plymouth when E-boats struck off Mounts Bay, sending *Wallasea* to the bottom along with two of her charges. In a similar attack off Beachy Head the trawler *Pine* also lost two of her flock and had her own bows blown off by a torpedo. She carried on fighting the E-boats until help arrived, only to sink when taken in tow.

In the North Sea the E-boat pack found easier prey in the mine-sweeping *Cap D'Antifer*, which they despatched within minutes.

However, the trawlers' overall losses at the beginning of the year were light, and for most Harry Tate vessels in home waters it was a case of plodding on with their usual unspectacular duties during the massive build-up for the Second Front. Like the old drifter *King's Grey*, based at Devonport; her routine consisted of Channel sweeping by day and putting into a different port each night, Brixham, Falmouth, Dartmouth, and then back to Devonport. It was a humdrum existence repeated hundreds of times on similar ships, but that a Second Front was coming at last was made evident by such scenes as the handing over of the old *Monique Andre*, a converted French trawler operating from Plymouth, to the Free French. Cook Scadeng:

'The *Monique Andre* was as dirty as they come, we'd lie in our bunks at night and hear the rats scurrying along the steampipes within six to eight inches of our faces. So there were no regrets when we were told she was to be returned to the Free French Navy.

'Never was there a greater ceremony. We spent days getting all the stores listed and ready to be returned to the depot. The turnover was ordered to take place at Ardrossan, not far from Glasgow, so we steamed our way there up the west coast.

'The great day came and everything movable was transferred

to the jetty, every pot, pan and item of stores, to be carefully stacked in a large covered van. Off went the van, and the skipper asked us all to get into a decent suit and get our personal gear on the jetty, ready for transport. "Now," he said, "when these froggies come along we have to line up along the jetty, facing the ship so as to witness the hauling down of the Ensign and the raising of the Free French flag!"

'What a performance. The French arrived in another covered van and piled out of the back. First, an armed guard of two French sailors who stood rigidly to attention while the standard bearer placed himself between them, then the French relief crew. Their officers arrived by car.

'We lined up facing the forward part of the ship while the French faced the after end. Simultaneously, and to commands of "Present Arms!" in French, and a modest request from our skipper to stand to attention, accompanied by some blasts from a French bugle, our Bunts hauled down our Ensign and the French hauled up theirs. A few handshakes and goodbyes were exchanged, the new crew climbed aboard, and we got into their wagon. Off we went, to a chorus of groans when, a few yards along the jetty, we passed the van with our ship's gear and stores still aboard and untouched going back to the *Monique Andre*, where the French were to take it all back again.'

In the spring of 1944 the Royal Naval Patrol Service reached a working strength of 57,000 officers and men. Overwhelmingly now its ranks were filled with hostilities-only ratings, but Harry Tate's Navy retained its spiky, pugnacious, defiant identity.

The old trawler *Clythness* had been a minesweeper at Dover, was at Dunkirk, and all in all had gone through a rather eventful time. Recommissioned as a water-carrier she had spent the winter of 1943-44 watering the landing craft assembled in Cromarty Firth. When she left Aberdeen on this task there was the moving scene of her skipper bellowing at his seasick sailors as they struggled to get the smallboat swung out. He had asked for seamen, he said, and been sent bloody farmers. A few days later he presented the messdeck with a brown paper parcel in which was a book from the comforts, entitled 'How to be a Successful Farmer'.

This skipper was a wiry ex-fisherman, a small man in his middle-thirties but with a powerful voice that could be heard all over the harbour. A thoroughly tough man, he nevertheless had a sentimental and generous side to his nature and his bark was generally worse than his bite. But there was fierce rivalry between him and the chief engineman.

There was the day *Clythness*, which had been steaming in the centre of a convoy, discovered at daybreak she was alone on the sea with the convoy a far-off smudge of smoke on the horizon. A destroyer flashed urgently from a discreet distance that *Clythness* was steaming through a minefield, or so the more pessimistic of the crew judged the signal to read. This was too much for the chief engineman, who afterwards drew up a 'round robin' petitioning for a new C.O. However, the skipper got wind of it and cleverly prevented his arch-enemy from going ashore; much to the secret relief of the chief, whose enthusiasm had waned.

When the 'bond' – the monthly supply of whisky and gin – came aboard, a skipper would throw a party for brother skippers from other trawlers, and they would get down to steady drinking for the next twenty-four hours until the liquor was finished. As one seaman describes:

'During these parties anything could happen. First they became mellow and sent a bottle down to the messdeck, whereupon someone would open a bottle of illicitly stored rum and another party would start there. Then the skippers became a nuisance, ordering the steward, or if he had conveniently disappeared, the member of the crew who was on watch, to dish up a meal for them, anything from a plate of sandwiches to a fry-up of bacon and eggs. After this they might get sporty and hold a shooting competition with the revolvers kept in the wardroom, when it was as well to keep below under cover. It generally ended up with a fight between a couple of the skippers and the cook chasing a seaman out of the galley with his carving knife; or, as on one occasion, the chief engineman trying to put a troublesome stoker over the side. Next day, after a twelve-hour lie-in, everything would be back to normal.'

Very occasionally a determined attempt would be made to shake some sterner discipline into the Harry Tates, as at Granton, on the Firth of Forth, when an RN commander assumed command and looked with jaundiced eye on the motley collection of Patrol Service craft which included a fair complement of little motor minesweepers or 'Mickey Mouses'. Taking a leaf out of the book of old 'Monkey Brand' Stephenson at Tobermory, the commander, along with a working party, raided unguarded ships and dismantled parts of their guns – a bit off an Oerlikon here, a little off a 12-pounder there – had them all labelled and dispatched to his office, and sat back to await the inevitable result, a steady stream of furious skippers to retrieve their losses.

One sight to cap all others was that of the skipper of a whaler going ashore three sheets to the wind, coat slung over his shoulder, cap at an angle of 45 degrees, his pet Alsatian bounding along beside him, giving loud voice to blistering remarks about the RN which were exciting in their inventiveness and a revelation to the ears of the Wrens.

But perhaps no better illustration of the root spirit of Harry Tate's Navy, undiminished by four years of war, could be the experience of a party of senior naval brass who set forth from Scapa Flow one fine afternoon, bent on a fishing expedition to Hoy. Admiral Burnett, in HMS *Belfast*, flagship of Cruiser Squadron 10, had organised the party and a drifter arrived to transport them. The crew were no doubt impressed by HMS *Belfast* but hardly by the relaxed group of men in old jackets and flannels, led by an elderly, red-faced man in a cap and dirty raincoat.

To the flag lieutenant's inquiry, 'Who is the captain of this driftah?' there was no reply, so Admiral Burnett reverted to the Buchan dialect and asked, 'Fa's skipper o' this boatie?'

A youth eventually looked up from the drifter's wheelhouse and said slowly and very deliberately: 'This iss a Stornoway ship, and we're aall captainss here. . . . '

In the Mediterranean, minesweeping had been stepped up in all areas. Ships were constantly busy, like the whaler *Satsa*, working on the Italian minefields at Pantelleria, Sicily, Sardinia, and along the coast of Italy. *Satsa* did the sweeping at night for the landing on Elba, and when dawn broke, found herself surrounded by twenty-seven floating mines, a sight that froze the blood of her crew at the thought of their hairbreadth escape.

The trawler *Hornpipe* was in at the Anzio landing. Extracts from Lieutenant Dormer's diary describe the build-up at Naples, and afterwards.

'The typhus has spread, and we are not allowed ashore at all. Nor can laundry be sent. We have all been issued with anti-louse powder. Some "enterprise of great pith and moment" is in the offing. The port is crowded, heavy air-attacks are expected, and we close up at dawn and dusk. The burning question is, are *we* going? Will the steering be repaired in time? We coaled today, a hopeful sign, since there had even been talk of digging our coal out. They brought a coal barge to *us* . . . never before. Confinement on board is no joke. Some of the sailors have even taken to writing letters to each other for the benefit of the censor . . . me.

They tell each other what they think of "Jimmy-the-Bastard" ... me.

'*Tuesday.* We are very likely to go on the party now, so there is a crescendo of excitement, and grim jokes. The whole area is in a fever of preparation. German reconnaissance planes have been over, so they'll probably be waiting on the beaches. The only question is, where? Funny to think that some unsuspecting little town or village will, in a few days, be world famous.

'*Wednesday.* The steering is mended, and excitement increased so much that people worked overtime without even remembering to grumble. At last, extricating ourselves with great difficulty from the mass of ships and landing craft, we sailed to Castellamare for the night, with best wishes from the stay-at-homes. There, as soon as dusk fell, every sort of flap arose ... human torpedoes, E-boats. ... But nothing happened, though we spent the evening at action-stations with a boat full of bombs patrolling round the ship.

'*Thursday.* Checked up on everyone's lifebelts and tin-hats. Issued field dressings and checked every detail of organisation and equipment. The C.O. went to a most secret conference, of which no details are to be released until actually under way. Let's get cracking, waiting is a strain. Only four trawlers are concerned, we are lucky this time ... I wonder if we shall say "lucky" later?

'*Friday.* "Never sail on a Friday", but we did, about noon, behind a big convoy of landing craft. The officers were only told of the plan in the evening, though Sparks, a leading telegraphist, has known all along. So far, at 2000 hours, all is well. We can see gunflashes, as usual, from the Minturno area, and various aircraft are about.

'*Saturday.* 1100. The night passed quietly, but the landing craft were hard to see, and by 0300 the convoys were in a fair state of confusion. At 0500 the course seemed wrong, and the speed too slow. I asked the nearest LCI ... we were with the wrong convoy. Cracking on we found our flotilla of fleet sweepers at daybreak, and spent a hectic day picking up dan buoys. We had hardly ever done this before, and found it difficult. I spent much of the day in the sea, swimming to shackle on wires.

'*D-Day.* A lovely, calm, sunny day, almost cloudless blue skies. The multitude of ships off the beaches look more like a review than an invasion. The sweepers cut several mines, one of which damaged the A/A cruiser *Palomares*. We are now about to escort her back to Naples, in tow of tugs. There are a few columns of smoke rising from the shore, and every now and then a dull thud. Sometimes a cruiser does a bit of bombarding or a few enemy planes approach. There are constant red warnings, but no attacks yet.

'*D-Day plus 2.* Escorted the tug *Evenshaw*, towing two lighters to Anzio, but had to sink one of them by gunfire as it broke adrift and the sea was too rough to recover it, in spite of using oil. Arrived off the American beaches at 1500. The town was being heavily shelled, and shells were bursting on the beaches and in the sea. Return fire from U.S. warships was landing quite close inland. At 1600 three dive-bombers attacked the HQ ship, without result, but one American vessel was sunk, with its bows sticking out of the water. At dusk, just as we were setting off with a Naples-bound convoy, the Luftwaffe arrived in force, and the next two hours were a terrific muddle of flares and tracer and bombs in all directions. We hardly fired at all ourselves, but I saw four aircraft go down in flames and the destroyer *Janus* badly hit and burning. We had a nasty half hour later, well out on our own, having lost the convoy in the confusion. Enemy planes dropped dozens of flares in a circle round us, but we made smoke and were not attacked.'

On the fourth day after the landing *Hornpipe* arrived at Anzio again – 'just at dusk, the worst possible time, with the convoy of LSTs disorganised by a gale. There was a heavy air attack which lasted three hours. A Heinkel attacked us with a torpedo, which I saw drop. We had a go at him but missed, as the ship was rolling in a heavy sea. There were attacks about every half hour all next day as we hung about in the anchorage. I attempted to have a wash, but a stick of bombs came down just ahead as soon as I got my shirt off. At 1500 the BBC boasted about "our complete mastery of the air over the beach-head". There were two formations, each of 12 aircraft, cruising overhead, all silvery in the sunshine. We felt nice and safe, until they peeled off and attacked, one after the other. One of them dived straight into the sea, it all looked too like the films to be real. We were very worried about the evening, but the sun went down in a glory of crimson and gold, and it got dark without anything happening. No one dared to be the first to say "I don't think they're coming." And so it went on.'

The trawlers were switched from escorting convoys to Anzio to make anti-submarine patrols between the Pontine Islands. The aim of this was to seal off the inshore shipping route, but it was not a success, the cruiser *Penelope* being sunk by a U-boat inside the 'sealed off' area. The trawlers resumed their journeys to the beach-head.

'One could see for miles, all the beach-head, and the Alban hills, the poplars of the Pontine marshes, and the great snow-capped mountains beyond. All around the perimeter little white puffs appeared, grew into tall columns, and faded away. Against the dark of a leafless wood, we could see the flashes of our own artillery.'

The Germans had perfect observation from the Alban hills; Dormer later saw enemy photographs in which one could easily pick out an individual trawler. The Germans also had one or more very long range guns known as 'Anzio Charlie', which made life hotter all around.

'The afternoon was quiet until the Jerries noticed an LST that had anchored away from the rest. They started shelling it with a most enormous great gun whose shell sent waterspouts up some 150 feet. After the fifth shell, at exactly three-minute intervals, the LST was seen to be moving. The sixth shell was close astern of her, but after the seventh they gave up. We, and the merchant shipping, remained several miles off shore, the latter unloading into DUKWs.'

Later on, the beach-head was kept perpetually shrouded in smoke, and mines were the main problem. *Hornpipe* went on to dan-laying.

'One day we were looking forward to provisions from a fleet sweeper, but they unfortunately hauled up a mine in their sweep which killed their first lieutenant. "Oh dear," said my C.O., "we can hardly ask them for 40 pounds of fresh meat now."

'Near the end we arrived in the smoke screen one morning, simultaneously with several German midget submarines. They hadn't a chance, being clearly visible in a glassy calm.

'Finally, just before the breakout from the beach-head, we had to get our own sweeps out, to sweep a convoy into Anzio. All the sweeping gear was stowed away, and we had forgotten how to use it. Surprisingly we got it running, but most of the sweep was done in a thick smoke screen, where none of us could see each other, and the convoy did not follow in the "swept" water anyway, so the whole thing was a bit of a farce.'

Work went on off West Africa, and it was these waters which saw the end of one of the most notable ships sailed by Harry Tate's Navy.

Southern Pride was a big whaler of nearly 500 tons. Under construction at Blyth at the beginning of the war, she was taken over on the stocks for Admiralty service, and when completed in 1940 she and *Southern Gem*, of the same tonnage, were the largest whale-catchers in the world.

Southern Pride arrived at the Belfast trawler base late in 1940. With a very low well-deck constantly under water – she had a nine-inch freeboard when fully loaded – she was the prototype of the Flower-class corvettes, and did twenty knots on trials with a bronze propeller. She had been designed to reach South Africa on her way to the whaling grounds without refuelling, travelling rather like a submarine, and the effect of the addition of a four-inch gun, ammunition, depth-charges and the rest was very nearly disastrous on her first convoy trip into the Atlantic. After losing the convoy a few days out in heavy weather, *Pride* was forced to heave-to for forty-eight hours, during which time her boats were damaged and the charthouse structure on the upper bridge wrecked. She subsequently never took on her full capacity of oil fuel; except once, in the South Atlantic, and then she was nearly driven under.

The middle of 1943 saw *Pride* operating from Freetown, she and *Southern Gem* working as a pair, taking merchantmen round to various surf ports on the West African coast, where the ships were unloaded by surf boats, and escorting cable ships. On one such tour of duty *Pride* crossed the Atlantic to Pernambuco, Brazil, with a cable ship, patrolling round and round her charge while the vessel hauled up and repaired undersea cables. Then *Pride* had the task of escorting across to Dakar, via Freetown, about twenty little motor fishing vessels built in the US. The MFVs mostly seemed to be manned by retired Army officers, including three full colonels. One of the boats broke down on the equator, crossing the line dizzily back and forth all night, and *Southern Pride* with it. Finally *Pride* towed the boat back to Pernambuco.

At this stage the whaler's number one, Lieutenant Allan Waller, had a recurrence of ear trouble and had to go into hospital. On recovering, and with *Southern Pride* gone, he attached himself to the US Navy, along with an engineman from *Pride* now fit again after breaking a leg while playing football, and the first lieutenant of *Southern Gem*, who had been to hospital to have his tonsils out. The USN tried to arrange passage to the States for the trio. However, the whaler *Buttermere* turned up bound for Freetown, and so the three men joined her. She was only a year older than *Pride*, but she put the fear of God into the passengers. She had been in Rio for a couple of months refitting, and the ship's company of thirty-six was highly demoralised; some thirty of them had got VD, or were just getting over it.

Buttermere was loaded up with quartz for asdics and was also escort for eight MFVs. She had not been long out at sea when the helmsman reported to the officer of the watch: 'Please, sir, the wheel's come off'. The O.O.W's reply was, 'Well, put it back on again!' which they did, fixing it in position with the marline spike of a pusser's dirk. After a few days the ship stopped completely, the chief engineer mournfully telling the captain 'The whole job's fucked, sir.' A pump had broken down in the engine room. Help came from a totally unexpected quarter when an engineer of one of the MFVs, Lieutenant (E.) Lance Harrison, RNVR, brought his boat alongside the stranded whaler in the flat calm. He climbed aboard *Buttermere* and made repairs using two galley stove lids, one from the whaler and one from his own boat. And so they made it to port – and never were the three passengers more grateful to get back to their own ships. Unfortunately, for the two men of *Pride*, it was not for long, though Allan Waller, the 'Jonah of Parkeston Quay', had no idea that he was soon to have a third ship go down beneath him.

In June 1944 *Southern Pride*, in company with a trawler, was escorting a merchant ship to a Liberian port, but never reached there. Off Marshall Port, about thirty miles from Monrovia, she ran on to a shoal. The time was four minutes past 7 p.m. Lieutenant Waller:

'I was sitting with the chief engineer outside the wardroom on the starboard waist when the ship struck. It felt as if she had been mined by an acoustic ground mine. I seized my lifebelt and hurried to my action-station on the bridge, while the chief ran aft. There were more shocks as I arrived on the bridge, like exploding depth-charges this time.

' "We're hit," said the captain – "Unprime depth-charges!" While we were doing this the ship rocked heavily but was not sinking, and seemed to have stopped. There were more shocks, and it now seemed we were striking either rock or hard sand. In four minutes the depth-charges had been made safe and I was back on the bridge. A signal was sent to the trawler *Pict* and I tried to fix our exact position – we were about three miles from shore in shark infested waters – but this was impossible in the failing light.

'The cox'n took over the wheel and the captain tried to move the ship at slow-ahead, without success. The engines were then tried at slow-astern. The wheel would not answer, but the ship appeared to move very slowly. Soundings were taken and two fathoms reported; the bangings and grindings ceased. The captain decided to anchor, as the ship seemed to have cleared the rocks and was riding well, but the chief engineer reported that the pumps were unable to cope with the water and it would soon be necessary to draw the fires. The captain then decided to try to beach the ship, and we began to heave in the anchor, but before this could be done the chief said that the engine room would have to be abandoned. More cable was let out and the anchor secured. The ship was still rising buoyantly and was well out of the water, though she had in fact been holed right under the Scotch boiler. The asdic well had been made watertight.

'It was now two hours since we had struck the shoal and there was not much more we could do. I helped the captain to decide on the ship's position and compose a signal to senior officer West Africa which we tried to send off over our own set, an attempt which was abandoned when the lights failed and power was low.

'Rum was issued, all hands gathered on the well-deck to hear a reassuring talk by the captain, and a sing-song was organised to help keep up morale. Some men broke into the wardroom spirit locker, and one troublesome seaman had to be shut up in the heads.

'Watches were organised, those off watch trying to rest. Still the ship showed no signs of sinking, though water was rising slowly in the engine room. Shortly after midnight several shocks were felt and the ship suddenly began to settle port side aft. We had already lost one boat, so a few of us now tried to build rafts by lashing together empty oil drums. There were four of us, Sub-Lieutenant Dunn, Lieutenant (E) Johansen, the chief engineer. Telegraphist Roberts and myself. But there was a heavy swell running, and just as we had completed one raft the ship lurched heavily to port and lay over at an angle, a huge sea came over and carried away our raft and all other floatable gear on the boatdeck. We ourselves escaped by each selecting a funnel guy and, when the sea came over, swarming up it, though I suffered a badly lacerated leg. A Carley float with three native stokers on it was also swept away, but kept afloat.

'I went down to the main deck to see if everyone there was all right. The ship was now listing to an angle of about 30 degrees; most of the hands were sitting on the starboard rail, which was well clear of the water. I remembered the seaman we had shut up, and making my way forward with difficulty because of the angle of the ship, found him lying completely unconscious outside the heads, the tapes of his lifebelt wound round his neck. Shaking him did no good, so in desperation I kicked and punched him. At last he came round a little and started raving. With the help of two men I sat him up with his lifebelt well inflated and securely fastened round his chest, then got him to the rail, where he seemed to realise to some extent his danger. I left him hanging over a rail with a rating on either side, satisfied that if he kept only slight control he would easily save himself, for at that end the ship was only about four feet under water.

'Scrambling back along the ship I then tried with Signalman Stone to get a message to a boat from *Pict*, which seemed to be having difficulty in finding us, and in the process was nearly washed over the side. *Pride* was righting herself quickly and the rising waters forced us to climb upwards to the lower bridge veranda and the Oerlikon and four-inch platforms. *Pict*'s boat finally took off the first load, and as the lower bridge was crowded I climbed to the upper bridge, and from there on to the searchlight platform on top. There was nothing to do now but wait to be taken off. *Pict*'s boat came over four or five times for new loads, during which time the swell moderated and it grew lighter.'

On the top bridge were Paddy Swanson, the assistant cook, and Seaman Field, an asdic rating. Paddy could not swim and had anxiously equipped himself with three lifebelts. Field promised faithfully to jump into the water with him when the boat arrived, which he did, but in swimming to the boat Paddy reached a speed which astonished everyone and was hauled aboard well ahead of his shipmate.

Finally the boat made its last journey to pick up the remaining six people aboard: the captain, chief engineer, engineman, telegraphist, Sub-Lieutenant Dunn and Lieutenant Waller. 'We abandoned ship from the port side and I looked at my watch before I jumped; it was 5.17 a.m., ten hours since we had struck the shoal. The captain followed me into the water and after a short swim we reached the boat and were pulled aboard.'

Only one man was lost, and this a seaman who was swept away despite the best efforts of his comrades to save him; the three stokers washed over earlier with the Carley float drifted safely ashore. Even the ship's dog managed to swim the three miles to the beach, though the ship's cat and three kittens were never seen again.

Adding to the melancholy of the disaster was the loss of the cash in the wardroom safe, for *Southern Pride* had been due to make another crossing to Pernambuco, and so they had bought all the cruzeiros available in Freetown and put them in the safe – which now lay abandoned under water. However, there was a bright sequel when, on returning to the wreck with a salvage party from a tug, Lieutenant Waller managed, with help, to get down and rescue the cash, and spent most of one day drying it out.

In the same week that saw the ignominious death of *Southern Pride*, the trawler *Birdlip* also met her end off the West African coast. *Birdlip* was one of three trawlers escorting a merchantman from Takoradi to Freetown when she was torpedoed by a U-boat. Half of her company, including the captain, were lost, the remainder managing to reach the shore on two rafts.

Birdlip's swift fate was very much on the minds of the crew of another escort trawler, the *Duncton*, as she approached those same waters less than a month later. *Duncton*, based at Freetown, was returning north from Capetown after a three-month refit when she broke down. Her number one was Lieutenant Arthur Miles.

'A few days out of Walvis Bay, where we called for repairs to our W/T transmitter, the engines were stopped owing to leaking boiler tubes. Spare tubes were fitted, but more leaks developed. Our transmitter remained out of order so we couldn't wireless for help, and it was a case of improvising as best we could to stop the leaks, which now affected a great number of the tubes. Several times the boilers were refilled by hand pump, all hands from the captain to the cook taking a spell, but steam was raised only to produce further leaks, and repairs had to be started all over again.

'Fortunately the weather was perfect, whales and sharks playing around our silent ship. One evening a sing-song on deck came to an abrupt end when the lookout sighted mysterious green flares, and action-stations was sounded. Nothing happened, but we felt like sitting ducks, remembering the fate of *Birdlip*.

'Food and water were now rationed, no fresh water at all for washing, and everyone grew beards. Somebody joked "Why don't we sail her?" and very soon the idea was being taken seriously. The big foredeck awning made a good mainsail, and every bit of canvas aboard, together with some pretty odd bits of bunting, was hoisted until the ship was festooned with "sails". As one of the crew described it, we looked like the washing on the Siegfried Line. There was a steady wind on the beam and the quartermaster steered from the auxiliary wheel aft. By Dutchman's log *Duncton*'s speed under sail was a good one knot! The wind blew steadily off the coast so that we could not, with our unwieldy rig, even tack towards it, and the best we could manage was to continue heading north.

'Every day our dinghy put off on a practice cruise in preparation for sending a volunteer crew hundreds of miles north to the Portuguese island of Sao Tome, to fetch help. This would have been very much a last resort, and luckily the most they did was take snapshots of us – the last sailing man-o'-war. For at last steam was raised and our engineers' makeshift repairs enabled us to limp slowly into Lagos after about a fortnight without engines. We learned that aircraft had made several fruitless searches for us and our next-of-kin cards had already been taken out at the base. We were back from the dead.'

16

The Last of 'Lord Austin'

Flotilla upon flotilla of Patrol Service minesweepers, together with scores of anti-submarine trawlers, were among the thousand warships that led and supported the great invasion of Normandy on D-Day – June 6 1944.

For some it was a dangerous front seat, given the hair-raising task of sweeping ahead of the mammoth invasion fleet. Like the old trawler *Ijuin*, whose tottery engines mustered a full nine knots with her safety valves screwed tightly down. She was danlayer to a flotilla of fleet sweepers ordered to sweep and light a channel from St Catherine's Point, Isle of Wight, to Normandy, then to clear an anchorage close inshore for the invasion force to Juno beach-head.

Signalman Leonard Stent:
'We left anchorage at St Helen's Bay at dusk on June 5 and carried on with our job until the change of tide, when during the hours of slack water we lay quietly waiting to stream oppositehand sweeps for the remainder of the journey. As we rested for this brief spell a motor launch came close by to greet us with "Hey there, don't look now but you're being followed!" We all strained our eyes through the gloom until a frantic yell from Leading-Seaman George Swallow froze us all with fear, for right under our counter lay a mine, and as we pitched, so the thing rolled back and forth, the horns at times only two or three feet from contact with our hull. George tore along the deck, grabbing a long-handled deck-scrubber as he went, and hung over the stern to fend off almost certain destruction, until the chief engineman, with coolness and presence of mind, strolled down to his control position and gave the engine a kick ahead, the turbulence causing the mine to drift clear but with agonising slowness. Of all the stories of minesweeping I'm confident that our George was the only man who used a broom successfully.'

In the great offensive some trawlers earned their battle honours early, like *Grenadier* on D-Day. She was off Arromanches when she fired at an enemy plane, causing it to drop its bombs in a hurry. One bomb hit *Grenadier*, making a great hole in her side, but they coaxed her back to Portsmouth, where her wound was fixed up with a concrete patch.

Other Harry Tates pressed on with humbler tasks. The trawler *Clythness*, carrying fuel oil and petrol, left Poole harbour on the night of June 5 for the Normandy beaches. All next day, D-Day, she was at sea, having become separated from the convoys of the night before. Seaman Thomas:

'By nightfall we anchored in a small cove under the cliffs somewhere on the French coast. We were alone except for a barge which we had found broken down and taken in tow. The young sub-lieutenant RNVR commanding the barge had gratefully accepted the skipper's offer of the tow in spite of the dire warning he received from our chief engineman, who spent more time on deck than in the engine room, that our Old Man had lost the convoy and would get us all blown up. Next day we found the invasion beaches proper at Arromanches, and the Sub., overjoyed at his safe arrival, invited us all across to splice the mainbrace, a rather peculiar little "party" on the edge of battle. But not for long, for very soon we received orders to proceed to Omaha beach, where the fighting had been fiercest.'

The trawler *Cevic* had returned from the Mediterranean, where she had been water-carrying, to have her tanks refitted for carrying oil to the Normandy beaches. Skipper Thorpe:

'We arrived in Portsmouth Harbour on D-Day plus one to see notices stuck up all round the harbour saying "This is D-Day". We had to pick up 120 drums of oil as deck cargo, distributing them evenly each side of the ship. When loaded, however, I found we had sixty drums on the port side but only fifty-six on the starboard side, and demanded to know where the other four had gone. It turned out that the lorry driver had been trying to keep them for himself. It stuck in my mind for days, how he could come to do such a thing when so many men were being killed on the beaches.'

Incredibly, though the trawlers took a thrustful part in these early stages of the Normandy invasion and many had their scars to show for it, only one was sunk. Hers became a lone statistic among the losses of hundreds of landing craft and several small warships. The date was June 24, and the trawler the veteran *Lord Austin*.

Austin had returned, very thankfully, from her last Russian convoy six months before, in December 1943; by sweeping coal dust from every nook and cranny she made enough steam to get up the Mersey and dock at Birkenhead at midnight. She paid off, the crew departed on leave, and for the Hull trawler it was the end of her rigorous life in the northern seas. When recommissioned she was a greatly altered ship and had a new captain, though he was no newcomer to the vessel. Lieutenant E. S. Terence Robinson, RNVR, had joined *Austin* as a 'new boy' on Northern Patrol, and his promotion to command followed service as her number one.

'We now had an open bridge. We had radar, and had lost our trawler mast; we had large sponsons on the wheelhouse deck with Oerlikons, and stripped Lewis guns on the bridge. We also had radar operators and coders, and were nearly a large enough crew to have a Naafi manager. But we still made only ten knots flat out except when going downhill, and we still made lots of smoke except when burning good Welsh coal.

'After several training work-ups we were ordered to the Clyde to pick up some dumb-barges – barges without means of propulsion – in company with two other trawlers. We found ourselves towing a barge filled with water-tanks for the invasion; it was fully as big as *Lord Austin* and we had to take it down to Falmouth. On the journey we got mixed up in a bit of a battle in the Bristol Channel when some E-boats got rough with our motor gunboats, but I decided we were non-belligerent. I named our barge "Fanny" and for the most part she behaved herself well.

'We arrived in Falmouth with Fanny, but nobody wanted us. Instead we were ordered on to Southampton, where we arrived eventually after a number of adventures. Here again, nobody seemed very enthusiastic about Fanny, but by this time I'd had enough of her and gave her to the Sea Transport people, receiving, almost in exchange, my sealed bag of orders for Operaton Neptune – though no one thought to tell me that I was entitled to open it. Eventually I did so, weighed anchor from close in to Seaview, Isle of Wight, and picked up the right convoy of tank landing ships bound for Juno beach. The sea was much smoother than on the day originally planned for the invasion, nevertheless at dawn the next day I could see the unfortunate troops hanging over the sides of their ships being thoroughly seasick. We closed the coast and the LSTs went ashore in turns to land their follow-up troops.

'It was certainly a wonderful sight. Heavy ships carrying out bombardments, ships everywhere and the sky dominated by the RAF. What a change from our convoy PQ17 to Russia, and my own earlier memories of the French coast in 1940 at Dunkirk and after.

'Towards the end of a long day I was ordered to take a tank landing craft in tow. She had struck a sea-defence mine on the way in to the beach, and although badly damaged had somehow managed to get her tanks ashore. We took her in tow and beached her near Portsmouth. Back we went again, and soon we were spending our days patrolling on anti-submarine and E-boat work.

'Then came the great gale. I hadn't liked the look of the weather when we anchored for the night, and had put down both anchors. I went up on the bridge at midnight to have a last look round before turning in, and found we were dragging. We got under way, found we were an anchor short when we weighed, and manoeuvred somehow all night without hitting anything. There were plenty of casualties among the landing craft but we were lucky, except for one of the stewards who hurt his back so badly I had to get a doctor over from a destroyer.

'On most nights the enemy planes came over dropping mines and the odd bomb but the battleships and cruisers kept very quiet to avoid giving away their positions. We tried to mark the position of some of the mines with dan-buoys, and often this was a help to the sweepers in the morning.

'One night while we were anchored a plane came over low. One of the gunners asked permission to open fire with the Oerlikon, but as we were anchored near a big ship I ordered him not to fire. The plane dropped a bomb which we heard coming down, and it went off alongside, so disposing of a theory I had held that you never heard the bomb that hit you. It made a great mess, putting our radar out of action and making a hole in the ship's side near the engine room, but we were able to plug this successfully and were lucky to escape without casualties. My cabin was a shambles. The radiator had been torn off the bulkhead and lay flat on the deck; in the bathroom my shaving brush had been lifted off the shelf, blown out of the door, and the door then shut after it. Blast did some extraordinary things.

'Each morning at dawn we weighed anchor and set off to patrol the lines. As the minesweepers started their work the battleships took up positions for long-range bombardment, and it was an incredible sight to be able to pick out 15-inch shells at the height of their trajectory and see them quite clearly.'

The big ships were the *Rodney* and *Nelson*, which bombarded the shore batteries at Le Havre and drew the enemy's fire in reply. During all this spectacular shooting match a Marine band played encouragement on the deck of one of the battleships. Shells landed so near to *Lord Austin* that her crew had to duck to dodge the water-splashes. German spotter-planes flew over very high, but before dark *Rodney* and *Nelson* moved anchorages – leaving *Austin* to endure a rain of bombs intended for them both.

'One day we saw our first flying bomb. No one knew what to make of it and all ships were ordered not to fire. It seemed to circle the anchorage and then turn inland, probably coming down on the Germans themselves.'

And then it was Saturday, June 24. A warm day that broke with blue skies and a fairly calm sea. *Lord Austin* weighed anchor at 5.30 a.m. She had ten miles to go to take over patrol round the anchorage, and the watch-below was asleep.

Parachute mines had been dropped in the night, and soon after getting under way *Austin*'s asdic operator, George Edwards, reported he was 'pinging' mines. When they neared the trawler *Northern Reward*, Lieutenant Robinson called over to her: 'My asdic operator reports this place is lousy with mines.'

'Yes,' replied *Northern Reward* – 'don't touch 'em.'

Only minutes afterwards a mine went off right below *Lord Austin*. The time was 5.55 a.m. Lieutenant Robinson:

'Because of the distance we had to go to take up our patrol I had been hurrying; had we been making seven knots or less we might not have triggered off the acoustic mine. When the explosion came we were thrown about heavily on the bridge, the ship's siren was jammed wide open and making a terrible din, and the engines stopped dead. I rushed to the voice-pipe but there was only a roaring sound of steam from the engine room.'

The mine had struck in the engine room, where some of the men must have been killed instantly. *Austin* heeled over to port. She had barely ten more minutes to live.

When those on the bridge had scrambled to their feet Lieutenant Robinson ordered a boat away, but in the explosion both boats had been smashed and the davits and tackle bent and twisted. Liferafts were got away and scrambling nets dropped over the side, some men leaving before the order to abandon ship was given. Others followed orders and ran to remove the primers from as many depth-charges as they could. Among these men was George Edwards.

'I ran down and looked into the messdeck, but it was half full of water with no sign of life. With another of the crew I ran to the engine room, but we could see nothing except steam. Then we heard cries of "Help!" coming from the "fiddley" – the engine room grating. We opened it and hauled up a stoker so badly scalded that as we pulled him up by his hands all the skin came off his fingers, but we managed to get him into a raft.'

The ship's confidential papers were dropped overboard and now the rest of her company hurried to leave the quickly dying *Lord Austin*. Just before she struck the mine, George Edwards had gone below to make an adjustment to the asdic gear, and on passing through the messdeck had noticed his lifebelt hanging over his bunk. Normally he did not bother to wear it on the bridge, but this time without thinking he took it and put it on. This action undoubtedly saved his life later, as he could not swim. After jumping into the sea he struggled on until an officer thrust him a piece of board, on to which he and another man clung as the ship started to go down.

Lieutenant Robinson was the last to leave the ship. 'I carefully took off my shoes, they were nearly new and I hated losing them. I then went down to the sponson and did a swallow-dive. The group of us swimming together were anxious to get farther away as the ship was going down fast by the stern and we didn't want to be sucked down with her.'

After heeling to port, *Lord Austin* righted herself and heeled to starboard, then straightened up again and sank quickly stern first, bows up. There were two more explosions as she went down, possibly the boilers going up.

One seaman who could not swim, and was without his lifejacket, clung to a liferaft which was secured to the ship by a lanyard, and was dragged down with the ship to drown because he had no knife to cut the raft free.

As the ship sank, smooth and ladylike to the end, with scarcely a ripple, Edwards thought a mast would hit him and his companion on the plank, but it just missed them.

'Other men in the water were shouting to me to get away from the suction of the ship, but I *was* sucked down and could only see foam and bubbles as I fought to get to the surface. Suddenly I saw a clear picture before me of my wife and baby standing over my own grave. Then I got clear of the water, breathless.'

Seven of *Lord Austin*'s company were lost. Her portly old chief engineman, the engineman and a stoker were either killed or trapped by the explosion; the other losses were two seamen, the assistant steward and the leading steward, who, still recovering from the back injury received in the gale, had been caught lying helplessly in his bunk. All the survivors were rescued within minutes by an American coastguard cutter, which later transferred them to *Northern Reward*. A number of injured were then passed to a destroyer, which in turn transferred the more seriously hurt to *Rodney*. Lieutenant Robinson:

'*Reward* was very good to us, fitted us up with survivors' clothing, dried our clothes, fed and consoled us, and had to carry on with her normal patrol in addition. *Rodney* sent across eighty loaves of bread in a whaler. During the morning we saw a "Mickey Mouse" motor minesweeper also blow up on a mine; when the smoke cleared there was nothing left, just pieces of wood. Later we passed the cruiser *Scylla* under tow. She, too, had struck a mine early in the morning, and although they got her home, her back was broken and that was the end of her.

'Eventually *Reward* transferred us to a Blue Funnel liner being used as an accommodation ship. Here I had a stand-up row with the naval lieutenant-commander who wanted to keep all our company aboard his ship as crew replacements. I told him I wanted us landed on the beaches and we'd find our own way home. In the end, after we had spent a night in the ship, he reluctantly had us put ashore.

'I walked along the beach until I saw an American tank landing ship with her ramp down, and asked the captain if he could give us a lift home. "Sure, skipper," he said – "hitch a ride with us." They were a very hospitable lot.

'We had one or two scares on the way back, and one in particular I wasn't likely to forget. Among my survivor's clothes I had been given a pair of combinations. These had a "trapdoor" in the stern which was very difficult to operate. At quite the wrong moment a mine went off rather close, and my nerves not being very steady I leapt out of the heads and arrived on deck in a considerable state of disarray. It was a long time before I was able to get back to a state of decency.

'On a more serious note, the ship was carrying some German prisoners from the First Panzer Division, and during the night one of my petty officers came to me and suggested, quite soberly, that we should dispose of the prisoners – "Let's put the bastards over the side". He was not alone in his bitter feelings, which took some calming down. When your ship is sunk, and your shipmates with her, it can prove too much.'

They were landed near Southampton, Germans and all. The crew were then sent off to Lowestoft while the officers went to Portsmouth to report the sinking.

'*Lord Austin* was a fine, stout vessel, a wonderful seaboat. I had been in her for three years, we had experienced many adventures together and had got through safely. It was a terribly sad thing when she went below, because I loved her. Some fine men went down with her, too.'

All through the early landings and in the months afterwards, Patrol Service ships were involved in every describable operation and service at sea.

It fell to the old trawler *Ijuin* to help sweep in the combined British and American fleet to bombard Cherbourg. Signalman Stent: 'Our task completed, we prepared to lay off and watch the "real navy" do their stuff, but try as they might, the Germans refused to play. Every enticement was offered to the enemy shore gunners to open fire and so disclose their positions, but all to no avail. So the Admiral ordered our flotilla of sweepers to offer ourselves as bait, which we did, almost to the point of thumbing our noses. The poor German gunners, their patience exhausted, let fly at us at last, the cruisers and battleships replied, and there we were, caught in the middle of a king-sized duel. Our flotilla leader hoisted "Retire independently" and retire we did; the *Ijuin*, her ancient engines leaking steam from every pore, lifted her skirts and rapidly fled the scene with a bow-wave like a destroyer, closely followed and sometimes overtaken by very large H.E. shells, which happily all missed. We were told afterwards that we'd clocked nearly 12 knots!

'We then had a grandstand view as our naval gunners proceeded to show our American cousins how to reduce shore defences to rubble.'

BYMS 2188 arrived at Cherbourg to suffer a surprise blast of shells from the one remaining fort, which the US army had said was cleared. Chief Petty Officer Davies: 'Next day the fort was in rubble, thanks to the work of RAF Tempests, and the job of clearing Cherbourg harbour began. Every night the Germans would mine the entrance, and next day our flotilla would go out and clear it. For three days the body of an American soldier face down in the water, floated back and forth on the tide inside the breakwater; as it floated past us yet again, an ironic voice would call out "Hi, Joe!" The body was eventually recovered and I trust laid in peace somewhere in the Cherbourg Peninsula.'

The little *Fisher Boy* earned further honours at Cherbourg. When a bargeload of mines was sunk at the entrance to the harbour she anchored over it and recovered the mines, so re-opening up the harbour. Later she went up one of the German rivers, where various forms of obstacles had been sunk or moored, and cleared the lot.

In late July the Harry Tates suffered a heavy loss when the trawler *Lord Wakefield* was bombed and sunk by German aircraft while working off Normandy. Twenty-six of her company were lost, including her commander, a skipper-lieutenant, and two skippers.

Then came the battle for the River Scheldt, with small motor minesweepers doing excellent work as part of a large force which sailed for Walcheren Island, the key to the Scheldt. It was vital to clear the river to Antwerp to allow the supply ships to get right in behind the advancing armies. Chief Petty Officer Davies:

'In the early dawn our fleet of sweepers under the guidance of the base ship, *St Tudno*, hove-to and waited for the *Warspite* and *Black Prince* to finish their pounding of the town of Flushing. When they had spent their deadly cargo and came speeding out, their massive black shapes made us feel rather proud and patriotic, and at the same time made our small wooden ships seem very insignificant, until word was spread that *Warspite* had made the signal: "My part was easy, yours is vital, good luck and God speed."

'Our objective was to get to Terneuzen and Breskens, which were in British hands, on the other side of the estuary from Walcheren, but we only managed to stream sweeps and get a couple of mines before it was realised the Germans were far from finished at Flushing – they let us know of their presence in no uncertain manner. Word was sent to Army headquarters to bring fire to bear on the town to enable our fleet to make a dash for the harbour, such as it was, of Terneuzen. We made it, though not without casualties on some of the ships. Then came a waiting period while the Marine commandos went across and stormed the fortress-like wall of Flushing, and the RAF, with Dutch approval, blasted the dyke and flooded the island. After this our work began without interference and we cleared the Scheldt from Flushing right into Antwerp with the loss of only three ships, a small price to pay when reckoned against the sight of the big merchantmen immediately sailing up with urgent supplies.'

On November 29 1944 a special signal from General Eisenhower congratulated the minesweepers on the successful conclusion of the operation to open up the Scheldt and the arrival of the first convoy at Antwerp. . . . 'The work has been completed in the face of adverse weather conditions in almost a week less than the estimated time, which reflects great credit on all concerned.'

Chief Davies: 'For us, it was a case of well, the job's finished, how about a run ashore to see what the girls are like? We did not mean to be unsympathetic or uncaring for the casualties; we weren't tough, we were scared and alive, and so our relief took this form.

'There was an amusing experience involving our petty officer engineman. During the brief visit ashore in Terneuzen he found himself a lady friend who was married, and was caught by the husband's unexpected return. On being chased out of the house he was told in broken English to the effect: "I don't mind you sleeping with my wife, but leave your shoes on the doorstep like any good Dutchman." '

One of the Mickey Mouse sweepers which helped in the Scheldt operation was MMS 44. Afterwards she went on to Ijmuiden, where the Germans were still around. Cook Scadeng: 'The watch ashore found an abandoned German officers' canteen with its well stocked wine and spirit cellar, and came back very, very drunk.

'In a few days Captain Hopper arrived in *St Tudno*, the base vessel, to demonstrate that he, too, could take a leading part in the mopping-up activities. Together with the commander of the Canadians he arranged a drumhead service and the troops of a Scottish regiment beat a retreat on the jetty. All this was to impress the Germans, who were being marched off in their thousands, disarmed and disillusioned.

'After Ijmuiden we were based in Amsterdam. Captain Hopper promised us leave for Christmas, and just before we sailed, our number one, Sub-Lieutenant "Lucky" French, came to me to discuss Christmas dinner. He had some inside information which resulted in he and I going ashore to bargain with a local small-holder for a couple of geese in exchange for a carton of duty free cigarettes. Our Sparks and a seaman volunteered to pluck the geese on the way over and stowed themselves away in the ship's small air-raid shelter to do the job.

'It was a lovely sight as we made for home, the *St Tudno* steaming ahead with her two minesweeping flotillas following in two single lines astern, reminding us of a big swan with her cygnets trailing behind. Halfway across the Channel Captain Hopper made the signal "Leave to one watch from the day before Christmas", and everyone cheered up immensely. It was a bright day but with a stiff breeze blowing. I peeped into the air-raid shelter to see how the two lads were getting on with their plucking and was astonished at the pile of white feathers they'd made, they were standing in them up to their waists. They wouldn't be long, they said. The fleet sailed on for another half an hour, when suddenly the pluckers opened the shelter door. The breeze caught the feathers and soon a whole fleet of sweepers was steaming through what looked like a snowstorm, a beautiful sight. Our skipper nearly blew his top.'

Christmas for others was spent at the rear of the big push into Europe. *Clythness* arrived at a small village about twenty miles upriver from Brest, where she worked completely on her own for the next three months. After carrying oil for the invasion her tanks had been cleaned out and now she resumed her earlier role of water-carrier, taking fresh water to the American ships in Brest harbour. Seaman Thomas: 'Brest was a shambles, all the water-mains broken and the town in ruins, the nearest quay with fresh water being the small village of St Nicholas, where we used to load up. During this period we were isolated from all contact with the Navy and hadn't been paid for weeks.'

All the ship's company enjoyed some very lively nights ashore – especially the skipper.

'One night he returned aboard and found no quartermaster on duty to welcome him. From the messdeck he sent a search party to find the erring seaman. A blank being drawn in the galley and stokehold, the favourite places for a quartermaster on a cold night, he left a message that if the miscreant hadn't fallen overboard he would deal with him in morning. A new quartermaster was appointed and he helped the skipper to his quarters, switched on the light and disclosed the missing man sound asleep in the skipper's armchair, an empty bottle of the skipper's whisky by his side.' Next day the skipper had forgotten the whole incident.

Bartering occupied the attention of many of the Harry Tate crews at this time, as indeed it did the rest of the Forces. Like on one old minesweeping trawler from Dover, as told by her gunner.

'We had to go across to sweep off Dunkirk and the French coast, operating from Calais and Boulogne, returning every fortnight to Dover for stores. In Dover we spent all our fortnight's pay on cocoa or anything that would sell in the black market and in this way earned thousands of francs, which enabled us to live it up well over there. Then we were offered English pound notes for English tea, and as I was friendly with the steward we were able to pull off this deal, only to discover on our way back that the notes were all counterfeit. However, on going ashore in Dover we took a trip on several buses and to quite a number of pubs, and changed the lot.

'Another time we were not so lucky. We spent our fortnight's pay on cocoa, ready to go back to France. Then the ship broke down on her way across and had to be towed back. After repairs we were told we were going to Plymouth, so there we were with all that cocoa and no ready money. It was mid-evening. We collected all our kitbags containing the cocoa, knocked up all the shopkeepers and asked them to buy it back. They did so – after all, we had been good customers. We then had a good drink and went off back to the ship, only to be told that our orders had changed again and we were leaving for France after all. . . . '

In the Mediterranean in 1944 it was the same story of trawlers, drifters and motor minesweepers assisting in almost every operation as the tide of war turned heavily in favour of the Allies.

One 'invasion' with a difference was that of a trawler group which swept the channel into Heraklion, Crete, and were the first ships to enter harbour there. This was in late November. The group, led by the trawler *Staffa*, was a mixed force of six trawlers and whalers, two motor minesweepers, two motor launches and a dan-layer. Crete was still largely in the hands of the Germans and when the sweepers' senior officer, Lieutenant-Commander Geoffrey Syrett, RNVR, went ashore with two other officers he entered a cafe which, the proprietor told him, was frequented by the local German commander, who was very fond of a game of chess. However, Commander Syrett decided that such a meeting might not be quite the most suitable way of ending the war in that locality, and he did not stop to meet the German.

In mid-December there followed off Northern Italy a unique action in which a group of trawlers, so accustomed to taking the defensive role, were actually used as an attacking force against an enemy convoy. The action took place north-west of Spezia, and became known as the Battle of Mesco Point. One of the five trawlers involved was *Hornpipe*, whose number one was Lieutenant Dormer.

'Earlier in 1944 our trawler group had moved up to Leghorn, south of Pisa, as soon as it was taken, and spent a very dull period doing patrols off the harbour and to seaward of the front, which became static a few miles north. There was little or no enemy activity at sea, though the Germans were running coastal convoys from Genoa to Spezia. British and American coastal forces attacked these regularly, but had trouble with the very heavily armed German flak-lighters.

'One night Lieutenant-Commander W. B. T. Bate, RNVR, our senior officer, in *Minuet*, was on the northernmost patrol when he intercepted a signal from an aircraft that an enemy convoy of four barges was approaching Spezia. Being always a very enthusiastic warrior he requested permission to leave his patrol and attack, but was, of course, refused. Strangely enough, that same night I dreamed of *Hornpipe* attacking an enemy convoy. As, up till then, no one had ever thought of trawlers doing such a thing, this seemed an odd coincidence, but months later, in December, the operation was at last laid on.

'After a preliminary sweep to clear and mark a passage through the enemy's offshore minefield our five trawlers – *Hornpipe*, *Minuet*, *Twostep*, *Ailsa Craig* and *Gulland* – plus a number of motor torpedo boats were to waylay an enemy convoy. The trawlers were to engage with gunfire at long range, to distract attention, while the MTBs attacked. The RAF wanted to join in too, by firing the coastal forest and silhouetting the enemy against the flames. But the Navy had little enthusiasm for this idea, as I'm afraid we thought they'd be just as likely to bomb us too.

'In the event the MTB's didn't carry out their torpedo attack, though Commander Allen, senior officer of the Inshore Squadron, controlled the whole affair with his high-class radar.

'Before the operation we had an intensive work-up in which we learned to keep station in line ahead at 50-yard intervals, which was not easy. I, as first lieutenant, handled *Hornpipe* throughout, leaving the C.O. (Lieutenant-Commander H. de Legh, RNR) free to look at the wider picture. The effort of station-keeping was so intense that I hardly had time to be frightened, and rarely to look round.'

Lieutenant Dormer wrote the following account of the battle on *Hornpipe's* way home afterwards.

'Just after dark we arrived off the enemy coast, met our coastal forces and stooged slowly in. Suddenly starshell burst just short of us, and we had a nervous half-hour while the German shore batteries searched and searched. It was eerie, shells whistling over us, gun-flashes along the coast, and starshell all over the place. I don't think they saw us . . . at least, nothing solid came near. We heard asdic transmissions, and thought an enemy force had come out to intercept, but they kept away. We closed the coast to about two miles and stooged around until 0200 hours. Several times there were false alarms, as our scouting MLs and MTBs made contacts.

'We had just about given up hope – I had long ago taken the cotton wool out of my ears and let the air out of my lifebelt. We were simply manoeuvring around at 50-yard intervals, everyone rather tired, bad tempered, and longing to go home. Then ... ALARM GREEN 100. ... "Oh, just another false one." But no, the range is given over the R/T ... OPEN FIRE.

'The first salvoes of starshell, from the 12-pounders of *Ailsa Craig* and *Gulland*, stationed at each end of the line, burst short; nothing to be seen. Then ... there they are ... several low, beetle-like objects in the glare, with splashes rising among them as the four-inch guns of *Minuet*, *Twostep* and ourselves open fire. But stuff is coming back, bunches of gentle-looking tracer shells come sailing over to accelerate and pass with a whoosh, or splash in the sea alongside. The fire becomes heavy. One flak-lighter is pouring out so much muck that it looks like a bloody catherine wheel. Shells of all sizes, 88mm., 40mm., 20mm., even down to .303 or somesuch are whistling and splashing all around as shore batteries and land ack-ack sites join in.

'FULL-AHEAD ... We had been going dead-slow, even astern ... then "turn in succession straight towards the enemy". I thought it was a mistake – we are third in line and I am praying hard: "Our Father, which art" ... steer two degrees to port. ... "Hail Mary" ... 45 revs ... "God Almighty" ... Whoosh, bang, crackle, splash ... the Bofors come in groups of five. One can tell pretty well where they will land. Of one group three went over, two fell short. *Ailsa Craig*, leading, pours a long burst of 20mm. into the nearest small craft. The craft, actually an R-boat (German motor launch) burst into flames, whereupon the Germans started pouring tracer into it also. ...

'We were steaming now at full speed straight for the shore. *Ailsa Craig* yelped something over the R/T about being 800 yards off. ... RED 18. ... Turn about together. ... Maximum speed. ... Make smoke ... off we go. Never have trawlers gone so fast, under a blaze of enemy starshell, with heavy stuff from the shore batteries splashing all around. A storm of red-hot splinters passes my face from a near-miss to starboard.

'The C.O. had scarcely needed to say a word throughout. Now he ordered me to steer for the shell splashes, to put the enemy gunners off, but I was more worried about finding the gap in the minefield and mutinously clung to the course provided by our DR plot. Commander Allen was checking up. ... "Report state, puppies." "Titus O.K." "Harry O.K." "Jack injured, No. 1 in command." "Andy on fire aft, no casualties." And so on.

'At last we were out of range and by a miracle not hit. It only remained to get the force into some sort of order and go home. We thought the affair had been a complete failure, the gunners said they had hardly been able to see their targets for the smoke and glare, and we were tremendously surprised when Commander Allen announced success – "A gallant and determined fight against heavy odds" he called it in a signal. Apparently there were eight enemy ships in all. Three of our trawlers had fired about 100 four-inch rounds between them, the other two only providing illumination. Our only casualty was the C.O. of *Twostep* (Lieutenant J. Nye, RNR) who had his right arm broken by one of eight rounds which hit their bridge. On *Hornpipe* we merely collected one hunk of metal, just where I'd been standing.'

Away to the east at this time the trawler *Moonstone* was patrolling the Greek island of Corfu. On Christmas Eve in harbour *Moonstone* wore a festive air, with home-made trimmings in place and the galley stove working overtime; but what promised to be a quiet Christmas was rudely interrupted. At 9 p.m., with her shore party recalled, *Moonstone* steamed off in answer to an emergency call from the Greek mainland, where civil war now raged, and in the early hours of Christmas Day met up with two Greek ships crowded with refugees. A pitiful avalanche of wounded, sick, cold, starved and malaria-ridden people clambered aboard the trawler. Seaman Albert Owen:

'Every inch of space in the old lady was taken up and, women and children sick down below, we set off on the return journey to Corfu. Our passengers' stomachs, through lack of food, must have felt like gaping wounds, but they still suffered from seasickness and everything was a mess and a shambles. As they began to recover, our Christmas fare became a story of forty loaves and fishes; all the food was given out and chocolate rations became the refugee children's presents as we played real Father Christmases in the most pathetic circumstances. We reached the island of Paxos at early light, and what a welcome we received; the inhabitants had a diet of what appeared to be dark bread dipped in the local ouzo, very potent. There was some wonderful singing that night in the local tavern.'

While on patrol in this area *Moonstone* was also successful in capturing a Greek vessel employed on smuggling guns and ammunition to the rebels. Her commander was a much-wanted man with a few murders behind him, and a grateful government official later visited *Moonstone*, shook hands with all, and presented medals to three members of the crew.

For another trawler, *Sheppey*, acting as dan-layer to a group of fleet sweepers working off Piraeus, life was neither so eventful nor so adventurous. In a largely monotonous routine, 'flogging' was the main occupation of the day. One of her crew: 'We flogged all sorts of gear to the Greeks – stores, ship's equipment, clothing, comforts. Someone got the equivalent of £7 for a pullover with a large burn hole in it; I got £14 for an old overcoat. When we went to sea afterwards we couldn't swing the smallboats out as all the ropes had been sold.'

No medals in this case; but that's how it was.

Meanwhile, away across in the Far East, a far flung group of little BYMS sweepers worked as industriously as their sisters in Europe. One of these craft was BYMS 2006, engaged on special duties with the Army during the campaign in Burma; in naval slang she was 'chaung hopping', doing any job along the Arakan, working the river and salt water inlets. Tough as her crew were, one special incident made them feel just a little queasy, as Petty Officer Coxswain Charles Ridsdale describes.

'After the landings at Myebon we were ordered to ferry troops of the 25th Indian Division to Akyab. These were mainly men of the Yorks-and-Lancs, Gurkhas, and some Punjabs, and by a strange coincidence I found that one of the soldiers in the Yorks-and-Lancs belonged to Hartlepool, as I did, and I knew him well. He was a sergeant in Army intelligence.

'During the trip we nattered together for hours, and he introduced me to his "oppo", a corporal in the same regiment. This lad looked a kind and gentle youth, something like my idea of a young Mr Pickwick, but was actually a real tough nut. One evening, while we were having a quiet smoke, my friend asked the corporal to show me what was bulging his pocket out, and quite casually the corporal withdrew a fairly big bundle wrapped in a filthy bloodstained rag. When undone it proved to be full of gold teeth, which puzzled me until my friend gave the grisly explanation. It appeared the corporal always managed to have himself included in burial parties, especially those of dead Japanese, and by some means arranged to leave a marker where the body was buried – a hand or a foot protruding from the soil. When the chance came he went back to the grave, scraped the soil away, knocked the gold teeth out of the corpse's jaw and added them to the store in his pocket.

'Months later, while in Singapore, I learned from a friend that the corporal had made a considerable sum by selling the teeth to Chinese dentists.'

17

Take My U-Boat

Northern Isles, a big and sturdy Grimsby trawler, had been among the first vessels of the Patrol Service to put to sea on the outbreak of war. The start of 1945 found her with a splendid, unblemished record of long years on the Northern Patrol, followed by escort and patrol work off the US coast, and now, in South African waters, with two years' good work round those tropical coasts to her credit.

Good work, but monotonous work, such as steaming out of Durban on loop patrol, on which duty she was engaged on the morning of January 19 1945, working under the direction of the South African Navy. Because of the humdrum, largely unhurried nature of her job, *Northern Isles* would often fish. Telegraphist James Brown: 'We did this to help with our rations. We were on canteen messing; any money not spent at the end of the month was disbursed among the crew to augment our wages. Therefore the more fish we caught, the less food we had to buy, and the more beer money for the lads at the end of the month.'

So on the morning of the 19th, because the fish were close inshore, *Northern Isles* went in after them. She had three spinners and fishing tackle over the stern; the spinners belonged to the captain, which was not unusual as many trawler captains did their own share of fishing, it was a common practice. Unfortunately for *Northern Isles*, in her preoccupation with following the fish she ran on to the rocks at the Bluff. Telegraphist Brown: 'She struck the rocks at 9.45 a.m. As soon as it became obvious she was stuck fast, I wirelessed for tugs, but they could not budge her. The constant swell hindered matters and the tugs were scared to get too close to us in case they should suffer a similar fate and pile up alongside.

'When the tugs retired, the captain ordered all non-essential ratings to leave in the ship's two lifeboats, which left about a dozen of us remaining on board. I asked if we were likely to get any of our personal gear off, to which the captain replied, "You'll be bloody lucky to get off yourself!" For the ship was well and truly stuck, and heeled over at a steep angle.

'At 2 p.m. the signal station on the Bluff started flashing. I was now the only one on board who could read the light, my good friend the Bunts having conveniently decided he was non-essential and gone with the boats, so I had to make the difficult climb to the bridge and take the message. It was from the South African Navy, telling us to place ourselves under the orders of the Royal Navy forthwith. In other words, they wanted nothing further to do with us.

'When it was clear nothing could be done for the old *Northern Isles* the captain asked me to send for the lifeboats to come and take us off. This I did, and got the alarming reply that the sea was now too rough for them to risk coming alongside. Ever since we'd stuck, a party on the beach had been trying to fire rocket lines out to us, but the wind always blew the lines off course. We hadn't been paying much attention to their efforts, but with this development we started to take them much more seriously. Seaman Sandy Reid, one of the smattering of peacetime sailors found on most RNPS ships, tied all our heaving lines together, secured a lifebelt to one end and threw it over the side, letting it drift ashore successfully on the flowing tide. Under Sandy's expert guidance a breeches buoy was then made fast. Determined to save the best of my personal gear, I dressed in my number ones and took my seat in the breeches buoy looking more as if I was going on a long weekend from Sparrow's Nest rather than a dip in the Indian Ocean. Our wise Chief, Jock Cowie, put his watch in a Durex and tied a knot in the neck before taking to the breeches buoy. I had a waterproof watch and so I didn't bother. But when we got ashore my watch had stopped, while Jock's cheap ten-bob effort was still going strong.

'After we'd dried ourselves out we were taken to a camp along the front at Durban. About 4 a.m., the unearthly hour when the continuous Durban swell was at its quietest, I was awakened with some other men and we set out in the ship's whaler under the command of the captain, in an attempt to get back on board. But the sea was still too rough and the attempt had to be abandoned.

'Our confidential code books had been put in weighted bags and cast over the side as per pusser's procedure, but to our mortification one of the bags was cast up on Durban beach. The swell got the blame, but our crew was promptly organised to mount a 24-hour watch along the beach. We didn't find anything more and the watch was only just called off in time before some of the wilder sparks planned to get back on board via the breeches buoy to recover the contents of the ship's spirit locker.'

At separate courts-martial the captain of *Northern Isles* and the officer of the watch were found guilty of negligence and received sentences which included each to be 'dismissed his ship'. As *Northern Isles* had, in the meantime, died miserably in sight of shore, the formal naval language seemed ironic.

As for Telegraphist Brown, he managed to wangle himself aboard the trawler of his choice, *Le Tiger*, famous for her killing of a U-boat off the US coast, but at this time more noted for a special survivor she had snatched from the sea. A bitch called Pruddie.

'*Le Tiger* picked her up from a piece of wreckage in midAtlantic. A survivor from some torpedoed ship, she adopted *Le Tiger* and some wit christened her Pruddie. I say wit because she was anything but prudent, being almost constantly in whelp. When the South African newspapers got to hear about Pruddie's adventure, they pestered us all for the details. This was at rum time, and some of the accounts given the reporters were pretty lurid. One had the rescue taking place in the midst of a howling gale, with the captain calling for volunteers and the crew stepping forward to a man! There must have been some red faces in the Durban newspaper offices next day when the highly-coloured and conflicting reports appeared.

'When Pruddie had pups she would allow no one on board who was not crew. One day our group commander came down to inspect us. We were lined up on deck and the old boy was stepping down on deck with his hand up at the salute, when Pruddie dashed out of the foc'sle and sunk her fangs into his well-fed calf. For a second or two we didn't know what to do, and simply stood to attention as the commander hopped about the deck with Pruddie hanging on like a limpet. Then a seaman, who was Pruddie's special favourite, broke ranks and persuaded her to relinquish her grip.'

The loss of *Northern Isles* coincided with other melancholy losses among trawlers and drifters early in 1945. *Golden West*, foundered off Aberdeen, *Computator*, lost by collision off Normandy, and *High Tide*, foundered off the Welsh coast. Mines, too, continued to claim their toll, from the *Arley*, mined in the North Sea, to the *Treern*, which went down thousands of miles away off Greece. And four vessels were torpedoed by U-boats. *Haybourne Wyke* and *Ellesmere* both fell victims in the Channel, while *Nordhav 11* was torpedoed off Dundee, and the whaler *Southern Flower* plunged to the bottom off Iceland.

On March 3 1945, the day *Southern Flower* died, the patrolling *Northern Sun* was detached and ordered to an area south of Reykjavik to hunt the whaler's killer, though without success. Lieutenant Geoffrey Howarth:

'*Southern Flower*'s Skipper Brown was a great friend and frequent visitor to our wardroom. He was a quiet, inoffensive little man, completely opposite to the usual run of skippers, and out of uniform could easily have passed as a country parson. Our information was that *Flower* had gone down in seconds and there was only one survivor. We learned on returning to port that it was Brown. Sitting up in bed in hospital he was a very sad man and extremely lucky to be alive. He told us he was leaning out of the bridge window when the ship was hit, and as she went down beneath him, miraculously he was sucked to the surface and saved.'

Northern Sun had recently come through a very rough round of 'met' reporting trips in the middle of the winter-bound Atlantic. Trawlers given this duty spent three weeks on station, which in the rigorous weather conditions was a daily nightmare. Only when two Wallasey-based trawlers limped back to base having burned their mess furniture to keep up steam was the stint shortened. Lieutenant Howarth:

'On one occasion we knew that two U-boats were engaged on similar work in the same area. I was on watch when the wireless operator handed me an immediate priority message from the Admiralty, which said they had intercepted a U-boat transmission to Bremerhaven in which our sighting had been reported. Weighing up our chances we thought it likely that the Germans' own met reporting would be considered more important than risking a brush with us, and so it turned out, for we saw nothing of them.'

Another winter adventure of *Northern Sun* happened when she was ordered to take over the escort of an auxiliary floating dock, off the south coast of Iceland. The dock, built in the US, was intended for the war in the Far East, and *Northern Sun's* job was to escort it to Gibraltar, on the second stage of its trip across the world. An earlier attempt to get one of these huge docks across the South Atlantic had ended in disaster when the well escorted convoy, which included an armed merchant cruiser, was attacked by U-boats. The dock broke its back and was lost. And so, because of the desperate need for a floating dock in the Far East, the Admiralty had decided to risk the next one in the North Atlantic in wintertime. AFD 17 reached Iceland safely but then hit bad weather, and the tow broke. The dock wallowed around for days but amazingly stayed afloat. Lieutenant Howarth:

'We met it off the south of Iceland and relieved the escorts, which were low on fuel. The two ocean-going tugs also needed to refuel, so they detached in turn to go to Falmouth for oil. While only one tug had the tow, no progress was made and the most that could be done was to keep the dock head to sea. It was the best part of a week before the double-tow was resumed and seventeen days later we reached Gibraltar, having taken well over a week to get through the Bay of Biscay. The most serious mistake we made was in joining the T. 124-crewed tugs at a celebration party on the Rock; it was surprising the length of time it took the bloodstream to absorb a mixture of Export Guinness and port.'

After the casualties among Patrol Service vessels in the early months of 1945, April was a quiet period. Though there was no let-up in duties at sea, the war in Europe was coming to a close. When, on the last day of April, Hitler committed suicide, Germany's unconditional surrender was only days away.

Berlin surrendered to the Russians on May 2. That day also saw the last loss in action among the Patrol Service ships operating in home waters. The minesweeping trawler *Ebor Wyke* was working off the east coast of Iceland when she was attacked by an E-boat, torpedoed and sunk. Only one man survived; a particularly grim loss considering that it was all over less than a week later.

In these last days of hostilities trawlers were still showing their teeth against the U-boats. *Arab*, the VC veteran of the Norwegian campaign so long ago, made a U-boat contact off the Minch and steamed in to attack, but a depth-charge went off on the surface, breaking just about every pipe in her engine room. She was towed into Tobermory by one of the destroyers on work-up there, arriving in the early hours of the night to be greeted typically by the fiery 'Monkey Brand' Stephenson firing dozens of snowflakes to light up the harbour while a tug took her to a buoy. By the time *Arab* was repaired the war in Europe was over.

What must have been virtually the last attack on a U-boat was that made by *Northern Spray*. It happened off Garosskagi, a promontory in the approaches to Reykjavik, and the awful place on which ships would try to make a landfall on the way in, if the compass did not spin off by up to 25 degrees because of magnetic variation. Commanding *Northern Spray* was Lieutenant Geoffrey Thorpe.

'I was senior officer of the escort force based on Reykjavik, escorting in a small homebound convoy including a tanker, the *Empire Unity*, when we were attacked just off Garosskagi. The tanker was hit and the crew abandoned ship.

'*Spray* was astern of the convoy when we sighted the U-boat's periscope only a cable away. We went hard over and full-ahead and dropped a shallow-set pattern of depth-charges. We must have been close, as we subsequently found we were without our asdic dome – it had presumably been knocked off by the U-boat's conning tower or wire cutter. We never heard what finally happened to that U-boat, as the end of the war in Europe was declared the next day.

'We picked up a boat containing *Empire Unity*'s chief engineer. He told us that the tanker's engines were all right as he had actually stopped them, so we decided to re-board the derelict; her captain and deck officers had been picked up by another trawler and were already on their way to the UK. I put our coxswain and a small boarding party aboard the tanker, plus her chief engineer and some of her engine crew. In minutes she was under way and we successfully took her in and anchored her at Hvalfiord.

'Full of hope we slapped in a salvage claim, assessing the ship and cargo at £2 million! Unfortunately, due to some technicality the ship was said to be owned by the Ministry of War Transport, and all we got was fourteen days' pay. My coxswain got the BEM and I got a Mention in Despatches, but I often thought of the £2 million that got away. I didn't understand at the time why *Empire Unity*'s crew had abandoned so quickly, but I learned later she either carried aviation gas, or had carried it immediately before, and they obviously expected the ship to go up. We, in our youthful ignorance, knew no better.'

Up on the north coast of Scotland, off Loch Erriboll, Skipper-Commander Billy Mullender, DSC, was finishing the war as he had begun it, on the bridge of an asdic trawler. He was steaming *Stella Canopus* on patrol when suddenly a U-boat surfaced not far off. Mullender boldly turned to the attack. The trawler's guns were swiftly manned and they had a shell in the breech when, to their skipper's surprise, the U-boat hoisted a black flag of surrender. Mullender steamed alongside and ordered the U-boat commander to hand over his sextant and chronometer. 'But captain,' protested the German commander, 'I am giving you the whole ship!'

It was the day of Germany's surrender and Mullender didn't know it. *Stella Canopus*, however, was cheated of her final glory. Before Mullender could take the U-boat in, an armed yacht with a senior officer on board raced up and took possession of the prize.

Now followed the mass surrenders at sea, and to the trawler *Guardsman*, which had been on west coast convoy duty, came a signal honour: she was ordered to the Kyle of Lochalsh to represent Western Approaches trawlers in an escort of the first surrendered U-boats to arrive. On reaching Lochalsh, *Guardsman* found representative destroyers, sloops, frigates and corvettes already gathered round four U-boats, and next morning the convoy sailed for Londonderry. But, shades of Harry Tate to the last, because of her slower speed, slower even than the U-boats, *Guardsman* was soon left miserably behind and, losing the convoy altogether, turned despondently for Greenock. A little later she did actually escort a big U-boat on a short voyage, and her best moment, representing the asdic trawlers, came when in Wallasey Dock she stood alongside a U-boat placed on view to the people of Liverpool and Birkenhead. The sight of the German, and the kind of vessel that had helped to hunt such killers for nearly six years, was an eye-opener. Then away went *Guardsman* to Devonport, to join trawlers coming in from all parts of the world to tie up at buoys below Saltash bridge.

Just what they had been up against in their counterparts in the enemy fleet came home to the Harry Tate crews who assisted in rounding up the German armed trawlers. For the trawler *Skomer* it was a proud moment when she took possession of the surrendered German minesweeping flotilla based at Jersey. The German crews brought their ships to within ten miles of Plymouth under Royal Marine escort, then a British officer and signalman took over each ship to bring her into Plymouth harbour. The resplendent trawler which *Skomer*'s captain and her signalman K. N. Williams took over was a stunner. Signalman Williams:

'When *Skomer*, being a coal-burner, was at full-ahead we could rely on 12 knots with a fair sea. So when my C.O. gave the order for full-ahead on the German trawler you can imagine his feelings and mine when the stern went down and the bow came up like a motor launch. As for armament, she had some kind of rocket-firing equipment right on the bow, a four-inch quick-firing gun on the foredeck and numerous machine-guns all over her. On her funnel were the silhouettes of various RAF aircraft.

'To negotiate the boom defence at Plymouth we had to stop the trawler's powerful diesel engines and proceed by trial and error. Meanwhile the people of Plymouth and Devonport had learned of our approach and collected all along the cliff walks and quays to cheer us in – a very proud moment indeed.

'For a time, *Skomer* helped to escort German prisoners-of-war from Jersey via LCTs, and we spent some time ashore viewing their defences and the huge camouflaged naval guns sited on top of the highest hill. These guns were at least 16-inchers, but I don't think they were ever fired. On Jersey we were able to buy creme-de-menthe by the glassful for sixpence, for there was nothing else available in the way of food or drink. The inhabitants were living on rats, cats, or anything that moved in the animal world, and we were offered carrots as sweets! There was a woman on the island whose husband, the authorities discovered, had been an inmate of the notorious Belsen concentration camp. We had the glad task of bringing her to the UK to be with her husband again.'

In September came the Japanese surrender, but even yet it was not all over. The Patrol Service's last three trawlers were lost in October 1945, ending an eventful summer of further casualties from mines, collisions and bad weather in the minesweeping operations that had to be continued in the wake of victory.

When the last entry was made, Harry Tate's Navy had lost well over 400 trawlers, drifters and whalers, while the casualties among other RNPS-manned craft including motor minesweepers, motor fishing vessels, BYMS sweepers, armed yachts and small auxiliary vessels took the total to almost 500.

They were losses far in excess of those of any other branch of the Royal Navy, and were actually more than the combined losses of destroyers, sloops, corvettes, frigates, fleet sweepers, motor torpedo boats and motor gunboats.

No Grave But The Sea

On a June day in 1956 Lieutenant Roger Geary-Hill, RNVR, commander of the trawler *Staffa* at war's end, put on his wartime uniform again and caught a train for Leiston, Suffolk. He took with him the flag of Admiral Cunningham, Commander-in-Chief Mediterranean, which *Staffa* had flown for four days at Algiers in 1943. *Staffa* had now been sold to the depleted Italian Navy; Geary-Hill had taken the flag which hung in her wardroom and decided the best home for it would be Leiston, in appreciation of the town's generosity in adopting *Staffa*, whose three-inch gun had been made in a local factory. So, with permission from the Admiral and the Admiralty, he presented the flag, and copies of signals, to the assembled town council.

Some other Admiralty-built trawlers like *Staffa* went into service with the Italian and other foreign navies; many more were sold for mercantile use. As for the requisitioned fishing vessels, most were stripped of their guns, asdic and sweeping gear, refitted, given back their trawls and returned to their peacetime owners. And Harry Tate's Navy was no more.

At Sparrow's Nest the White Ensign was lowered. The sentries vanished from the gates, the wartime buildings were removed or altered, and grass began to grow on the lawn again. The seats went back into the concert hall and the first seaside show returned. Across at the Oval, the training huts were dismantled, and they began to think again of cricket.

When all the naval trappings had gone from the town the Royal Naval Patrol Service might never have existed, except for the new addition to the landscape made in 1953. This was a memorial, a tall, fluted column, topped by a bronze ship, erected high above Sparrow's Nest with a clear view out to the grey North Sea. It was unveiled by the First Sea Lord, revealing seventeen bronze panels set in its broad circular base, bearing the names of 2,385 officers and men of the Royal Naval Patrol Service aged from sixteen to the late sixties, fathers, sons, brothers, cousins, who died in the service of their country and found 'no grave but the sea'.

So it stands today, in the busy little fishing port where traffic still stops in the main street while trawlers sail across it, through a retracting bridge. This memorial, and some wooden panels listing men and ships, set in the interior walls of the concert hall, are all that remain to show that 'Harry Tate's Navy was here'.

Holidaymakers loll in their deckchairs in the summers at Sparrow's Nest, the flower-beds a mass of colour and the turf evergreen. But to many men who revisit it with their families, men in possession of a somewhat worn silver badge about the size of a shilling, the scene reverts in fresh memory to one of bare earth flattened by the marching and trampling of a million feet, while once again the air is punctuated by the raucous voice of the loudspeakers issuing a constant stream of commands. . . . 'Attention – D'ye hear there? – The following ratings report to the Drafting Master-at-Arms – Men under punishment to muster on the stage – All ratings who have rejoined the depot and not passed the doctor, fall in on the roadway outside the concert hall at once – By the right, men of the Royal Naval Patrol Service quick march!'

For such visitors, to stand at the base of the memorial in Belle Vue Park and read the long register of names, is to think of those men, as with kit-bags over their shoulders, they piled into the lorries for Lowestoft station, bound for destinations all over Britain to join the small ships in home waters, or take passage for the Patrol Service bases in the Mediterranean, Africa and the Far East, never to return.

Harry Tate's Navy had its shortcomings and its frustrations, and was bloody-minded to the end. It also had a special brand of determination and sheer guts.

It is remembered with pride.

Acknowledgements

The authors gratefully acknowledge the generous help given to this book by officers and men of the Royal Naval Patrol Service, the Royal Naval Reserve, the Royal Naval Volunteer Reserve, and the Royal Navy. In particular they thank the following for their valuable contributions:

Seaman George A. Adams.
Lieutenant G. James Allen, RNR.
Lieutenant-Commander Stanley F. Archer, RNR.

Telegraphist Eric H. Bardsley.
Chief Engineman George R. Beasley.
Lieutenant-Commander F. N. Bentley, RNVR.
Leading-Telegraphist A. Blakeburn.
Lieutenant Ralph Boddis, RNVR.
Lieutenant Colin F. Brown, RNVR.
Telegraphist James Brown.
Seaman Patrick Bryant.
Seaman Norman Burgoyne.
P.O. Telegraphist Thomas E. Burn.

P.O. Edmund Carroll.
Captain R. V. E. Case, DSO, DSC, RD, RNR.
Leading-Seaman T. A. Charge, RN.
Lieutenant Peter H. Clarke, RNVR.
Coder Jack S. Clegg.
Lieutenant Leslie Clements, RNVR.

Chief P.O. William J. Davies, RNR.
Lieutenant-Commander Geoffrey Dormer, RNR.
Surgeon-Lieutenant Allan Douglas, RNVR.
T.O. Telegraphist E. F. J. Edards.
P.O. George Edwards.
Skipper-Lieutenant W. G. 'Billy' Euston, RNR.

Engineman Douglas Finney.
Seaman (SD) Leslie Forster.
Lieutenant-Commander S. G. 'Jim' Fowler, RNVR.

Lieutenant Rupert L. Garratt, RNVR.
Lieutenant Commander Roger M. Geary-Hill, RNR.
Seaman-Gunner Lionel Gordon Gray.

Lieutenant A. L. Hargraves, RANVR.
Lieutenant-Commander Bryan W. Harris, DSC (and Bar), RNVR.
Commander Guy Harris, OBE, RN.
Hon. Lieutenant-Commander John E. Harwood (QC), RD, RNR.
Acting Leading-Signalman Frederick Hazell.
Leading-Signalman Gordon Hooper.
Lieutenant J. B. Hornby, RNVR.
Lieutenant Geoffrey R. Howarth, RNVR.
Telegraphist Fred H. Howson.

P.O. Coxswain Sid A. Kerslake, RNR.

Lieutenant-Commander Stanley W. Lock, RNVR.
Seaman-Gunner G. R. Lunn.

Leading-Seaman Harold McCall.
Chief Engineman John P. Mair, RNR.
Lieutenant H. G. F. Male, RNVR.
Leading-Seaman Arthur W. Mallett.
Lieutenant Arthur H. G. Miles, RNVR.
T.O. Telegraphist J. A. Mitchell.
P.O. Robert H. Muir.
Commander William J. O. Mullender, MBE, DSC, RD, RNR.
Lieutenant T* John Oakey, RNVR.
Seaman Albert Owen.

P.O. John S. Paterson.

Leading-Seaman J. P. Rampling, PSGL.
Lieutenant-Commander James G. Reeve, RNVR.
P.O. Coxswain Charles Ridsdale.
Cook William Riley.
Lieutenant E. S. Terence Robinson, RNVR.

Leading-Cook F. J. Scadeng.
Signalman L. B. Smith.
Leading-Seaman Coxswain Raymond Smith.
RDF Rating T. Roy Sparkes.
Signalman Leonard Stent.
Chief P.O. Amos W. Sumner.

Seaman Robert Thomas.
Lieutenant-Commander Geoffrey Thorpe, RNVR.
Skipper-Lieutenant William H. Thorpe, RNR.

Leading-Seaman S. D. Varley.

P.O. Engineman Walter Walker.
Lieutenant-Commander Allan Lansley Waller, VRD, RNR.
Seaman James Waterson.
Lieutenant-Commander E. Leslie Wathen, DSC, RNR.
Lieutenant-Commander Richard F. Wattam-Bell, RNVR.
Chief-Skipper Sidney A. White, DSC, RNR.
Signalman K. N. Williams.
Leading-Coder David Willing.
Signalman E. Neville Wilson.

Leading-Seaman Coxswain Ernest Claude 'Lofty' Yallop.

The authors thank Mrs Jean de Pass, wife of the late Captain Daniel de Pass, CBE, RN (Commodore of the RNPS, Lowestoft, 1940-44) for kind assistance with information and photographs; Mrs Frieda Shillan, wife of the late Lieutenant-Commander A. A. Shillan, RNVR (photographs); Lieutenant T* John Oakey, RNVR, Secretary of the Irwell Association, and Lieutenant-Commander E. B. West, RNVR, VRD (and Bar), for providing the official Scrapbook of the Association; Mrs Hilda Mothershaw (Wren Hilda Ralph); Fireman Joseph Willis, Merchant Navy; Mr David A. J. Pugh; Northern Trawlers Ltd, Grimsby; together with the *Grimsby Evening Telegraph*, *Eastern Daily Press*, *Hull Daily Mail*, and many newspapers which kindly helped in the search for 'Sparrows' from the Nest.

NEL BESTSELLERS

Crime

T005 801	RIFIFI IN NEW YORK	*Auguste le Breton*	30p
W002 750	FIVE RED HERRINGS	*Dorothy L. Sayers*	30p
W002 848	CLOUDS OF WITNESS	*Dorothy L. Sayers*	35p
W002 845	THE DOCUMENTS IN THE CASE	*Dorothy L. Sayers*	30p
W003 011	GAUDY NIGHT	*Dorothy L. Sayers*	40p
W002 870	BLOODY MAMA	*Robert Thom*	25p

Fiction

T009 548	SUEDEHEAD	*Richard Allen*	25p
W002 755	PAID SERVANT	*E. R. Braithwaite*	30p
T007 030	A TIME OF PREDATORS	*Joe Gores*	30p
T009 084	SIR, YOU BASTARD	*G. F. Newman*	30p
T009 769	THE HARRAD EXPERIMENT	*Robert H. Rimmer*	40p
T010 716	THE ZOLOTOV AFFAIR	*Robert H. Rimmer*	30p
T010 252	THE REBELLION OF YALE MARRATT	*Robert H. Rimmer*	40p
W002 918	THE ADVENTURERS	*Harold Robbins*	75p
T011 798	A STONE FOR DANNY FISHER	*Harold Robbins*	60p
T011 771	NEVER LOVE A STRANGER	*Harold Robbins*	70p
W002 653	THE DREAM MERCHANTS	*Harold Robbins*	60p
T011 801	WHERE LOVE HAS GONE	*Harold Robbins*	70p
T010 406	NEVER LEAVE ME	*Harold Robbins*	30p
T006 743	THE INHERITORS	*Harold Robbins*	60p
T009 467	STILETTO	*Harold Robbins*	30p
W002 792	THE KILLER	*Colin Wilson*	35p
W002 822	GILLIAN	*Frank Yerby*	40p
W002 479	AN ODOUR OF SANCTITY	*Frank Yerby*	50p
W002 860	FAIROAKS	*Frank Yerby*	40p

Science Fiction

W002 844	STRANGER IN A STRANGE LAND	*Robert Heinlein*	60p
T009 696	GLORY ROAD	*Robert Heinlein*	40p
W002 838	BETWEEN PLANETS	*Robert Heinlein*	30p

War

W002 686	DEATH OF A REGIMENT	*John Foley*	30p
W002 484	THE FLEET THAT HAD TO DIE	*Richard Hough*	25p
W002 805	HUNTING OF FORCE Z	*Richard Hough*	30p
W002 423	STRIKE FROM THE SKY—THE BATTLE OF BRITAIN STORY	*Alexander McKee*	30p

Western

T007 340	TWO RODE NORTH	*J. D. Brady*	25p
T010 619	EDGE—THE LONER	*George Gilman*	25p
T010 600	EDGE—TEN THOUSAND DOLLARS AMERICAN	*George Gilman*	25p

General

T011 763	SEX MANNERS FOR MEN	*Robert Chartham*	30p
W002 531	SEX MANNERS FOR ADVANCED LOVERS	*Robert Chartham*	25p
T010 732	THE SENSUOUS COUPLE	*Dr 'C'*	25p
T007 022	NEW FEMALE SEXUALITY	*Manfred F. De Martino*	50p
W002 584	SEX MANNERS FOR SINGLE GIRLS	*Dr. Georges Valensin*	25p
W002 592	THE FRENCH ART OF SEX MANNERS	*Dr. Georges Valensin*	25p

NEL P.O. BOX 11, FALMOUTH, CORNWALL

Please send cheque or postal order. Allow 5p per book to cover postage and packing (Overseas 6p per book).

Name..

Address ....

....

Title ....
(DECEMBER)